The Road to Revolution

MAURICE LEE, JR.

The Road to Revolution: Scotland under Charles I, 1625–37

UNIVERSITY OF ILLINOIS PRESS

Urbana and Chicago

This book is printed on acid-free paper.

LIBRARY OF CONGRESS CATALOGING IN PUBLICATION DATA

Lee, Maurice.
The road to revolution.

Includes bibliographical references and index.
1. Scotland—History—Charles I, 1625–1649. I. Title.
DA803.3.L44 1985   941.106'2   84-8750
ISBN 0-252-01136-8 (alk. paper)

This book is dedicated to all my friends and
colleagues in the historical profession,
past and present, here and abroad, who have
made membership in our guild such a continuous
pleasure for me for so many years. Ave.

Contents

Preface

IN DECEMBER 1632 Sir Robert Kerr of Ancrum wrote a long letter to his son William, earl of Lothian, about the rebuilding of Ancrum House and the planning of its policies and gardens. Most of Sir Robert's suggestions went on the assumption that the domestic peace which Scotland had enjoyed for a generation and more would continue. There was one cautionary note, however. The outer walls of the tower should not be weakened by enlarging its windows, he wrote, "because the world may change again."[1] The world did indeed change again, more rapidly and completely than Sir Robert anticipated; he was to die in penniless exile in Holland. This book is the story of that change. It is a sequel to the account of Scottish politics after the union of the crowns of England and Scotland in 1603 which I began to tell in *Government by Pen: Scotland under James VI and I*. It covers the years from the accession of Charles I in March 1625 to the riot in Edinburgh in July 1637 which was the first link in the chain of events that led ultimately to civil war in Charles's three kingdoms and to the temporary overthrow of the Stewart monarchy. It ends where it does because the recent books of David Stevenson, *The Scottish Revolution 1637–1644* (1973) and *Revolution and Counter-revolution in Scotland 1644–1651* (1977) cover the civil war period very well. I do not agree with all of Dr. Stevenson's conclusions, but his work is both judicious and thorough, and obviates the need for telling the story so soon again.

In my preface to *Government by Pen* I pointed out that there was no chronological narrative account of Scottish politics after 1603. Surprisingly enough, this is also the case for the reign of Charles I prior to 1637. The one book devoted to the subject, David Mathew's *Scotland under Charles I* (1955), is a series of essays on various topics rather than a political narrative. Stevenson provides a good analytical chapter at the beginning of his first book, and Gordon Donaldson has written a splendid fifteen-page summary in his volume in the *Edinburgh History of Scotland* series. Given the limited space at their disposal, both scholars quite properly dwell on the features of the years 1625–37 that were the most prominent causes of the troubles that erupted thereafter. In so doing they, and the other scholars who have written about this period, are following the lead provided by their seventeenth-century predecessors. The two major contemporary (or near-contemporary) historians of these years, Clarendon and Burnet, both writing after the traumatic experience of the civil war, were naturally concerned with explaining how the war came about. The much briefer accounts of John Row and William Scot, and the chronicle of Sir James Balfour of Denmylne, Lord Lyon King of Arms, are all bitterly hostile to Charles's religious policy, though on other subjects Balfour is not unfriendly to the king. In short, there is no narrative, contemporary or modern, which tells the story of the reign as it unfolded, without any sense of impending doom—and, as is well known, Charles himself had no premonition of disaster. In June of 1637 he described himself to his nephew as the happiest king in Christendom.[2]

The following pages constitute an attempt to tell that neglected story. It has had to be pieced together from the surviving documentary evidence, mostly government records and official and private correspondence, and there is not as much of the latter as one would wish. There was a greater volume of letters in James's day, when the Scots at court were much more numerous and more influential, and the king himself kept in touch with his friends in his ancient kingdom. For the availability of much of what correspondence does survive, all historians are heavily in the debt of Sir William Fraser, that indefatigable Victorian genealogist and compiler of the histories of Scottish noble families, which he published along with massive appendices of documents from their muniment rooms; the notes to the following chapters will indicate how much this account owes to Fraser's work.

What my piecing together shows is that, after a disruptive and difficult opening phase which lasted approximately two years,

The Road to Revolution

Charles's regime in Scotland settled down, owing to the rise to power of William Graham, earl of Menteith, a man whom historians have completely overlooked. This neglect has been so total that at first I could not believe what the sources were telling me: there had to be some mistake. But there is no mistake. For about five years, from 1628 to 1633, Menteith was the most influential man in Scotland, and during those years Charles's government was moderately successful. But Menteith, like his master, brought ruin upon himself. In 1633 he fell from power, and thereafter the king and his advisers made one mistake after another, culminating in the decision to introduce the new service book in 1637, a decision which led directly to disaster. It is, of course, impossible to assert that if Menteith had retained his influence there would have been no explosion in Scotland, no Long Parliament, no civil war, no Cromwell guilty of his country's blood. But Menteith's brief political career is certainly the stuff of historical might-have-beens, and if there is a hero of the melancholy tale these pages have to tell, that hero is Menteith.

There remains the question of the larger picture. Since what happened in Scotland led directly to revolution and the overthrow of the Stewart monarchy, these events are, presumably, a part of all those happenings that go to make up the so-called "general crisis" of the mid-seventeenth century, even though the formulator of the theory of general crisis, Hugh Trevor-Roper, excluded Scotland as "largely irrelevant" to his hypothesis.[3] As Preserved Smith once remarked in another connection, however, every dogma has its day, and I own to considerable skepticism as to the validity of Trevor-Roper's theory. T. K. Rabb is certainly correct in pointing out that the last third of the seventeenth century is vastly different from what had gone before, and that this difference requires explanation. But it is not altogether convincing to argue from this that there was a "crisis" which began somewhere in the 1620s and ended in the 1660s. On the whole I prefer the more cautious formulation of J. H. Elliott, who argues that there are many analogies between the 1560s and the 1640s.[4] The temptation to expand on these matters is considerable, but will be resisted here, though there are some observations in the final chapter.[5] A proper discussion of the "crisis" theory would unduly lengthen this account, and disproportion it to boot. I have therefore eschewed any systematic attempt at comparative analysis, though comparisons with Charles's government of England are occasionally made. It seemed enough in this book to tell the hitherto untold Scottish story.

No historian is an island, and I, like others, owe much to many people and institutions. My thanks go first to Rutgers University and its research council for their generosity with both time and money; next to the University of Edinburgh for an appointment to its Institute for Advanced Study in the Humanities which greatly facilitated my research; to the libraries of Rutgers University, Princeton University, the University of Edinburgh, the Princeton Theological Seminary, and the University of Guelph; to the British Library; the National Library of Scotland and especially to its Keeper of Manuscripts, Dr. Ian Rae; the Scottish Record Office and its Keeper, Dr. John Imrie, and Assistant Keeper, Dr. Athol Murray; and to the S. F. A. Mr. Ian Cranna of the University of Edinburgh, who was most helpful in providing transcriptions of certain documents from the National Library of Scotland. Much of the first chapter of this book appeared in somewhat different form in *Albion* in 1980; I am grateful to the editor, Dr. Michael Moore, for permission to reprint. Many friends and colleagues have provided counsel and read sections of the manuscript to its advantage, notably Professors Gordon Donaldson, Sidney Burrell, Edward Cowan, and Richard Schlatter, and Dr. Kevin Sharpe. The University of Illinois Press was, as always, agreeable and efficient; I want to thank especially Ms. Margaret Laff, my copy editor, who picked up my usual large number of inconsistencies and fixed a lot of messy grammar. And, of course, my wife—she managed to keep her temper throughout, which must have been difficult at times, and for this, as she knows, I am deeply grateful.

The Road to Revolution

NOTES

1. *A&L* I, 63.

2. C. V. Wedgwood, *The King's Peace, 1637–1641* (New York, 1955), p. 21.

3. Trevor Aston, ed., *Crisis in Europe, 1560–1660* (New York, 1967), p. 123.

4. T. K. Rabb, *The Struggle for Stability in Early Modern Europe* (New York, 1975). J. H. Elliott, "Revolution and Continuity in Early Modern Europe," *Past and Present,* no. 42 (1969), 35–56.

5. For my views see M. Lee, Jr., "Scotland and the 'General Crisis' of the Seventeenth Century." *SHR* LXIII (1984), 136–54.

Abbreviations frequently used in the notes

A&L	*Correspondence of Sir Robert Kerr, First Earl of Ancram, and His Son William, Third Earl of Lothian,* ed. David Laing, 2 vols. (Edinburgh, 1875)
APS	*The Acts of the Parliament of Scotland,* ed. T. Thomson and C. Innes, 12 vols. (Edinburgh, 1814–75)
BL	British Library, London
CSPD	*Calendar of State Papers, Domestic Series, of the Reign of Charles I,* ed. John Bruce *et al.* (London, 1858–97)
CSP Venetian	*Calendar of State Papers and Manuscripts Relating to English Affairs Existing in the Archives and Collections of Venice,* vols. XVIII–XXIV, ed. A. B. Hinds (London, 1912–23)
HMC	Historical Manuscripts Commission, London
M&K *M&K Supp.*	HMC, *Report on the Manuscripts of the Earl of Mar and Kellie* (London, 1904); *Supplement* (London, 1930), both ed. H. Paton
NLS	National Library of Scotland, Edinburgh
RCRB	*Records of the Convention of the Royal Burghs of Scotland,* ed. Sir J. D. Marwick, 6 vols. (Edinburgh, 1866–90)
RMS	*Registrum Magni Sigilli Regum Scotorum,* ed. J. M. Thomson *et al.,* 11 vols. (Edinburgh, 1814–1914)
RPCS	*The Register of the Privy Council of Scotland,* 1st and 2nd series, ed. J. H. Burton, D. Masson, and P. H. Brown (Edinburgh, 1877–1908)
RSCHS	*Records of the Scottish Church History Society*

SHR	*Scottish Historical Review*
SHS	Scottish History Society, Edinburgh
SRO	Scottish Record Office, Edinburgh
Balfour	*The Historical Works of Sir James Balfour,* ed. J. Haig, 4 vols. (Edinburgh, 1825)
Laing	HMC, *Report on the Laing Manuscripts,* vol. I, ed. H. Paton (London, 1914)
Row	John Row, *The History of the Kirk of Scotland from the Year 1558 to August 1637,* ed. D. Laing, Wodrow Society (Edinburgh, 1842)
Scot	William Scot, *An Apologetical Narration of the State and Government of the Kirk of Scotland since the Reformation,* ed. D. Laing, Wodrow Society (Edinburgh, 1846)
Stirling	*The Earl of Stirling's Register of Royal Letters Relative to the Affairs of Scotland and Nova Scotia from 1615 to 1635,* ed. Charles Rogers, 2 vols. (Edinburgh, 1885)

NOTE

Dates are given Old Style, save that the year is taken to begin on January 1 (as it did in Scotland starting in 1600). Money is given in pounds Scots; where pounds sterling are meant, the word *sterling* is used. The ratio of pounds Scots to sterling was 12:1. A merk was two-thirds of a pound. The spelling and punctuation of quotations have normally been modernized.

The Road to Revolution

1

The End of the Jacobean System

On Sunday, July 23, 1637, there occurred in the city of Edinburgh the most famous "uproar for religion" in all of British history. The occasion was the introduction of the new service book, "Laud's liturgy" as it came to be called; its reception had been carefully prepared. What happened is well known—how, when the dean of Edinburgh began to read from the new book in St. Giles cathedral, the insults and imprecations began, especially on the part of the women, followed by physical violence within the church and without, both during and after the service. Jenny Geddes may never have existed, but those who felt and behaved as legend says she did were present in force. The bishop of Edinburgh, wrote the future deviser of the Covenant, Archibald Johnston of Wariston, with grim satisfaction, "after the forenoon's sermon was almost trampled underfoot, and (in the) afternoon . . . was almost stoned to dead; the dean was forced to cage himself in the steeple. . . . This uproar was greater nor [than] the 17 of December, and in all history will be remarked as the fair, plausible, and peaceable welcome the service book received in Scotland."[1]

"The 17 of December" had been the last great religious riot in Edinburgh. It had taken place over forty years previously, in 1596, when a Protestant mob, whipped up by clerical extremists, demanded that King James VI cease what it believed to be his coddling of Papists and dismiss his allegedly Popish officials. The riot was an utter failure. Not only did the king not alter his course, he also compelled the citizens of Edinburgh to pay heavily, financially and otherwise, for their disobedient behavior, and he seized upon the occasion of this fiasco to begin his campaign to get control of the church, which eventually led to the revival of diocesan episcopacy.[2] But now, in 1637, King James's son faced something far more serious than a city mob led by a handful of radical ministers and political malcontents. He confronted a nation whose people were overwhelmingly resolved on resistance to his regime, by force if need be, as the sequel to the events of that memorable July Sunday was to show.

That such a situation could or would develop would have seemed almost inconceivable when King James died in March 1625. He had been an enormously effective and successful ruler. He had reduced both aristocracy and kirk to obedience; he had brought a considerable degree of law and order to the borders and even to the highlands; he had provided peace and prosperity for the better part of forty years; he had created a governmental machinery and had found ways to make it work effectively even after he became an absentee king in 1603. He was well served, to be sure; but then, he showed a considerable talent for picking capable subordinates. James had not solved all of Scotland's problems, of course. The enemies of episcopacy had not been wiped out, and the recent changes in religious practice embodied in the five articles of Perth were unpopular. Not every class in Scottish society had prospered. The poor were still legion, and the machinery for dispensing poor relief was elementary. By the beginning of the seventeenth century rural tenants had greater security of tenure than before, but they and many smallholders in the country and lesser burgesses in the towns had no great share in the expanding economy. It was from these classes, and the sons of the manse, that the clerical Covenanting leadership came.[3] The Scottish treasury, like that of almost every other European state, was usually empty, and James's profligacy repeatedly spread despondency among his financial officers. In 1621, however, as a consequence of the situation in the Palatinate, parliament had enacted a new tax on a hitherto untouched source of wealth: the net income of annualrents (interest on loans or mortgages). Many people who up to this time had paid no or very little tax now had to pay,[4] and others had to pay more. If it could be made permanent, this new levy promised virtually to double the government's receipts from direct taxation.

In little more than a decade after James's death all his good work had been undone, and Charles I found himself facing the united ranks of that coalition of landowners and kirkmen which had ruined his unfortunate grandmother and was to ruin him. Historians have usually explained this by pointing to Charles's ignorance of Scotland, which led to perfectly avoidable blunders such as the decision to impose the new service book, and to his character, which was most unsuitable for the role he had to play. There is surprising agreement as to Charles's qualities and defects. He was a very private man, with many private virtues: he was devoted to his family, cultivated, devout, a genuine connoisseur of art. He was also nervous, shy, and unsure of himself, which caused him to adopt a public manner which was reserved, taciturn, formal, chilly, and ungracious. He had a stubborn and authoritarian temperament, and was both secretive and impatient, a very unfortunate combination of characteristics in a king. He seldom troubled to explain his orders; he simply issued them and expected instant compliance. His own sense of duty, of his obligation as a king to govern his people according to his vision of what was best for them, was very acute, and what he expected of himself he also expected of others. He assumed that loyal service was his due and gave no hint of appreciation to those who rendered it, so he generated in his servants neither affection nor respect. His mind moved slowly, and was inflexible and legalistic; "with the key of the laws he seeks to open the entrance to absolute power," commented one Venetian agent in England.[5] Those who opposed him did so, he believed, for personal reasons, so it was not necessary to keep faith with them. Hence the duplicity which became such a pronounced characteristic of his public behavior, especially in difficult times, and which in the end led him to his death.

Charles never publicly criticized his father, though in character he was very unlike James, who was a garrulous, learned, quick-witted, gregarious, argumentative man, personally sloppy in all kinds of ways, and whose court was raffish, undignified, and scandal-ridden. Charles, writes the gossipy Bishop Gilbert Burnet, "was much offended with King James's light and familiar way, which was the effect of hunting and drinking, on which occasions he was very apt to forget his dignity, and to break out into great indecencies: on the other hand the solemn gravity of the court of Spain was more suited to his [Charles's] own temper, which was sullen even to a moroseness."[6] But there were resemblances between father and son. They both loved the chase. They both, in their different ways, loved that disastrous man, the duke of Buckingham. And they both firmly believed in the doctrine of the divine right of kings. Charles, however, drew from it more extreme conclusions than James ever had. Charles believed that "because he was their anointed king his subjects would accept without resentment the curtailment of their power by him."[7] James knew better than that, and was well aware of the practical necessity of compromise and occasional retreat. Charles had no such awareness, and his previous experience and upbringing had not served to provide him with any. Unlike his father, he had never been the victim of an aristocratic coup or been trapped on the privy in his own palace by a rebellious nobleman. He had never faced an angry mob in the national capital or a rebel army in the field or an overwrought clergyman who pulled at his sleeve and called him "God's silly vassal." His view was that once he had issued his orders, both servants and subjects must put aside their private judgments and obey him, simply because he was king.

Temperamentally, then, Charles was most unsuited to rule, and he did make a number of unnecessary mistakes. But it is by no means clear that Charles could have avoided trouble in Scotland. Once the old king was dead, some sort of confrontation with the Scottish aristocracy was very likely to occur, sooner or later. The nobles had only recently been brought under control by King James; they had a long tradition of independent action and local supremacy, and they were underemployed. The union of the crowns had created political and social strains which were beyond the skill of James, or of any king, entirely to assuage. The union had eliminated the court in Edinburgh and deprived most of the aristocracy of regular personal contact with their absentee king, and his vastly increased power made them uneasy. "Doubtless our king will do what he can to curb the nobility of Scotland, and to diminish their power, thereby to conform them to the custom of England," wrote Sir Robert Gordon of Gordonstoun to his young nephew, the earl of Sutherland, about five years before James's death. "It is not now with our noblemen as when our king was resident in Scotland. Hardly then could the king's majesty punish any of our greatest nobility when they had offended, by reason of their great dependencies and friendship. But now, he being absolute King of all Great Britain, the cause is altered. He may, when he listeth, daunt the proudest and mightiest of you all." Indeed some contemporary royalists explained the events of 1637 and thereafter in terms of an aristocratic conspiracy. The nobility, wrote John Spalding, a member of the episcopal bureaucracy in Aberdeen, suborned "a number of rascal serving women to throw stools at the reader and perturb the kirk. . . . They begin at religion as the ground of their quarrel, whereas their intention is only bended against the king's majesty and royal prerogative."[8] Though the details of Spalding's allegations of conspiracy are absurd, the thrust of his argument is sound in one particular: the fundamental problem of the Scotland of Charles I was one of government rather than religion. Furthermore, difficulties were bound to arise because the governmental system which obtained at the end of the reign of James VI could not long survive his death. As it turned out, the actions of the new king were to provoke a crisis at once.

King James's death came at a very awkward time for Scotland. The country was just beginning to emerge from three awful years of crop failure, floods, murrain, and famine, which brought on what one scholar has called "the most serious demographic crisis of seventeenth-century Scotland."[9] She was perhaps at war with Spain, or about to be, though no one had officially said so—the country had not been at war for more than two generations, and officialdom's response was understandably uncertain. The three leading Scottish officials were men whom neither Charles nor Buckingham knew very well; for whatever reason, the great duke had thus far made no effort to engross Scottish patronage. Two of the three were old and trusted friends of King James: John Erskine, earl of Mar, "Jock o' the Slates," James's old schoolfellow, lord treasurer since 1616, and Thomas Hamilton, earl of Melrose, "Tam o' the Cowgate," a lawyer who had been a member of the bureaucracy for over thirty years and was now secretary of state and president of the court of session, the highest Scottish civil court. The other member of this triumvirate, Sir George Hay of Nethercliff, lord chancellor since 1622 and a busy entrepreneur with an interest in a good many business ventures, was somewhat younger than the others, with less than ten years of service in office. He owed his present eminence to the patronage of the marquis of Hamilton, Buckingham's friend and, arguably, James's favorite Scottish courtier during the last years of his life. Hamilton's sudden death at the age of thirty-five, just a few weeks before that of James, was a matter of considerable importance; it meant that there was now no London Scot who both possessed the new king's confidence and knew the leading men in Edinburgh.

Mar, Melrose, and Hay ran a government by consensus through the instrumentality of the privy council, following the methods worked out during the decade of dominance of the late Lord Chancellor Dunfermline, whose colleagues they had been. They received the king's instructions, persuaded him to alter them when necessary, either by writing to him direct or by using one of their allies among James's Scottish entourage at Whitehall, and presented him with proposals of their own, which he usually accepted. They and their colleagues on the council governed Scotland for James, and he let them do so, because he knew them and everybody else of importance in the kingdom personally, and because he trusted them: they were his old and loyal friends as well as his servants. This system had the advantage of minimizing the strains inherent in the removal of king and court from Edinburgh in 1603. Scottish magnates and other people of importance in Scotland might have lost continuous personal contact with the king, but they could still command his attention, either through the council collectively or as individuals, or through one of the Scots at court. James's officials came mostly from the ranks of the lairds, the lawyers, and the younger sons and cadet branches of aristocratic families. For the most part he avoided giving office or political power to great nobles or to his revived bench of bishops; Mar's case was exceptional. It was James's personal, intimate knowledge of the Scottish scene which Charles lacked. If the existing governmental system was to continue, Charles would either have to acquire that knowledge or accept his councillors' recommendations on faith.

Prior to his accession Charles had shown very little interest in Scotland—"*your* nation," he called it in a letter to the council in October 1625, a phrase James would never have used.[10] He knew the courtier Scots, of course, men like his father's old servants John Murray of Lochmaben, earl of Annandale, keeper of the privy purse, and Mar's cousin Thomas Erskine, earl of Kellie, captain of the guard. These two were the council's chief pipelines to the court. Charles did not much care for them, and at least in Kellie's case the feeling was reciprocated: Kellie deplored Charles's behavior in encouraging attacks on the royal prerogative during the English parliament of 1624, and he regarded Buckingham's influence as pernicious.[11] But there were some Scottish courtiers to whom Charles did pay attention. Two of these were more important than the others. One was Robert Maxwell, earl of Nithsdale, a Catholic, who had restored the family fortunes after the execution of his elder brother by marrying one of Buckingham's cousins. He was arrogant, quarrelsome, stupid, deeply in debt, and much disliked by the ruling triumvirate in Edinburgh. The other was the poet Sir William Alexander of Menstrie, James's master of requests and a gentleman of Charles's bedchamber. He was the principal promoter of the scheme for the colonization of Nova Scotia, which was to be forwarded, financially and otherwise, by the sale of baronetcies on the Ulster model. Alexander's closest Scottish associate in this scheme was the director of the chancery, Sir John Scot of Scotstarvet. He was a greedy man and a troublemaker—in Sir James Balfour's words, "a busy man in foul weather, and one whose covetousness far exceeded his honesty."[12] He was also a learned and plausible debater, whose ability to influence the king was to have most unfortunate results.

Charles was known to be interested in the Nova Scotia scheme: he had written to the privy council in its support, and Alexander dedicated a promotional pamphlet to him.[13] Charles had also been making inquiries into the rights of the various sorts of landholders in the Principality of Scotland; in January 1625 Kellie informed his cousin the treasurer that Charles was planning to issue an act of revocation some time before he reached his twenty-fifth birthday in November, and that he had written to Hay and Melrose about it.[14] It was generally understood that a king, in order to protect himself from the consequences of misgovernment during a minority—and for two centuries every Scottish ruler without exception had succeeded as a minor—could, before he reached twenty-five, revoke anything done in his name before he reached the age of twenty-one. Charles apparently was planning to extend that principle to the property included in the Principality of Scotland. Apart from these two matters, however, no one in Edinburgh knew what Charles's intentions were or what his policy would be, when word of James's death arrived. So little was known of the new king's views that some of the opponents of James's ecclesiastical measures were hopeful that Charles would alter the policy of what the earl of Rothes called the "imposing of certain novations upon the Kirk." Rothes was referring to the five articles of Perth, which he had opposed in parliament in 1621. These consisted of changes in the practices of the Scottish church which James had imposed in the final years of his reign as part of his campaign to bring the Scottish church into conformity with that of England. The articles met with considerable hostility and resistance, in particular the requirement that communion be taken kneeling, which many people regarded as Popish. After 1622 the primate, Archbishop John Spottiswoode of St. Andrews, virtually gave up attempting to enforce them.[15] In James's last years there had been occasional speculation in Scotland that Charles might be more sympathetic to the kirk's traditional practices than his father, but in the months after his accession, opinion swung abruptly the other way, largely on account of his marriage to a French princess. In January 1625 James had authorized a policy of leniency toward Catholics in connection with Charles's marriage festivities, and rumors of royal double-dealing on the Catholic question were rife in London. "You cannot believe the alteration that is in the opinion of the world touching his Majesty," wrote Kellie to Mar late in July.[16] Charles had to order the council to issue a statement denying that he was soft on Catholics or that there would be any changes in the church as he found it. The disappointed presbyterians resented being lumped together with Papists in this proclamation as non-conformists and potential disturbers of "the peace either of religion or present Kirk government." Charles's attitude in this matter, wrote one of them, "made many honest people to have harder thoughts of the King than they had before."[17]

It behooved the Scottish leadership to get to London promptly—though Melrose, for one, went reluctantly—both to make themselves known to their new master and to pay their last respects to the old. Superficially the visit went well enough; Charles was cordial and had already continued them in their offices for life.[18] There were several indications of trouble to come, however. Despite his councillors' request that he act, Charles postponed his decision on the makeup of the new council, and it was reported that he planned to drop the judges of the court of session from its membership.[19] Lord Chancellor Hay, under some pressure, surrendered his profitable tack of the Orkneys. He was well compensated, and he calculated that his enemies would have one less handle against him—his patron Hamilton's death had left him vulnerable.[20] At King James's funeral, Archbishop Spottiswoode was a conspicuous absentee. He had insisted that he would march in the procession only beside his fellow primate of Canterbury; Charles conceded this point, but then ordered him to wear an English surplice. He refused, and did not march at all. "This carriage of his is much commended here, and I doubt not but will endear him to his country," commented Gilbert Primrose in a letter to his father, James, the clerk of the privy council, who had remained in Edinburgh.[21] But it must have grieved Spottiswoode to be unable to pay a last tribute to the old king, whom he had greatly admired and with whom he had collaborated so closely for over twenty years. Charles's order was an indication that he was not going to reverse his father's policy of assimilation of the Scottish church to that of England—that, if anything, he would intensify it. It also became apparent that Charles was not going to abandon the revocation. One of Gilbert Primrose's tasks in London was to draw up a draft under Melrose's supervision.[22] The substantive clauses of this document, which applied only to the Principality of Scotland, were straightforward enough, but the preamble asserted that the king had the power to revoke grants made during his minority, "or by our predecessors in their times," which were prejudicial to the kingdom.[23] Whether this was a rhetorical flourish or a portent of further action was not at all clear, and it contributed to the sense of uncertainty and unease.

The sense of unease was further heightened by Charles's comments on and responses to a proposal from the magistrates of Edinburgh on the question of the organization of the town's churches. This issue had arisen after a pre-communion meeting in 1624, when a group of dissidents publicly accused one of the ministers of softness on Popery and urged that communion be celebrated in the old manner, which had been outlawed by the five articles of Perth. James was very angry; the consequence was a long negotiation between the town magistrates and the government, which the magistrates' proposal was designed to settle. In his response to this proposal, Charles's tone was peremptory. He insisted that each minister should have a house and a salary of 2,000 merks, brushing aside the town's argument that it could afford no more than 1,200; he ordered the town to pay the larger amount by 1626. The Edinburgh practice of holding a meeting to try and censure the conduct of the town's clergy on the Tuesday before communion Sunday horrified Charles, who called it an Anabaptistical frenzy. "What a Reformation that was, and how evil advised!" he commented.[24] He followed these remarks with a chilly letter ordering the town to elect only religious conformists as magistrates. Archbishop Spottiswoode undertook to mediate between the parties, and in September 1625 an agreement was reached which incorporated the town's figure of 1,200 merks as the ministerial stipend.[25] Then, in June 1626, Charles unexpectedly began to insist that the town pay the ministers £100 sterling (1,800 merks) as, he said, it had agreed to do. In Charles's behalf it should be pointed out that Edinburgh's habit of paying the ministers a 300-merk bonus each year indicated that the town could afford more in salary money, and gave the town government a grip on its clergy which the king wished to end. The town government continued to drag its feet; the issue became entangled with some of those involved in the revocation, and for some years the matter slept, with Edinburgh paying 1,200 merks.[26]

The general uncertainty as to the king's intentions had not been dispelled when the convention of estates met on October 27, 1625. Charles's letter ordering the meeting had given no indication of his purposes,[27] though it was generally expected that he would ask for money. This was indeed the first order of business. Charles requested a tax to pay his father's debts, the expenses of his coronation, which, he said, would take place next year, and the costs resulting from the current "estate of the affairs of Christendom"—i.e., the war. The estates promptly voted the same tax which had been adopted in 1621, including the extraordinary 5 percent levy on annualrents, and the council immediately wrote Charles a fawning letter informing him of that fact.[28] Both the swiftness of the estates' action and the letter were unfortunate. There had been no bargaining of the sort Charles had just had to put up with in England; the estates had not even waited to discover what else Charles wanted before voting this very large tax. The letter was the kind which the council had become accustomed to writing King James during the chancellorship of Dunfermline, who was a master of the adulatory phraseology best calculated to please the late king. But James, fond though he was of hearing his praises sung, never lost touch with the realities of Scottish political life. Since Charles was ignorant of those realities, the vote and the letter, taken together, led him to assume that in Scotland all he had to do was to issue orders, issue them firmly, and obedience would follow.

Charles might have learned the erroneousness of this opinion from the way the estates treated the rest of his program. They instantly rejected his proposal to forego the tax, except for the amount needed to pay for his coronation, in return for paying for the maintenance for three years of 2,000 men, with the shipping necessary to transport them; the country, they said, was much too poor to afford that. The controversial items on a long list of royal proposals, most of which had to do with economic issues and the way in which the court of session conducted its business, were referred to the appropriate bodies for action or advice, save two, which were rejected. The geography of Edinburgh militated against the judges' coming to court on horseback, they explained—James would not have needed to be told that—and the proposed duty on coal exported in foreign ships would ruin the trade: foreign buyers would go elsewhere. The estates did not say so, but the implication was that this proposal was designed to benefit English coal owners. The estates also took a number of actions on their own initiative, three of which, adopted at the request of the lairds, were apt to anger Charles. They accused Scotstarvet of extortion and publicly ordered him to adhere to the approved schedule of fees for the work of his office. The lairds bitterly complained of the precedence the king had granted to the Nova Scotia baronets. Alexander was well aware of the sensitivity of this issue.[29] He explained that the precedence was necessary to induce people to contribute to the plantation by taking up the rank; the estates rejoined that "if it were found meet by his Majesty and the Estates," they would undertake the costs of the plantation themselves. And, finally, the estates addressed themselves to the rumor that Charles was planning some alteration in the court of session, whose meeting had been repeatedly postponed on Charles's orders. Since the court had been established by act of parliament, the estates asked Charles to proceed in the same way if he proposed to make any changes.[30]

More was to come. On November 3, the day after the estates adjourned, the council received the king's commission for the new council and promptly decided to return it to him with a request for three changes. The quorum, which called for eight members plus the officers of state, was too large; it should be cut to five. The councillors did not want immunity from legal action for nonpayment of debt; this would set a bad example, and anyhow it would be harder for them to raise loans if their potential creditors had no redress at law. Finally, the king had named Melrose president of the council, with precedence over everyone save the chancellor, the two archbishops, and the treasurer. Melrose did not want this job: the nobility would be jealous of him, and the king's business would suffer as a result. He could do better from his accustomed place at the council table.[31]

Two weeks later, on November 17, while Charles was still

digesting all this, the council wrote again, a letter very different in tone from that of three weeks earlier reporting the vote on the tax. The chancellor had produced a series of documents to which the great seal was to be attached, among them, apparently, a statement authorizing a new act of revocation, perhaps summarizing it, but providing no text. On October 12 the revocation had apparently passed the privy seal in just this way.[32] Hay and his colleagues protested. No one knew exactly what was in the document, and there was universal fear that "all . . . former securities granted by your Majesty and your royal progenitors were thereby intended to be annulled, and that no right hereafter to be made in the majority of kings could be valid." They hinted very strongly that they believed the revocation to be illegal, except as it applied to the Principality. All but one of the other documents "involved the establishing of new judicatories and introducing of novelties without any seen necessity," and were illegal in their opinion. In this connection they asked the king to designate one or two of the councillors who had served under James to come to London to confer with him in order to provide a fuller explanation. And finally they protested against Charles's designation of Alexander Strauchan, laird of Thornton, one of the first Nova Scotia baronets, as a member of the council and of the various commissions which Charles was planning to continue or create. This was indeed a bizarre appointment, given Thornton's reputation. He had seduced the second wife of the fifth earl Marischal, persuaded her to live with him, and with the aid of her son by Marischal had looted Dunnottar Castle of its tapestries, furnishings, and valuables during the earl's absence. So thorough were they that when the old man returned he had to borrow a bed—"an old clouted" one—to sleep in.[33] After her husband's death, Thornton married the lady, and was sued by the sixth earl, the son of his father's first marriage, for, among other things, having committed these acts of robbery. The suit was settled before James's death, but there had been a tremendous scandal, and the councillors felt aggrieved at having to associate with such a character, whose "sincerity in religion," they said, was also in doubt.[34]

That the councillors should write such a letter, in the face of the recent warning to Lord Erskine, Mar's eldest son, that "when he [Charles] has once resolved to follow any course, there is no means to draw him from it, or alter the least jot of his resolution,"[35] indicates the depth of their anger and concern. The comprehensive nature of Charles's plans was now apparent. Though they had not seen the revocation, their information as to its contents was accurate enough. The king's plan was to revoke all grants made since 1540 of land which had belonged to either the crown or the kirk, whether or not the grant had been made during a royal minority. The amount of property involved was enormous; virtually every landowner of any consequence would be adversely affected if the king carried through his scheme. Among the most seriously threatened were the families of men like Melrose, the loyal servants of the crown upon whom James had depended to run his government and whom he had rewarded with pieces of the church property annexed to the crown in 1587. These were people whose support Charles could ill afford to lose.

The scope of Charles's action was completely unexpected. Given his father's well-publicized aversion to what he had called, in *Basilikon Doron*, "that vile Act of Annexation" of the temporalities of benefices to the crown—subsequently repealed—there had been some anticipation that the crown might attempt to recover their property for the bishops. "Few noble men in Scotland can free themselves from robbing the church in some degree," wrote Sir Robert Gordon of Gordonstoun in 1620. He advised his nephew the earl of Sutherland to forestall future difficulty, if he could, by exchanging his feus of the temporalities of the bishopric of Caithness, acquired by his great-grandfather from his then brother-in-law the bishop between 1557 and 1560, for land not previously in the possession of the church.[36] But Charles's act went far beyond the temporalities of sees. The landholding classes became panicky and mistrustful, and their mood was not improved by Charles's order of October 22 that all recipients of pensions appear before the council to disclose the cause and the amount of the grant. This kind of order usually foreshadowed a winnowing of the list.[37]

The king's other changes, though nowhere near as widely resented, were also unpalatable to those whom they affected. There was to be a complete separation between the council and the court of session; furthermore, no nobleman was to sit on the court any more.[38] There was to be a commission of grievances, with wider authority and greater power than that created by James in 1623, which had dealt almost exclusively with economic issues. The new commission's principal functions were to hear complaints of official misconduct and to investigate people who spoke or wrote against the government. This commission was particularly alarming to the burghs because it could summon people accused of usury and of exporting bullion. Sir James Balfour described it as "nothing else but the star chamber court of England under another name, come down here to play the tyrant, with a specious visor on its face."[39] There was to be an exchequer commission with the power to do exchequer and treasury business; Mar and the treasurer depute, Sir Archibald Napier of Merchiston, could not act without the consent of the commission, but the commission could act without them.[40] Mar, who evidently had not known of this until Hay produced the commission in council on November 17, vehemently protested to the king. He had warned Charles that his enemies would try to blacken his reputation, he wrote, and evidently they had succeeded. This commission would destroy his credit, "and yet never put a penny in your purse." This was no way to treat an honest old servant: he hoped the king would reconsider. Mar's sense of grievance was the more acute because Kellie had just written to him that Charles had promised to give him a hearing before giving credence to any unfriendly reports—and now this! Mar was right in thinking that his enemies were at work. He and his deputy, Napier, were not very friendly; when James died Mar's enemies wrote Napier asking for information to use against him. Napier, according to his own account, rejected this as dishonorable, but, he says, "I was evil requited," because Mar never learned of his noble conduct![41]

The attitude of the Scottish leadership did not sit well with Charles. At first he expressed surprise that some proposals which he thought would be popular evidently were not. He complained to Kellie that during their visit to London none of his officials had reminded him to make a revocation, which had to be issued before he turned twenty-five in November; Kellie professed ignorance.[42] Charles's surprise soon gave way to anger, however. He was convinced that the councillors were deliberately fanning popular fears concerning the revocation,[43] and he ordered their leaders to come to London to explain themselves. "The humor of our leading men continueth to oppose the king's directions," wrote Nithsdale to Annandale, now his political ally, but also one of the signers of the letter of protest of November 17. "Let them answer, when they come here, for it."[44]

In the king's eyes the chief culprit was Melrose. His refusal of the presidency of the council was insulting. He was the most active of the triumvirate—Mar and Hay suffered from periods of bad health—his was the legal brain, and he was behind all the protests, which dwelt on the legal issues raised by Charles's actions. He stood to lose the most if the king's plans went through; he was president of the court of session, where two of his brothers also sat, and his landed wealth and his very title derived from church property. He had inspired the demand that changes in the session be made in parliament and the protest over the Nova Scotia baronetcies; he could also be expected to challenge the legality of the revocation, since it was absolutely unprecedented to attempt to nullify the actions of sovereigns of full age. Equally unprecedented was Charles's proposal to remove judges from the court of session; they had their appointments for life—*ad vitam aut culpam*—and all the precedents of James's reign indicated that a king could not remove a judge merely because he wished to.[45] Charles believed, however, that if he was to accomplish anything at all via his revocation, he had to break the grip of the great landowners on the court of session, where, so he had been told, the key legal issues would be decided.[46] They not only had to be excluded from the court themselves, but their influence over it also had to be attenuated to as great a degree as possible. Hence the decision that in future neither noblemen nor privy councillors should be members of the court.

The exclusion of the councillors from the session was thus the key to the implementation of Charles's policy. Charles knew that he could not simply sweep all of his father's old servants out of their offices and the aristocracy from the council board. The experience of James's reign had shown that the council's power, cohensiveness, and independent-mindedness grew in proportion to the number of judges sitting there. These men were lawyers, members of a tightly knit society on its way to becoming a sort of *noblesse de robe,* made up of the sons of lairds, burgesses, and other lawyers, whose families intermarried a good deal. "No sooner had the legal profession as a lay profession been established," writes Gordon Donaldson, "than kinship, almost heredity, prevailed in it as it did in most walks of life in Scotland."[47] Johnston of Wariston's family provides a good example. His father was an Edinburgh merchant, his mother the daughter of the great feudalist Sir Thomas Craig. Two of his aunts and a sister were married to members of the court of session and an uncle married the sister of a fourth member. Both of Johnston's wives were lawyers' daughters; the second wife was the daughter of still another judge of session.

This closely connected profession was likely to follow the lead of the country's principal lawyer, Lord Chancellor Dunfermline, and then, after his death, Melrose, who had been president of the court of session since 1616. It was no accident that at the end of Dunfermline's tenure of power every member of the court of session was also a privy councillor. Nor was it accidental that Dunfermline's predecessor as James's *éminence grise,* Lord Treasurer Dunbar, who operated from Whitehall and therefore had an interest in a subservient council, consolidated his power by a reorganization which eliminated a large number of judges from its membership. A weak and docile council was what Charles wanted, one which would be impotent to resist his plans. He did not want the sort which would habitually write him the kind of letter it had recently sent, indicating unwillingness to approve a royal warrant on the ground that the special privilege it granted would set a bad precedent and cost the treasury £30,000, and implying that Charles was ignorant of the financial consequences of his action.[48] Elimination of the vast majority of the lawyers from the council, thus isolating Melrose and depriving him and other political malcontents of the weight of legal support for their arguments and objections, would promote weakness and docility there. Removing noblemen and councillors from the court of session and establishing the principle that judges were removable at the king's will would create docility on that body as well. A place on the court of session was very desirable since, among other things, it carried tax exemption with it; a lawyer who had reached the top of his profession would think very carefully about risking his seat on the bench by voting against the king. So court and council were to be separated, and the power of Melrose, the most important link between the two, was to be broken.

The meetings between the king and the Scottish leaders began on January 7, 1626, and lasted for a fortnight. They were acrimonious and unproductive. The military and diplomatic situation made the timing unfortunate. In December 1625 word had come of the disaster the English had suffered at Cadiz; in addition, Charles was now embroiled in a dispute with his French brother-in-law over the latter's treatment of his Protestant subjects. Charles's frame of mind, under the circumstances, could not have been of the best. The foreign situation affected the Scots as well. The country suffered from invasion jitters and was hopelessly unprepared, desperately short of gunpowder, and "not a craftsman to make a steel bonnet in all the land."[49] Melrose and his colleagues made very little impression on Charles, who seemed simply not to hear anything he did not want to hear; the old men returned home defeated and resentful—"in dudgeon," wrote the Venetian ambassador.[50] Only Archbishop Spottiswoode emerged with an improved position. He had not been present at the meeting of the council which had offended Charles; he had always been a strong supporter of the royal prerogative, and he now took advantage of various opportunities to endorse Charles's views. The king was obviously pleased.[51]

Discord began almost at once. Charles thanked his councillors for the prompt vote on the tax, but then charged that the rest of his program had failed, not on its merits, but because its spokesmen, Nithsdale and Annandale, were unpopular. Hay "in great choler" rejoined that the cost of supporting 2,000 men, on the basis of figures he had collected from sea captains, was so great that the estates would not hear of sending the matter to committee to work out some sort of compromise, as the king had thought could be done. Spottiswoode disputed Hay's memory of the sequence of events, claiming "in some little passion" that the leadership had decided not to send the proposal to committee before, not after, they put it to the estates, and a wrangle between the two ensued.[52] So the sessions went, with the triumvirate justifying its actions and engaging in sharp exchanges with the king's supporters—Spottiswoode, Nithsdale, Scotstarvet, and the bishop of Ross—and with most of the participants, including the king, making frequent displays of touchiness and vanity.

Charles proved to be very ill informed on the revocation. His position was that he had done nothing more than his father and grandmother had done, save for one clause he could not remember; he expressed astonishment that there should be such a fuss. Had he known more about past revocations, he would have been less surprised. That of James V had caused a good deal of trouble, partly because of the opportunities for extortion it offered to an increasingly covetous king, partly because the vagueness of its language—it revoked anything done as a result of "evil and false suggestion"—made large numbers of landholders tremble for the security of their possessions. Mary had issued a revocation in 1555, when she was in her thirteenth year, at the time of the transfer of the regency to her mother from the duke of Châtelherault, directed chiefly at the latter's grants as regent. Some historians have argued that the fact that the queen's twenty-fifth birthday was approaching and that she might be contemplating issuing another revocation was a factor in her overthrow in 1567. James VI's revocation, issued in 1587, covered a lot of ground but was drawn with considerable precision and caused no anxiety. Everyone understood that it could not be implemented, and it was ratified in the same parliament which annexed church lands to the crown, an action from which the landholding classes expected to profit.[53] Charles's revocation was a very different matter, and much more frightening. He had far more power to implement his revocation than his predecessors had had, and his document was of a very different sort. As Mar pointed out, since Charles became king at age twenty-four, he had done nothing as king which he could properly revoke. The text of Charles's revocation was at last produced and compared with his father's; the point which Hay and Mar emphasized repeatedly was that Charles was attempting to revoke acts of his predecessors made in their full age. If this act was ratified by parliament, no one could be sure of his property, now or in future: Charles's successors could revoke his acts. At the meeting at which the texts were compared—the only session from which the king was absent, although Buckingham was there—the only speech in favor of the revocation came, Mar wrote, from "that worthy judicious lawyer the bishop of Ross, who babbled all the time so far without sense or reason, as every indifferent man who heard him might easily perceive that his judgment was far short of that which the gravity of his beard did promise."[54] Hay, in summing up, boldly told the king that those who had advised him to issue the revocation had "made shipwreck of their own estates, and would now fish in drumlie waters by shaking all things loose that they may get some part to themselves; some of them having no wit at all, some of them but half witted, and neither of them (of) great honesty,"[55] a shaft aimed chiefly at Nithsdale and Scotstarvet.

The second great matter, having to do with the court of session, was left to Melrose, who, to avoid any charge of special pleading, indicated in advance that he was personally prepared to resign from the court as the king wished. The king's reasoning was that all offices vacated with the demise of the crown, and that he could therefore appoint whom he liked to the court. He also claimed that since the council was superior to the session, and no one disputed his right to appoint and dismiss councillors, his right to appoint and dismiss judges should be equally obvious. This case was argued by Scotstarvet, who by his own account had had his arguments endorsed ahead of time by Sir James Skene, a member of the court and Charles's choice to succeed Melrose as president. Skene was a man with no love for Melrose: in 1612 Melrose, then lord advocate, had prevented Skene from succeeding his father as clerk register and had briefly occupied the office himself. The argument of Skene and Scotstarvet was that when the court was founded, nothing was said about lifetime tenures, and that only two of the commissions issued before 1581 contained such a clause. Melrose's reply was based on precedent: there were no wholesale renewals when the crown changed hands in 1542 and 1567, and previous deprivations of individuals could be regarded as *ad culpam*. There was no clear-cut winner in this dispute. Scotstarvet in his account naturally gave himself the better of the argument. He also candidly admitted that personal animus against the current judges, especially Melrose, fueled his zeal—Scotstarvet disliked practically everybody, and made no bones about it. Mar, equally naturally, regarded Scotstarvet's reasoning as "feckless and to no purpose."[56]

Other matters took less time but were no less controverted. Charles was irritated that the council had sent the commission for the new council back instead of accepting it and asking for revisions. Mar and Melrose rejoined that it could not be accepted because the clause granting the councillors immunity directly contravened an act of parliament. The king's spokesmen could not make good on their claims that both council and session had ignored the statute in the past. The king's animus toward Melrose surfaced during this discussion, and also in his references to Melrose's refusal of the presidency of the council, an office which, Charles made it clear, he intended to fill. The king's annoyance here spilled over onto the earl of Morton, who reportedly had said that creating the office would mean one more vote for the king in parliament; Morton's denials were not very convincing. The egregious Thornton attempted to recover something of his lost reputation by accusing the lord chancellor of taking bribes. The alleged briber promptly denied this, and Hay struck back by accusing Thornton of arranging a bigamous marriage for his sister. Thornton's attempt to accuse Mar of oppressing him also backfired when Mar revealed the whole sordid story of his robbery of Marischal. Hay charged that the commission for grievances was in certain respects illegal; Mar declared that the treasury commission was not only illegal but also a personal slur on him: "I cannot but sorrow that in my old age that mark of distrust should be put upon me."[57] Nithsdale attacked Mar's handling of his office; Mar replied by accusing Nithsdale of oppression and corruption as a border commissioner. There ensued a slanging match, which Buckingham did his best to quiet down.

The last of the meetings took place on January 22, 1626. It dealt mostly with the court of session, and ended on a note of compromise sounded by Spottiswoode. There were seven judges whom the king wanted to replace: five officials, including Melrose, and two nobles, Lords Lauderdale and Carnegy, both of whom had claimed that they were entitled to remain on the bench. Hay had argued for the retention of Lauderdale and Carnegy on the basis of merit, and, indeed, their merit was not in dispute. Spottiswoode suggested that they be offered places as extraordinary lords. Charles, who had previously indicated that he wanted no aristocrats as extraordinary lords either,[58] agreed to this. But it quickly appeared that he was not willing to compromise on much of anything else. His interviews with Mar in February 1626 show how little his mind had changed; he repeated many of the allegations his councillors had been at pains to refute.[59] On January 26, 1626, a spate of letters, proclamations, and instructions went northward. A minatory letter went to the officers of state who were members of the court of session: resign from the latter or lose both jobs. The letter to Lauderdale and Carnegy was less harsh but no less firm: Charles asked for their resignations, not because they were aristocrats, but because he preferred to employ their talents on the council. In this letter Charles admitted that his vacancy theory was open to question, and in the end it was never put to the test, though Charles ordered it recorded in the session's books of *sederunt*. All the justices resigned, and the eight whom Charles wished to retain were readmitted. Oddly enough, their letters of renewal and the commissions of the new appointees made no mention of the question of tenure at all, and Charles never reopened it by again dismissing a Scottish judge.[60] As time went on, the lines of demarcation Charles had drawn became somewhat blurred. As has been said, he had agreed that councillors and aristocrats could serve as extraordinary lords. In 1628 the lord advocate, Sir Thomas Hope, proved to Charles's satisfaction that he had a traditional *ex officio* right to sit with the court; in 1634 the clerk register, Sir John Hay of Barro, became an ordinary lord. But these were exceptions rather than the rule. The situation that existed in Dunfermline's day was not repeated.

With respect to the revocation Charles attempted to allay his subjects' fears, which, he was now persuaded, were genuine, if misguided. He ordered the council to proclaim that his action was taken out of zeal for his subjects' welfare, to reduce the burden of taxation upon them by recovering property rightfully belonging to the crown. He also wanted, he said, to "free the gentry . . . from all those bonds which may force them to depend upon any other than upon his Majesty" by ending the feudal superiorities of the lords of erection, that is, of those laymen for whom King James had created—"erected"—a secular lordship out of what had once been church property; such a superiority was eventually defined as a position to which the titular of erection had no lawful property right. A superiority comprised the rights which the feudal lord, either the crown or a subject superior, enjoyed in the land held by his vassals. It was not a right to the use of the land, most of which, in the lordships of erection, was held in feu; it was, rather, a civil right to receive feu duties, and to feudal casualties. The feuar was liable for the public burdens of the feu, taxation and teind among others. Feuars who held their lands of subject superiors, such as the lords of erection, were not eligible to vote or sit in parliament. Those landholders who would now become the king's vassals were those who had received their infeftments from a beneficed man before the annexation of church property to the crown in 1587, a group which comprised the large majority of feuars, and those who had been enfeoffed by a lord of erection as lord of erection. Not only would they now depend directly on the king, they would also, by virtue of that fact, become more directly involved in public life by becoming eligible to vote for members of parliament, and to sit there themselves. The revocation had still another purpose: to benefit the church by providing each minister with an adequate stipend, and to put an end to the confusion and oppression to which the current condition of the teinds gave rise by "procuring . . . that every man may have his own teinds upon reasonable conditions."[61]

The problem of the teinds was one of staggering difficulty owing to the many complex and overlapping interests involved. First there were those who owed payment, either in money or kind, from a particular piece of ground: the landholder, either proprietor (heritor) or liferenter, and—if he leased out his land rather than working it himself—his tenant. The tenant's obligation might or might not be included in his rent. Then there were those to whom the payment was owed. In the vast majority of cases this was not the parish minister, for whose benefit the system had originally been created. It was probably a layman, either the titular, the person who had legal title to the teinds of a particular parish, or the tacksman, the person to whom the titular had either leased or, in some cases, feued his rights. In most cases, however, the titular or tacksman was legally obligated to pay a fixed stipend to the parish minister; this sum was usually a small fraction of the total revenue. A landholder might, of course, be either titular or tacksman of the teinds of his own lands, but most were not; the right to collect teinds on a piece of land had thus become a form of property right in the land which was separate from ownership or possession. The result was endless dispute, litigation, disorder, and, often enough, when collection time came, violence. Previous attempts at reform, some of which antedated the establishment of Protestantism, had all foundered in the face of the formidable difficulties involved in any kind of comprehensive change. Charles now proposed to tackle the problem by means of a general settlement which would eliminate the titulars and tacksmen, allow each landholder to collect his own teind, and at the same time arrange for increased payments out of the teinds to the parish clergy on the part of those landholders. This, said Charles, had been his father's intention. This assertion, however, was not altogether accurate. King James had had no objection to laymen, especially his favorites, holding tacks of teinds, as long as the minister's stipend was paid: for example, in 1622 Annandale got a tack of the teinds of the parish of St. Mungo, on condition that he pay the minister a 600-merk grassum and a stipend of £300 a year, as well as all taxes and the cost of maintaining the parish church.[62] In arranging increases in ministerial stipends, moreover, James had proceeded in a cautious, parish-by-parish fashion, not by a sweeping decree, and he had had considerable success.[63]

Charles declared that he had no intention of wronging anybody. He issued the sort of revocation he did because, not having had a minority in which the crown's patrimony could suffer damage, he felt obligated "for keeping of his royal prerogative to revoke what his predecessors had done to the hurt of the same."[64] But just what he intended to do, and how, was not disclosed. Though the earl of Winton, who was presiding over the council in the absence of the triumvirate, assured Charles that the proclamation was heard "to the exceeding great comfort of your Majesty's subjects," the disquiet, not surprisingly, did not diminish.[65] So in July 1626 Charles at last became specific. The revocation, he said, applied to all lordships of erection and to church property which had been annexed to the crown, other land or patronage which justly belonged to church or crown, the disposition of property mortified to pious uses, regalities, heritable offices, and property held of the crown which since 1540 had been changed from tenure by ward and relief, the old feudal tenure, to blench and taxt ward,[66] changes which were financially costly to the crown. The king's desire to make this last change might have been anticipated: in May 1625 he had refused to approve a tenurial change from ward and relief to blench which King James had apparently authorized but which had not passed the seals. Charles named a commission to work out appropriate compensation for those who surrendered their rights by January 1, 1627, and he promised to make a specific declaration as to the patrimony of the crown at the next parliament. Any revocation issued by his successors could apply only to that patrimony; all other property would be secure.[67]

This statement was helpful in some ways. Though the amount of property encompassed in it was vast and the commission's powers limited, the principle of compensation had been conceded, and the promised act of parliament would allay the fears for the future which Mar and others had so strongly emphasized. But almost everyone concerned found the statement disquieting in some way. The magnates would lose both income and power if feudal superiorities, regalities and heritable offices were eliminated, and with respect to the latter, at least, Charles's legal power to end them would be difficult to challenge.[68] The reformed church from the very beginning of its existence had laid claim to the whole of the teinds as its rightful possession; on this point there was no disagreement between bishop and presbyter. It was now apparent that Charles did not intend that this should happen, that bargains were to be struck with the current possessors of the right to collect teinds, whoever they might be, which would leave a considerable proportion thereof in lay hands. Where, as was normally the case, teind was paid in kind, titulars and tacksmen and, indeed, everyone who had the right to collect teinds would be especially hard hit by the loss of any part of the income from this source, since income in kind was such an excellent hedge against inflation. Even the heritors, for whose benefit Charles said he was acting, were dubious. The vassals of the lords of erection preferred to hold directly of the crown, as their actions during their brief period of comparative power in the late 1640s was to show. But many lairds were feuars, not only of the temporalities of bishoprics and monastic foundations, but also of kirk and chapel lands; Charles's apparent intention to improve clerical incomes and increase his own revenues out of the teinds was clearly going to cost them something, however much they might benefit from their new freedom from what Charles described as aristocratic oppression. Even many humble former tenants on ecclesiastical property who had feued their small holdings might have their titles called in question.[69]

A month after the issue of his explanatory statement Charles reverted to authoritarian tactics. He had asked the lord advocates to provide him with a plan for implementing his intentions; apparently without waiting for a reply he ordered the preparation of a summons of reduction (i.e., nullification) against all holders of church property, regalities, and hereditary offices. The holders of such property thus faced a nasty dilemma: they could either make a voluntary surrender by January and get compensation, or take their chances in court—either the council or Charles's newly constituted court of session—with the prospect of no compensation if they lost. The teind holders among them became the subject of sermons charging them with avarice.[70] There was, inevitably, considerable protest, fueled still further by Charles's order that the revocation be entered in the session's books of *sederunt,* thus giving it the strength of a judicial decree, and by his granting exemptions from the summons of reduction to those currently in favor at court.[71] There were calls for a parliament, especially from Melrose, and an aristocratic deputation made its way to London at the end of 1626 to express its fears, not only for the aristocrats themselves, but also for all those "who have at dear rates purchased from us and our predecessors large portions of lands and teinds . . . (who) may by the event of this action be in equal danger with us of irreparable ruin." Charles raged at this "as of too high a strain for subjects and petitioners," and threatened not to receive the deputation.[72] Clearly matters were approaching a crisis.

On the other matters raised at the January meetings Charles made adjustments to meet specific objections but gave no ground as to principle. He reiterated his insistence on the precedence of the Nova Scotia baronets, and exempted them from any fees to the heralds for registration of their patents. The commission for grievances went forward, still with its broadly defined powers independent of those of the council, including the authority to appoint agents in each shire. The commission did provide, however, that the same person could not act both as informer and as a supposedly independent witness, which, as Hay had pointed out, the provision for anonymous informing in the first draft would have made possible. The exchequer commission, of which Spottiswoode was president, also had wide powers, in the sense that the lord treasurer and his deputy could do nothing of any importance without its approval. The commission could not act without one or the other of them being present, however; the king thus met the most vehement of Mar's objections. The new council, weakened by the creation of these commissions and shorn of the members of the court of session, was constituted on March 23, 1626. Archbishop Spottiswoode's name led all the rest, even the chancellor's, and there was a lord president in the person of the earl of Montrose.[73] The quorum was not changed from that stipulated in the rejected commission of November 1625. It was unreasonably large and caused repeated difficulties in the ensuing years, as predicted, and so Charles gradually and reluctantly whittled it down.

The council's powers suffered further attenuation in July 1626, when Charles created a council of war to manage the feeble and underfinanced Scottish war effort.[74] Montrose presided over this council; the triumvirate was excluded. The key members were Nithsdale, Marischal, Treasurer Depute Napier, and the absentee Alexander. It was not very effective, save in the matter of raising regiments to follow various aristocratic captains overseas, and even here it had great trouble finding the money to keep the recruits from deserting. Once the invasion scare had passed, it was impossible to persuade anyone to make the financial sacrifices which Charles, remembering the alacrity of the vote on the tax, optimistically expected of his subjects.[75] The citizens of the royal burghs were the element in Scottish society most immediately affected by the war, since their trade suffered, and by the king's plans to raise money to fight it. The tax voted in 1625 was supposed to be spread over a four-year span, but Charles applied pressure to have the burghs pay their share all at once. Some, like Edinburgh and Glasgow, agreed; others, like Aberdeen, pleaded poverty and declined.[76] The burghs rejected Charles's request to provide warships for defense; there were no ships or seamen available, they said, and even if there were, the cost, which they estimated would come to £2,500 a month for a 300-ton ship with 100 men and 28 pieces of ordnance, would be prohibitive. They suggested that since defense was everybody's business, everybody ought to pay for it, an argument which the king was later to use in England in connection with ship money. The burghs went on to reveal their distaste for the war by urging the king "to make the seas peaceable, that trade and navigation may flourish."[77] Since the treasury also had no money to pay for warships, the king had to borrow on the anticipated tax revenues to provide three ships for coastal defense, and by the end of the year he was talking of stopping payment on pensions in order to bring in £60,000 a year.[78] By that time war with France as well as with Spain was in the offing, a much more serious matter for Scottish trade, and bound to be very unpopular and add still further to the difficulties of Charles's government.

As with measures, so with men: the January meetings did not cause Charles to lose confidence in those he had chosen as his advisers. He did refrain from appointing the offensive Thornton to the council, but Thornton was named to both the exchequer and grievance commissions. Charles appointed the almost equally offensive Nithsdale to be collector of the recently voted taxation. The king continued to find Scotstarvet's schemes plausible, and the council had continually to intervene in defense of the king's subjects, whom Scotstarvet was attempting to gouge on a really massive scale, allegedly charging fifty or sixty pounds for what used to cost two.[79] Archbishop Spottiswoode continued to enjoy an increasing measure of the king's favor, in spite of his and his episcopal colleagues' doubts as to the effect on the church of the king's revocation; furthermore, the king's insistence on the archbishop's precedence over the lord chancellor, the highest official in the kingdom, was disturbing to an aristocracy whose hostility to the involvement of clerics in politics had by no means abated. It seems likely that it was on Spottiswoode's advice that Charles took a moderate line respecting enforcement of the five articles of Perth and was lenient with some of those who were in legal difficulty for opposing them.[80] The archbishop carefully separated himself from the triumvirate, and made a confidant of the Catholic Nithsdale. "All things are loose here," Spottiswoode wrote in March 1626, "and the combination holds firm, which your lordship saw at court, which his Majesty's service will hardly endure."[81]

King Charles agreed. The chief target of his wrath was Melrose, who, besides losing his presidency of the session, was omitted from the commissions for the exchequer and for grievances and was forced in January 1626 to accept Sir William Alexander as joint secretary, with Alexander to be resident at court. Melrose was left with nothing of the office but an empty title; he displayed his annoyance by rebuffing Alexander's friendly overtures and treating him frigidly.[82] Mar, the ancient aristocrat, could not be handled as roughly as Melrose the *arriviste,* but he was subjected to pinpricks: his son was ousted as extraordinary lord of session; his authority as captain of Edinburgh and Stirling castles was undermined; and his expressed fears as to the impact of the revocation on his family's future were received icily by Charles. In addition to his other troubles he suffered a bad fall late in 1626 which left him permanently lame.[83] By the beginning of 1627 it was apparent that Mar would have to leave the treasury sooner or later and that his successor would be the earl of Morton. Morton was one of those people who was determined to be friendly with everybody, and was quite successful at it. He made up for his tactless comment on the presidency of the council by betrothing his son and heir to Buckingham's niece; he at once became Buckingham's candidate for the treasury.[84] Hay was less of a problem to the king because he had no real power base. Archbishop Spottiswoode, whose ambition for the chancellorship was of long standing and far from dead, cultivated Nithsdale, fed him stories that the council was responsible for the burghs' refusal collectively to agree to pay the four years' taxation in a lump sum, and urged him, for the good of the country, to move against Hay.[85] In the fall of 1626 Nithsdale tried to do this, and utterly failed; the charges were "so frivolous and of so small consequence," the archbishop wrote disgustedly to Viscount Stormont, that Hay's position was actually strengthened.[86] But the attempt frightened Hay. Earlier in the year he had shown some independence of mind and "crushed in pieces" various of Lord President Skene's proposals, endorsed by Charles, for revising the procedures of the court of session, proposals which would have allowed Skene to meddle in various aspects of the council's business under the pretense of taking "notice of such things as may advance his Majesty's service."[87] Now, according to the Venetian ambassador, Hay allowed himself to be bought.[88] Charles raised him to the peerage as Viscount Dupplin in May 1627; from then on he did as he was bidden.

Men who did as they were bidden, and gave advice only when asked, were ideal privy councillors in Charles's view—men like Patrick Lindsay, bishop of Ross, whose long-winded speeches infuriated Mar and Melrose. Ross had said, at the last of the conferences in January 1626, "that he wondered that any subject should deny the King's prerogative, for who doth so, he was no loyal subject."[89] Charles made him a privy councillor and an extraordinary lord of session. Charles had no use for his father's servants or his father's methods, and did not like to be reminded of them; he became very weary of hearing about Mar's gray hairs. These old men, he felt, were presuming on their age and experience, talking down to the inexperienced man he was. They would not have defied his father's orders so, he said to Mar in February 1626. "Alas, sir," replied Jock o' the Slates, "a hundred times your worthy father has sent down directions unto us which we have stayed, and he has given us thanks for it when we have informed him of the truth."[90] Charles found that state of affairs most unwelcome. He meant to rule as well as reign; he, not the council, would make the decisions. The power of the council to obstruct those decisions had therefore to be eliminated, and so it was, in that the morale and prestige and cohesiveness of the council as a body, and the *ex officio* power of the officers of state as individuals, were effectively destroyed. Instead of listening to his traditional advisers, the king now took counsel with men who were either unknown in Scotland and without influence there, like Alexander, or else well enough known to be disliked, like Nithsdale, Scotstarvet, and Thornton. Wherever possible he dropped James's old Scottish servants, men like Kellie and Annandale, who continued on at court, the ghosts of a past era, without respect or influence. In March 1627 Annandale was reduced to begging Secretary Conway to get his pension for him, "that the world may not take notice that he is neglected and forgotten."[91] Of the old king's advisers, the only ones, apparently, to whom Charles was willing to pay attention were the bishops.

Charles had overturned his father's system and turned his back on his father's servants in order to achieve the results he expected from the revocation. To this end he made his one excellent appointment to office, that of Sir Thomas Hope, an eminent lawyer and a long-standing associate of Melrose and Mar, as joint lord advocate with the aged Sir William Oliphant in May 1626 and sole advocate after Oliphant's death in 1628. Hope owed his appointment not to Melrose and Mar but to Annandale, whose protégé he was; this was the one permanent result of Annandale's brief political alliance with Nithsdale.[92] Hope was a cross-grained and difficult man, but he stayed in office because his expertise in land law and especially in the matter of the teinds was indispensable if the king's intentions with respect to the revocation were to be carried out. What these intentions were has sometimes been overstated. One scholar has recently described Charles's policy as revolutionary.[93] Another, more cautiously, writes that "the king's main interest was in increasing his own powers [and] . . . to limit the powers of the nobility."[94] The latter view is nearer the truth, but suggests more conscious, long-range political calculation than was, in fact, the case. Charles certainly wanted to make a display of his power, and he had become convinced that there was much amiss in Scotland; there is no evidence, however, that his thought had proceeded any further than that. As the sequel was to show, he did not intend to revolutionize the structure of Scottish landholding, or to engage in any wholesale resumption of crown lands, an idea which, in England, was being put forward by some members of the parliamentary opposition, doubtless as a means of embarrassing Buckingham. Charles saw the revocation as a lever which would bring about changes he regarded as desirable, such as improvement in clerical stipends, some regular income for the crown, the extinction of much heritable office-holding, the end not only of the confusion and oppression to which the existing state of the teinds gave rise but also of the dependence of lesser men on the great magnates. And he did have to hurry, to act before his twenty-fifth birthday. But his subsequent failure promptly to explain his purposes—a persistent error of his—or to provide machinery to implement them, and his use of maximum pressure with the summons of reduction, perpetuated the panic which his original action had touched off. What Charles was trying to do was difficult enough, and far more than his father had attempted. His efforts to disguise the novelty of his actions in this and other matters by appeals to past precedent and to James's intentions were unconvincing. He showed no sign, now or ever, that he understood or appreciated the wisdom of his father's remark in *Basilikon Doron* that "the most part of a King's office standeth in deciding that question of *Meum* and *Tuum* among his subjects."[95] Charles, far from safeguarding his subjects' property rights, was invading them. His abrupt tactics compounded his difficulties, and created both fear and mistrust.

So unpopular was the revocation that no one ever took responsibility for recommending it to the king, and to this day the recommender's identity is not known. Kellie, who was at court, opined that it was someone with a knowledge of the law. Whoever it was, wrote Sir James Balfour, should be accounted "infamous and accursed forever."[96] One possible candidate for this dubious distinction who, to the best of this writer's knowledge, has not been suggested before, is Sir James Skene. He was a lawyer and judge, the son of a distinguished judge and legal scholar who had twice been called on in King James's day to devise schemes for improving the royal income, schemes which included resumption of royal lands.[97] Skene was acquainted with his father's work; he was known at court; he was hostile to the triumvirate; he was friendly with Scotstarvet and Nithsdale and abetted their unsuccessful efforts to undermine Lord Chancellor Hay.[98] And of course he received his reward, in the form of the presidency of the court of session. The principal objection to this hypothesis is that if Skene were his mentor, Charles would have been properly informed about the implications of the revocation—unless he misunderstood what Skene told him. All this is speculation; there is no hard evidence to support it. But Skene was the most prominent lawyer of all the Scots with access to Charles's ear in 1625.

The revocation dominated the thinking of the political classes almost to the exclusion of anything else, but it was by no means the only source of discontent. The implications of Charles's action in separating the council from the court of session for the prestige of both bodies were clear to everyone in an age when, in the words of one scholar, "most major officials were judges and most judges were administrators."[99] No one took seriously the king's claim that he was merely carrying out the intentions of the court's founders, and there was some apprehension that the quality of justice would suffer. The commission of grievances got under way with considerable fanfare; the king referred a number of matters to it, and ordered a proclamation issued urging individuals to do likewise, but there is not much evidence that they did. "All sorts of people much repined," wrote Balfour. The burghs complained because the commission was authorized to investigate violations of the statutes on usury and the export of money; at the time of the voting of the tax in 1625, they said, Hay had promised them that Charles, when he came to Scotland for his coronation, would issue them a blanket discharge for such violations. The exchequer commission, like the council, had difficulties in obtaining a quorum and was further hampered because the language of the commission implied that when the minimum number (six, out of fifteen) was present their decisions had to be unanimous. The war served no Scottish interest and continued to be most unpopular. At the end of the year a delegation of clergy went to Charles to ask for a crackdown on Papists. The discontent was general. The country, wrote Sir Robert Gordon of Lochinvar to the council on August 20, 1626, is "so much grieved, what with revocations and yearly taxations, and now with penal statutes, that your Lordships can hardly believe how the people doth grudge."[100] Lochinvar was a new-made Nova Scotia baronet, and so not likely to exaggerate out of distaste for the regime.

By the end of 1626, then, the net result of Charles's activity was that he had seriously jeopardized his chances of ruling Scotland successfully. It was painfully apparent that he had little knowledge of his ancestral kingdom and no desire to learn about it. Treasurer Depute Napier offered to create and manage a network of correspondents to supply him with the information he needed, in return for a lucrative post at court, but Charles showed no interest.[101] The people who counted were unhappy with his policies, and he had deliberately destroyed the power of the council to govern effectively. Since the absentee kingship began in 1603, the council had been politically impotent once before, during the hegemony of the earl of Dunbar from 1606 to 1611. What Charles needed was a Dunbar of his own: a man who knew the ins and outs of Scottish politics, was politically acceptable to the people who counted, forceful enough to implement the king's policy successfully, and willing to undertake the labor necessary to achieve that success by traveling back and forth between Edinburgh and Whitehall. A measure of Charles's political ineptitude is that he destroyed his father's system of government before he had found his Dunbar. It was pure folly to rely on the egregiously incompetent Nithsdale, whom he repeatedly had to protect both from his creditors and from the penalties for recusancy, and the deracinated Alexander, who had been at court since at least 1608 and whose annual summer visits to Scotland had something of the character of a vacation.[102] But Charles was lucky. In December 1626 he found a potential Dunbar, and the one relatively tranquil period of his reign in Scotland was about to begin.

NOTES

1. G. M. Paul, ed., *Diary of Sir Archibald Johnston of Wariston 1632–1639,* SHS (Edinburgh, 1911), p. 265.

2. On this point see M. Lee, Jr., "James VI and the Revival of Episcopacy in Scotland, 1596–1600," *Church History* XLIII (1974), 50–64.

3. See the analysis of the origins of the clergy of the 1640s in W. Makey, *The Church of the Covenant 1637–1651* (Edinburgh, 1979), chap. 7. See also J. diFolco, "Discipline and Welfare in the Mid-Seventeenth Century Scots Parish," *RSCHS* XIX (1977), p. 181.

4. For example, residents of burghs of regality and barony, who were not liable for the burghs' share of national taxation (paid only by royal burghs and a few other communities, such as Glasgow, which were not royal burghs but were included on the tax roll because of their importance), had to pay the tax on annualrents.

5. Quoted by Mary Coate in C. V. Wedgwood *et al., King Charles I,* Historical Assn. pamphlet G 11 (London, 1949), p. 15.

6. Gilbert Burnet, *Bishop Burnet's History of His Own Time,* ed. M. J. Routh, 2nd ed. (Oxford, 1833), I, 34.

7. D. Mathew, *Scotland under Charles I* (London, 1955), p. 137.

8. Sir William Fraser, *The Sutherland Book* (Edinburgh, 1892), II, 357. J. Spalding, *Memorialls of the Trubles in Scotland and in England, A.D. 1624–A.D. 1645,* ed. J. Stuart, Spalding Club (Aberdeen, 1850–51), I, 79–80.

9. R. Mitchison, "The Making of the Old Scottish Poor Law," *Past and Present* 63 (1974), 65.

10. *RPCS* 2nd ser. I, 160–62. Italics mine.

11. *M&K Supp.,* pp. 200–201, 226–27.

12. *Balfour* II, 147.

13. Mar. 17, 1625, Charles to the council, *RPCS* XIII, 720–21. T. H. McGrail, *Sir William Alexander* (Edinburgh, 1940), p. 48.

14. *RPCS* XIII, 558–63, 716–18. *M&K Supp.,* p. 218.

15. Apr. 14, 1625, Rothes to Sir Robert Kerr, *A&L* I, 35–38. For the articles see I. B. Cowan, "The Five Articles of Perth," in D. Shaw,

ed., *Reformation and Revolution* (Edinburgh, 1967), pp. 160–77, and M. Lee, Jr., *Government by Pen: Scotland under James VI and I* (Urbana, Ill., 1980), chap. 5, esp. pp. 170–89.

16. *M&K Supp.*, p. 231.

17. *Row*, p. 340. J. Maidment, ed., *Letters and State Papers during the Reign of King James the Sixth* (Edinburgh, 1838), pp. 375–76. See also *Scot*, pp. 313–14; *RPCS* 2nd ser. I, 91–92.

18. Apr. 16, 19, 1625, Melrose to Morton, NLS Mss. 80, nos. 65, 66. Charles's letter is dated Apr. 13, 1625. Sir William Fraser, *Memorials of the Earls of Haddington* (Edinburgh, 1889), II, 88–89. The letters patent issued for Melrose on May 14, however, make no mention of a lifetime appointment. *Ibid.*, pp. 294–95.

19. *RPCS* 2nd ser. I, 10–11, 13–16, 649–51.

20. May 21, 1625, Gilbert Primrose to James Primrose, *ibid.*, pp. 654–55.

21. *Ibid.*, pp. 649–51.

22. May 17, 1625, G. Primrose to J. Primrose, *ibid.*, pp. 651–53.

23. The revocation is dated July 14, 1625, *ibid.*, pp. 81–82.

24. *Ibid.*, pp. 101–8. There is a full account of the events of 1624 in David Calderwood, *The History of the Church of Scotland,* ed. T. Thomson, Wodrow Society (Edinburgh, 1842–49), VII, 596–621.

25. M. Wood, ed., *Extracts from the Records of the Burgh of Edinburgh 1604–1626* (Edinburgh, 1931), pp. 275–76, 278. Oct. 2, 1625, Spottiswoode to Charles, D. Laing, ed., *Original Letters Relating to the Ecclesiastical Affairs of Scotland . . . 1603–1625* (Edinburgh, 1851), II, 788.

26. *Stirling* I, 50, 81. *RPCS* 2nd ser. I, 434, 438, 439, II, 1–3. Wood, *Extracts . . . 1626–1641* (Edinburgh, 1936), pp. 15, 40, 42. R. K. Hannay and G. P. H. Watson, "The Building of the Parliament House," *Book of the Old Edinburgh Club* XIII (1934), 28–29.

27. It is dated Sept. 7, 1625, *RPCS* 2nd ser. I, 132–33.

28. Oct. 28, 1625, the council to Charles, *ibid.*, pp. 151–53.

29. See his letter of Nov. 23, 1625, to Viscount Stormont, *Laing,* pp. 167–68.

30. For the proceedings of the estates see *RPCS* 2nd ser. I, xxv-xxxiii, 150–80. The official text of their acts is in *APS* V, 166–88.

31. *RPCS* 2nd ser. I, 182–85.

32. The date is given in the parliamentary record for 1633, *APS* V, 23. No trace of the document has been found in the privy seal register, and the keeper of the privy seal, Sir Richard Cockburn of Clerkington,

seems to have been in Edinburgh in October. Whether or not a text was read in council at this time is not clear. On Jan. 7, 1626, Mar said that he had heard the document read once there, *M&K*, p. 135. The council's letter of Nov. 17, however, says that "none as yet has seen the same," which seems plain enough.

33. *M&K*, p. 137.

34. *RPCS* 2nd ser. I, 193–95.

35. *M&K*, pp. 132–33.

36. Fraser, *Sutherland Book* I, 112–13, II, 338–39. For James's remark see C. H. McIlwain, ed., *The Political Works of James I* (Cambridge, Mass., 1918), p. 24.

37. *RPCS* 2nd ser. I, 187–88. In June 1626 Charles ordered the treasurer depute a buy up what pensions he could at three years' purchase, a very low figure. BL Add. Mss. 23,110, p. 56.

38. Oct. 5, 1625, Kellie to Mar, *M&K Supp.*, p. 234. Oct. 22, J. Douglas to Lord Erskine, *M&K*, pp. 132–33.

39. *Balfour* II, 131.

40. Oct. 22, 1625, Charles to Hay, *M&K*, pp. 131–32.

41. Nov. 18, 1625, Mar to Charles, *ibid.*, p. 133. Nov. 7, Kellie to Mar, *M&K Supp.*, pp. 235–36. M. Napier, ed., *Memorials of Montrose and His Times* I (Edinburgh, 1848), 23–24.

42. Nov. 13, 1625, Kellie to Mar, *M&K Supp.*, p. 238.

43. On this point see *M&K*, p. 146.

44. Nov. 28, 1625, Nithsdale to Annandale, J. Maidment, ed., *State Papers and Miscellaneous Correspondence of Thomas, Earl of Melros* (Edinburgh, 1837), II, 593–94. The political connection between the two began in 1622, when Annandale, just after the death of his ally Dunfermline, arranged for a marriage between his daughter and Nithsdale's son, both small children. The connection ended by 1627, on whose initiative is not clear, and the marriage never took place.

45. See, on this point, P. G. B. McNeill, "The Independence of the Scottish Judiciary," *Juridical Review*, n.s. 3 (1958), 140.

46. See the council's letter to him on Mar. 15, 1625, on the affairs of the Principality, *RPCS* XIII, 716–18.

47. G. Donaldson, "The Legal Profession in Scottish Society in the Sixteenth and Seventeenth Centuries," *Juridical Review* n.s. 21 (1976), 9–10. See also Mathew, *Scotland under Charles I*, p. 59.

48. Sept. 27, 1625, the council to Charles, *RPCS* 2nd ser. I, 144.

49. *Ibid.*, pp. 185–87, 191–92. Dec. 7, 1625, Patrick Home of Polwarth to Sir Robert Kerr, *A&L* II, 481–82. For Charles's diplo-

matic problems in these months see Thomas Cogswell, "Foreign Policy and Parliament: the case of La Rochelle, 1625–26," *English Historical Review* XCIX (1984), 241–67.

50. *CSP Venetian* XIX, 335. The Venetian reports must be used with caution; the remarks about Scotland are often inaccurate.

51. The sources upon which the following paragraphs are based are the notes made at the time by Mar, *M&K,* p. 133–46, 153–55, and an account written thirty-five years later by Scotstarvet, dealing mostly with his controversy with Melrose over the tenure of the members of the session, printed in *SHR* XI (1914), 164–91. For Spottiswoode's views see his letter of Nov. 14, 1625, to Annandale, Sir William Fraser, *The Book of Caerlaverock* (Edinburgh, 1873), II, 72–73.

52. *M&K,* pp. 133–34.

53. The texts of the revocations are in *APS* II, 357–58, 500–501, III, 439–42. See also G. Donaldson, *Scotland: James V to James VII* (Edinburgh, 1965), p. 53; M. Lee, Jr., *John Maitland of Thirlestane and the Foundation of the Stewart Despotism in Scotland* (Princeton, 1959), pp. 135–36.

54. *M&K,* p. 139.

55. *Ibid.,* p. 140.

56. *Ibid.,* p. 143.

57. *Ibid.,* p. 142.

58. Oct. 25, 1625, J. Douglas to Lord Erskine, *M&K Supp.,* pp. 132–33.

59. *M&K,* pp. 144–46.

60. *RPCS* 2nd ser. I, 220–21, 234–36. *Stirling* I, 13, 14, 15–16, 46. McNeill, "Independence of the Scottish Judiciary," pp. 143–44.

61. *RPCS* 2nd ser. I, 227–32. NLS Adv. Mss. 32.6.8, ff. 92–93. Mar. 4, 1633, Charles to the commissioners of surrenders, *Stirling* II, 655–56. Margaret Sanderson, *Scottish Rural Society in the Sixteenth Century* (Edinburgh, 1982), p. 65.

62. Laing, *Original Letters* II, 704–5.

63. For James's policy respecting ministerial stipends see W. R. Foster, "A Constant Platt Achieved: Provision for the Ministry, 1600–38," in D. Shaw, ed., *Reformation and Revolution,* pp. 124–40.

64. *RPCS* 2nd ser. I, 227–29.

65. Feb. 16, 1626, Winton to Charles, *ibid.,* pp. 234–36. Mar. 25, Charles to Mar, *Stirling* I, 31.

66. Blench tenure was tenure by payment of a nominal sum; in a

taxt ward tenure the casualties of wardship had been commuted to an annual payment.

67. *A&L* I, 40–41. *RPCS* 2nd ser. I, 351–53.

68. So said eight members of the council in May 1626, BL Add. Mss. 23,110, p. 10.

69. The researches of Margaret Sanderson, *Scottish Rural Society,* chap. 7, indicate that, in her sample of church lands, over 60 percent of the feuars were sitting tenants, and that at least half the feus were granted to men below the class of laird. This does not mean, of course, that they got half the land. How much they got is not clear. For lairds as feuars of kirk and chapel lands see *ibid.,* p. 118. David Stevenson, *Revolution and Counter-revolution in Scotland, 1644–1651* (London, 1977), pp. 137–39.

70. *Stirling* I, 57–58, 72. *Row,* p. 342.

71. E.g., Viscount Stormont. *Stirling* I, 100. *Laing,* pp. 173–74.

72. *Stirling* I, 86–87, 103, 109. *M&K,* pp. 151–53. *Balfour* II, 153.

73. Feb. 12, July 28, 1626, Charles to the council, *Stirling* I, 18–19, 68–69. *RPCS* 2nd ser. I, 241–43, 248–51, 265–67, 343–44. *M&K,* p. 141.

74. *RPCS* 2nd ser. I, 337–38. Charles further jolted his councillors by absentmindedly sending instructions to the council of war before naming it. *Ibid.,* pp. 333–35.

75. July 28, 1626, Charles to the council, *Stirling* I, 67.

76. *RPCS* 2nd ser. I, 364, 391–92. L. B. Taylor, ed., *Aberdeen Council Letters,* 3 vols. (London, 1942–52), I, 244–46.

77. *RPCS* 2nd ser. I, 362–63, 386–89. *RCRB* III, 233–34, 237.

78. *RPCS* 2nd ser. I, 366–68. Nov. 10, 1626, Charles to Mar and Napier, *Stirling* I, 92–93. The pensions reported in the survey ordered in October 1625 cost the treasury about £66,000 a year. *RPCS* 2nd ser. I, 201–5.

79. *RPCS* 2nd ser. I, 233–34, 517–18, III, 283–84. *Stirling* I, 17, 84–85.

80. *Balfour* II, 143–45. NLS Mss. 3,926, p. 355. *RPCS* 2nd ser. I, 305. July 12, 1626, Charles to the council, *Stirling* I, 62.

81. Fraser, *Caerlaverock* II, 73–74.

82. See Alexander's letters to Melrose in March 1626, Fraser, *Haddington* II, 145–47, and to Morton, Oct. 6, 1630, NLS Mss. 80, no. 40.

83. *RPCS* 2nd ser. I, 357. Mar. 25, 1626, Charles to Mar, *Stirling*

I, 31. *M&K Supp.*, pp. 240–43. Jan. 26, 1627, Erskine to Morton, NLS Mss. 79, no. 71.

84. Jan. 11, 1627, Morton to Mar, Jan. 24, Mar to Morton, *M&K Supp.*, p. 243.

85. See his letters of Mar. 14, Apr. 4, Aug. 12, 1626, to Nithsdale, Fraser, *Caerlaverock* II, 73–76, *RCRB* III, 217–19.

86. *Laing*, pp. 173–74. See also the correspondence of the Venetian ambassadors, *CSP Venetian* XIX, 559, 577, 594, XX, 24.

87. *Balfour* II, 136–38.

88. Feb. 2/12, 1627, Contarini to the Doge and Senate, *CSP Venetian* XX, 119–20.

89. *M&K*, p. 144.

90. *Ibid.*, p. 146.

91. *CSPD 1627–28*, p. 87.

92. Apr. 20, 1622, Melrose to Mar, NLS Mss. 3,134, no. 99. Jan. 8, 1631, Haddington to Annandale, Fraser, *Haddington* I, 177–78.

93. Makey, *Church of the Covenant*, p. 14.

94. David Stevenson, *The Scottish Revolution 1637–44* (Newton Abbot, 1973), p. 41.

95. McIlwain, *Works of James I*, p. 22. For the proposals for resumption of crown lands in England see Conrad Russell, *Parliaments and English Politics 1621–29* (Oxford, 1979), pp. 250, 283.

96. Nov. 22, 1625, Kellie to Mar, *M&K Supp.*, p. 239. *Balfour* II, 128.

97. See Athol Murray, "Sir John Skene and the Exchequer, 1594–1612," in Stair Society, *Miscellany I* (Edinburgh, 1971), pp. 125–55.

98. Oct. 13, 1626, Sir Robert Crichton to Viscount Stormont, *Laing*, pp. 172–73.

99. W. J. Jones, *Politics and the Bench: The Judges and the Origins of the English Civil War* (London, 1971), p. 16. Jones was writing about England, but his comment is equally true for Scotland.

100. Mar. 22, 1626, Home of Polwarth to Sir Robert Kerr, *A&L* I, 41–43. *RPCS* 2nd ser. I, 231, 359–61, 370–71, 678–79. BL Add. Mss. 23,110, pp. 18–19, 22, 52–53, 74, 76, 92–93, 117. *Stirling* I, 24, 38. *Balfour* II, 131–32. *RCRB* III, 235–36. Taylor, *Aberdeen Council Letters* I, 250–52. *Row*, pp. 342–43.

101. Napier, *Memorials of Montrose* I, 25–27.

102. *Stirling* I, 62–63, 142–43. *RPCS* 2nd ser. I, 552–53. McGrail, *Alexander*, pp. 172–73.

2

The Menteith Years:
the Revocation

Wᴵᴸᴸᴵᴬᴹ Gʀᴀʜᴀᴍ, seventh earl of Menteith, was a most improbable candidate for the role of Charles's Dunbar. He was in-
disputably an ancient aristocrat; he was nearer the king in age
than Charles's other Scottish advisers, having been born about
1591; and he was known as court. Prior to December 1626,
however, he had shown no interest in politics. He had succeeded
his father in 1598 as a boy, was served heir to his earldom in 1610
while not yet of full age, and in 1612 had married the daughter
of Patrick, Lord Gray, that veteran intriguer whose involvement
(when Master of Gray) in the death of Mary Queen of Scots destroyed his career. A dispute with his mother over her stewardship
of some of his property while he was a minor led Menteith in
1618 to inventory the contents of the earldom's charter chests; in
the following year he set out to recover all the lost properties and
rights of the earldom, a process which became a passion with him
and which eventually led him to ruin. In James's time his name
hardly ever occurs in the public records. He had a commission of
justiciary for the district of Menteith in 1621 which he appears
to have executed efficiently, and he had a reputation for the breed-
ing of terriers which once prompted King James to ask him for
some.[1] He had undertaken to increase the stipend of the minister
of Aberfoyle, and recover the parish's manse and glebe, in return
for the bishop of Dunblane's resigning the patronage of the
church to him; he was the sole heritor of the parish, and possessed

its teinds.[2] Otherwise Menteith was quite unknown when King Charles came to the throne.

Menteith was at court in December 1626 while the delegation of his fellow aristocrats was journeying south bearing the petition on the revocation which so enraged King Charles. Menteith sympathized with their views, and was convinced that Charles would be making a serious mistake not to receive them. So he intervened, via Alexander, with whom he was friendly—his brother-in-law was a Nova Scotia baronet—and persuaded the king to change his mind. "I believe some Scottish nobleman interfered," wrote the Venetian ambassador, "observing that his countrymen would be less exasperated at their departure hence without receiving satisfaction than at their return without having audience." According to William Forbes, the author of an early eighteenth-century tract on tithes—and there is no reason to doubt him—Menteith was that nobleman. On December 17 Charles indicated that he was willing to see the delegation, provided that its members apologized for the tone of the petition; on December 27 he made Menteith a privy councillor and a member of the exchequer commission.[3]

Charles received the delegation amiably, with an arch comment about the wily old foxes in Edinburgh sending the young into battle in their place—the three delegates, Rothes, Loudoun, and Linlithgow, were indeed young men, though they were all older than Charles. The king did more than that: he paid attention to the petitioners and to Menteith, and made a decisive change in his policy respecting the revocation. He laid aside the threat of legal action and appointed a sixty-eight-man commission, on which the lords of erection were well represented, to deal with the matters enumerated in the proclamation of July 1626; he did this, he said, at the request of the aristocratic deputation. The quorum was to be twelve, at least three from each of the groups represented in parliament, plus either the chancellor or the primate. There were two crucial aspects to the creation of this commission, apart from its make-up. First, Charles promised that he would accept the commissioners' decisions, a commitment he had hitherto not made. Second, it soon became clear that the commission was going to concentrate first on determining the value of the teinds for each parish, in money and/or in victual. This figure would then become fixed and unalterable, a great boon to the man who worked the land, whether proprietor or tenant: henceforth he would know the extent of his annual obligation and would no longer have to leave his harvest lying in the field until the possessor of the right to collect the teinds came to determine his share. The commissioners then were to assure the minister an adequate stipend from the figure thus determined, and see to it that the remaining portion of the teinds was made available to the heritors and liferenters for purchase. This would eliminate the titulars and tacksmen, who, in Charles's view, were responsible for the oppression of the landholding class, what Lord Loudoun called the "alleged bondage of tithes."[4] The crown was to profit also. It would receive an annuity from the teinds, a figure set in May 1627 at 6 percent, as well as a "reasonable increase of yearly rent" out of feu duties, and it stood to gain from restoration of the old tenure of ward and relief. Once the commission had done its work, Charles promised, there would be parliamentary ratification of its decisions, and no further action would be taken under either the revocation or the summons of reduction. The proclamation appointing the commission was issued on February 1, 1627; in March Charles wrote to the commissioners, specifically approving their decision to deal first with the teinds, on a shire-by-shire basis, and recommending that clerical stipends be fixed in victual rather than in money, which would be a considerable benefit to the ministers, in view of the continuing inflation.[5]

The nature of the commission and the order of its priorities were matters of great importance. In theory the commission's powers were to run for only six months, but they could be renewed, and it was obvious that they would be. The size of the commission meant that nothing could be hustled through by a small clique; more important, the fact that the tithes were being dealt with first meant that nothing at all was going to be done very quickly. Before there could be any change in the status quo, it would be necessary to determine the value of the tithes, and that was going to take time. For Charles's policy to succeed, ample time was essential—time to allow the landholding classes to recover from their panic, to become aware that Charles meant it when he said that he did not intend to overturn "confirmed feus or other lawful rights of any of the lands of the temporalities of benefices" obtained before the act of revocation.[6] The panic did indeed subside; men no longer feared, said Spottiswoode in July 1627, that the revocation would "call in question all men's rights since King Fergus."[7] There is no evidence that Charles ever understood the importance of going slowly; his letters to the commissioners over the years were impatient in tone, urging them to get on with the job. It seems likely, however, that Menteith did understand this.

Menteith was not a thoughtful or far-sighted man, though he had ambition and energy. He was, in fact, a typical member of his class, greedier than some,[8] sharing its outlook and prejudices, and understanding how it wanted to be treated. He was able to persuade the king that there was more to be gained by being agreeable to the nobility than by threatening them. So Charles granted special favors to Rothes, Loudoun, and Linlithgow. More important, he began to be pleasant to the triumvirate. Mar and Melrose received cordial letters in January, at the time of the decision to appoint the commission, asking them to cooperate in its work. In March Charles appointed Melrose to the exchequer commission and in April sent him a "free discharge" for whatever minor errors he might have made in performing his administrative duties, even though Melrose had not asked for it.[9] In February Nithsdale was removed as collector of taxation and was licensed to recruit 3,000 men to fight for that rather bedraggled Protestant champion, Christian IV of Denmark. Nithsdale was not overeager to undertake this mission, and the chancellor, for one, was not sure he should—"I say it had been a far less error to have suffered Nithsdale to misguide this country still than to name him general." But he went, and was replaced as collector first by his deputy, Mar's man Sir James Baillie of Lochend, and eventually by Lord Chancellor Hay, the newly made Viscount Dupplin.[10] The triumvirs all expressed their gratitude, which was undoubtedly sincere, to the king. Melrose also wrote a fawning letter to Buckingham and readily acquiesced when Charles, expressing a wish to "further dignify" him for his services, asked him to alter his style, from earl of Melrose to earl of Haddington. "The reason he never told me," wrote the new countess of Haddington to her eldest son, "nor I did not sper (ask); but it is thought it is to humor the King because it [Melrose] is an erection."[11] But the king's smiles did not presage a return to power. When old Sir Richard Cockburn of Clerkington, the lord privy seal, died late in 1627, Charles forced Haddington to give up his secretaryship and take this powerless office instead, thus disappointing Lord Erskine, who had wanted the job. Alexander's new colleague as joint secretary was the insignificant Sir Archibald Acheson, a recently appointed member of the court of session; Alexander's grip on the powers of the office was now secure.[12]

Menteith did not become Charles's *éminence grise* in Scottish affairs all at once in the winter of 1626. It took him about a year to establish his influence; he had done so by the beginning of 1628, when Charles appointed him president of the privy council, and of the exchequer in Spottiswoode's absence.[13] There is no direct evidence in the sources to indicate just how Menteith accomplished this; the most reasonable surmise is that Charles, who apparently already liked him, came to trust his judgment when it became clear that following Menteith's advice in the matter of implementing the revocation had considerably reduced the level of tension in Scotland. Menteith remained the king's chief agent for five years. Like his predecessor Dunbar he was not a policymaker; his chief concern was to find ways of implementing Charles's policies, even those of which he disapproved. And like Dunbar he was constantly traveling; he averaged two trips a year between London and Edinburgh, and in most years was present at less than half the council meetings. Dunbar's journeying ruined his health; Menteith's did not—he died in 1661, aged about seventy. Diet may have had something to do with it. Dunbar was fat, but, if a surviving expense account of Menteith's gives an accurate picture, he did not overeat. He had his bread and beer in the morning, and beer at night, and when he was not dining out he contented himself with comparatively simple food: mutton (at two shillings a leg), capon, flounder, the occasional partridge.[14] He apparently enjoyed the traveling.

In most ways, however, Menteith was not at all like Dunbar.

The latter had been a capable and efficient lord treasurer; Menteith was bored by administration and had little talent for it. In August 1631, for example, Alexander wrote him a rather reproachful letter indicating that Menteith had botched both some official business, which Alexander tried to cover up, and some personal business of Alexander's. The secretary concluded by "assuring you that I will only revenge myself of that carelessness of yours for me by being diligent for you."[15] Perhaps because of his lack of ability and interest, Menteith showed no signs of wanting one of the great administrative offices. He might have had the treasury, especially after the death of Buckingham, the patron of Lord Treasurer Mar's expected successor Morton, but he did nothing to disturb Morton's eventual succession to the office. Dunbar kept his fellow aristocrats and politicians in line by intimidating them; Menteith frightened nobody and was either unable or unwilling to prevent the constant political jockeying at Whitehall which went on all through his years of influence. This state of affairs, which was due in considerable measure to Charles's destruction of the prestige of the council, often led to administrative difficulties in Scotland. In April 1629 Haddington was impelled to tell Menteith that all the would-be power-brokers intriguing at court were doing the country no good; he should ask Charles either to send them home to do their jobs or find substitutes who would, "for many more seek employment nor (than) attend the timely discharge thereof."[16] Nor did Menteith endeavor to build up a party by means of consensus and the use of his family connections in the manner of the earl of Dunfermline. He was, in fact, not much of a politician. His assets were Charles's liking for and confidence in him, his friendship with Alexander, his good working relationship with Lord Advocate Hope, and his instinctive sense of what the people who counted in Scotland, meaning mostly his fellow landowners, would and would not support, which in turn led them to accept him as a trustworthy spokesman for their point of view.

The test of Menteith's stewardship, of course, would be the success of the commission for the revocation. Its appointment was well received. "It offers," wrote Melrose (as he still was) to the earl of Roxburgh, "great mitigation to parties chiefly interested

. . . much different from the first projects devised and pressed by some whose fortunes, overthrown by their follies and wickedness, not able to be repaired by lawful means, are sought by them to be made up by undoing of his Majesty's father's faithful servants, by depriving them of the generous recompenses of their services bestowed upon them by that blessed king."[17] The commission's first action caused no controversy: it set the minimum stipend for a parish minister at 800 merks or 8 chalders of victual, an increase of 60 percent over what had been regarded as the acceptable minimum ten years earlier.[18] But it immediately became clear that the commissioners' work would be neither smooth nor rapid, which was bound to annoy the impatient king.[19] The bishops promptly showed their hands, in the form of a protest on the part of the archbishop of Glasgow that anything the commission decided should not prejudice the rights of the church.[20] "It is still believed by many," wrote Melrose to Roxburgh in March, "that their chief aim is to destroy the erections granted by blessed King James . . . and to encroach to themselves all the teinds, which will be found too great a morsel for their greedy mouths." Melrose himself was not sure that they aimed this high. He thought that what they wanted was exemption "from granting rights of teinds to heritors within their churches" and retention of their superiorities. He urged Roxburgh to persuade the king not to allow this to happen, and to stress to Charles that favoritism of any kind toward the bishops would make the nobility most unhappy. Two months later he had changed his mind and decided that the many, who included the chancellor, were right. The clergy were going to argue to the king that their right to the tithe was God-given, he wrote to Morton on May 10, and that their lands should be exempted from the jurisdiction of the commission.[21] They also took the position that tithes in the possession of bishops should be exempt from the crown's annuity and that no heritor should have a perpetual right to his teind.[22]

These assessments proved accurate enough. In May the clergy sent Adam Bellenden, bishop of Dunblane, and John Maxwell, an Edinburgh minister and future bishop, to Charles to complain that his policy would permanently deprive the church of its right to the teinds and turn the ministers into "mere stipendiaries." If the crown needed income from the teinds, let Charles turn them over to the church *in toto* and then ask the church for money.[23] Charles reacted angrily. He wrote a blistering letter to the bishops, scolding them for suggesting that he or the commissioners would treat them unfairly, and adding that their sermons to the effect that no lay person, including the crown, can lawfully possess tithes were undermining his policy by discouraging would-be purchasers among the heritors. In the circumstances, his statement to Dunblane and Maxwell that he had no intention of harming the church was not reassuring. Characteristically, however, Charles combined his unsatisfactory response with a special favor to the principal messenger: he instructed the lord advocates to try to recover the benefices annexed to the chapel royal, of which Dunblane was dean, and the exchequer to pay Dunblane 3,000 merks a year until the chapel's rents were reestablished.[24] The bishops did not change their views respecting tithes as a result of Charles' letter, but they did shift their ground. In July Spottiswoode was arguing that it was incompatible with royal authority to try to limit future revocations, and equally incompatible with the welfare of the church to make tithes heritable.[25] The argument apparently made no impression on the king.

Charles was much more responsive to another delegation, this one from the lairds, who feared that the interests of the titulars and tacksmen of the teinds would predominate in the commission.[26] They asked Charles to make sure that the value of the tithes should not be set too high—if it were, the heritors might not be able to buy them—and for their own security they asked that purchases be made through the crown, which would make the actual purchase from the holder and sell to the heritor, thus guaranteeing the latter's title. Charles endorsed all this, and authorized a meeting of representatives of the potential buyers to hear the king's response to their petition and discuss strategy.[27] The king also received a deputation from the burghs asking that church lands once belonging to them be restored, and that where appropriate their ministers be supported out of the tithes of neighboring parishes. Charles referred these requests to the commission, with the comment that they seemed reasonable.[28] All this activity worried Melrose, who suspected collusion between the gentry and the clergy, even though, as he himself noted, their interests were very different, since the gentry wanted to compound for their teinds in perpetuity at easy rates, while the clergy wanted no grants in perpetuity for anyone but themselves. Melrose darkly predicted that the lairds would come to regret deserting the aristocracy—"to have rent their own body," as he put it—to join with the clergy, who had been regarded as greedy when they were celibate and were much worse now.[29] If the lairds succeeded in their scheme to get their teinds without compensation to the titulars, or if the clergy obtained the right to raise clerical stipends fixed by parliament or to divide parishes and make the heritors pay for two or three sets of "ministers, readers, clerks, schools, and musicians," there would be serious trouble.[30] The lairds' leadership denied any sinister intentions, and, indeed, the lairds had earlier joined with the nobility in voting, against the bishops, that all tithes should pay the royal annuity and that the heritors should have their own tithes in perpetuity.[31] The lairds' leaders declared that all they wanted was to increase the royal revenue and benefit the kingdom.[32] Melrose found this patriotic posture unpersuasive. He also warned Morton not to allow the burghs' delegates to get any special favors: the other estates were more useful to Charles than the burghs. All the other groups in Scottish society were meeting and deciding on how best to profit from the revocation, he said; the nobility should too, and not be "stepbairnes."[33]

Melrose's rather paranoid nervousness about the outcome of all this political infighting was in part owing to the financial stake he had in it. The terms on which the lords of erection would surrender their superiorities and feu duties to the crown were also under discussion in the commission, and privy councillors were supposed to set a good example. From Melrose's point of view the first offer, that of the earl of Lauderdale, set far too good an example; Lauderdale offered to surrender his feu duties at ten years' purchase and his superiorities *gratis*.[34] Mar, both stung and frightened by what he thought was the king's belief that he preferred his private welfare to the public good, publicly followed suit in a meeting of the commission, an action for which Charles thanked him with the assurance that he would not be the loser for it.[35] Hay, who was presiding, confidently turned to Melrose, "never doubting but what the Earl of Mar had done was after a common resolution taken betwixt these two"; to his surprise, Melrose balked, saying that "those who had erections from his Majesty might return them at an easier rate than he and others who had . . . bought . . . the same for great sums of money." After the meeting Hay attempted to apologize, saying that he would not have pressed Melrose if he had not believed that Melrose was resolved. Melrose retorted that Lauderdale's offer was far below the market price; Hay rejoined that the crown could never afford to buy up the feu duties at the market price, and would have great trouble at the lower rate. Melrose went away angry; next day he had his revenge. In the matter of the crown's annuity out of the teinds Melrose proposed that teinds in kind be valued at a very high rate—it is, perhaps, safe to assume that little of his own income came from this source. "I fear," wrote Hay, "he will rather terrify others from doing anything than find many followers." He told Melrose so; "he said, who could stop him to buy his own thanks at any rate it pleased him. . . . Your lordship never did see at any meeting such a number of distracted people as we are. We have some will talk hours on end without sense or reason, and to tell what I think, I believe there are but few who labor in this great work as either meaning or hoping that any good shall come of it. . . . It may be that wise men may find themselves deceived," but Hay, at this point, clearly did not think so.[36] And with justification: if the king's own officers of state behaved this way, other titulars were likely to be far more recalcitrant. Melrose continued to struggle, and at the end of June he won a temporary success: the commission voted that the crown should buy up the feu duties at fifteen years' purchase and accepted his proposal respecting the valuations of teinds paid in kind. Melrose then sent a formal letter of submission to the king, not without reminding Charles that his only lordship of erection had not been a gift from James, but had been purchased at a good price from the grantee, the debt-ridden John Ramsay, earl of Holderness, who had received it for his services on the memorable day in Gowrie House in August 1600.[37]

Melrose's ungracious and reluctant submission was due mostly to fear. The obvious reluctance of the lords of erection and titulars of teinds to make the kind of submission the king wanted produced a confrontation between Charles and the sellers' agents at court, Lord Balmerino and Sir John Stewart of Traquair. Early in August Charles sharply ordered them to produce suitable submissions from the sellers by September 1. Dupplin intervened, explained that geographical factors made this impossible, asked the king for more time, and summoned a meeting of the sellers for August 31. Traquair urged Melrose and his fellow lords of erection and teind-holders to submit, to stave off really punitive measures. The king, he wrote to Morton, was showing sympathy for the position of the buyers—an accurate assessment—and they, along with the egregious Thornton, were denouncing the lord chancellor as the most hostile of all the lords of erection to the king's purposes. Traquair did not expect Dupplin to be damaged, but it was true, he said, that the leadership in Edinburgh was almost friendless at court. "All we get from Sir William Alexander is bought for fear and not for love, and . . . there is no trust to be had in him."[38] Traquair, an ambitious man whose previous efforts to impress the powers-that-be at court had not been successful, now made himself enormously useful as the councillors' spokesman; he successfully ingratiated himself with them—and with Charles, by his diligence in persuading people to sign submissions—and thus began his rise to power.[39]

There is no record that the meeting of tithe-sellers ever took place. Charles changed his tactics once again and ordered the lord advocate to draw up a form which they all were to subscribe. The task was to be done by December 1; those who had not submitted by then were threatened with legal action. Charles repeated his commitment to the principle that every heritor was to have his own teinds upon reasonable conditions, and promised to decide all controverted cases himself.[40] He also accepted the sellers' argument that the tithe-buyers also ought to sign a form of submission, and acknowledged that there were many knotty individual problems to solve. What, for instance, was to be done about the lord of erection who was titular or tacksman of the teinds within his lordship, but whose possession of those teinds antedated the erection of the lordship in his favor? Such posses-

sion did not fall within the scope of the revocation; Hope argued
that it should be included in the submission made by the lords of
erection who were so situated, however, or the heritors involved
would have no way of obtaining the right to purchase these
teinds.[41]

Needless to say, the deadline of December 1 was not met. The
form of submission was not fully worked out until January 1628,
and the process of collecting signatures from all concerned went
on for the rest of the year. The most recalcitrant were the bishops.
In April 1628 not one of them had signed—as late as June 1629
the archbishop of Glasgow still had not done so—and their failure to attend meetings of the commission often led to adjourn-
ment for lack of a quorum.[42] It proved to be equally difficult to
get accurate information about the tithes in each parish, such as
what they were worth, who owned what, and who had the right
to collect it. The first plan, implemented in April 1627, was to
use the machinery of the church: the presbytery was to see to it
that in each parish the minister and two inhabitants evaluated
the condition of the parish and informed the moderator of the
presbytery, who in turn would report to the commissioners.[43]
Heritors were to report also, and Treasurer Depute Napier was to
make up a rental book of the tithes and feu duties of the lordships
of erection.[44] Repeated prodding failed to produce enough of the
necessary information, and what did come in, if the surviving
reports are representative, was very hard to use. By the end of
1628 the commissioners obtained Charles's approval for a plan
which authorized the appointment of subcommissioners in each
presbytery to carry out the valuation, with increased power to
deal with, and if necessary to by-pass, local obstructionism,
and—pessimistically—with power to establish a series of fines
for themselves for non-attendance at meetings. There was some
argument over whether appeals from the subcommittees' decisions ought to lie to the full commission, or to king and parliament. The council opted for the former; Charles did not agree,
on the ground that knowing that their decisions were apt to stand
would encourage the subcommittees to do their work. There were
the usual delays in getting the subcommittees appointed; some
presbyteries had to be threatened with horning, and in one case,

that of Orkney and Shetland, the privy council had to intervene and appoint the subcommittee itself.[45] By the summer of 1629, however, the machinery was in place and the returns began to come in.

In 1628 and thereafter, Charles, by contrast with his earlier behavior, began to exhibit a considerable degree of patience. Though he was still prepared to use legal pressures on obstructionists and those who deliberately went against his policy,[46] he no longer required impossibly rapid responses to his orders. The deadline for submissions was repeatedly pushed back. Finally, in June 1628, he indicated that he was prepared to wait a year and a half longer for all the submissions to come in; in the meantime he would make his decisions as to the details of the settlement.[47] This change in attitude coincided with the increasing influence of Menteith, who now began to travel back and forth regularly between Edinburgh and Whitehall, and to spend substantial amounts of time at court on each occasion. He made the round trip at least nine times in the five years between the beginning of 1628 and the end of 1632, staying, on an average, about three and a half months each time. Though his recommendations to the king usually counselled patience,[48] Menteith was not averse to prodding the commissioners himself, "to waken them and make them go at a better pace,"[49] and prodding was certainly necessary. One letter from the king urging them on, dated October 28, 1628, was not recorded in the commission's proceedings until March 1631.[50] Alexander could still complain occasionally about the "vexations and divisions" which this business caused, and about fierce factional infighting,[51] but the intensity of that infighting diminished notably, as it became apparent that Charles disliked it, was using Menteith as a conduit in order to avoid it, and was relying heavily on Menteith's advice.[52] The usual procedure was for Menteith to carry the king's written instructions to Scotland, then, after an interval, return to Whitehall to report.[53]

In September 1629 the king published his decisions, in the form of four decreets arbitral.[54] The crown agreed to buy up the surrendered superiorities and feu duties of the lords of erection at the rate of ten years' purchase; the lords could continue to collect the duties until payment was made. Teinds would be bought up by the crown from titulars or tacksmen at nine years' purchase and resold to the heritors or liferenters of the property from which they were due. The value of the teinds was calculated at one-fifth of the "constant rent," or 8 percent of the annual value of the property, but what this figure amounted to in each individual case would have to be determined. In calculating the value of what was available for purchase by the heritors, allowance would have to be made for the stipend paid to the parish minister. The existing rental on any given piece of property might not be the same as the constant rent, though the commission decided that it would work on the assumption that the two figures were the same, barring evidence to the contrary.[55] The position of the tacksman was not always and everywhere the same; account would have to be taken of the length of the lease and the rate at which the tacksman paid the titular. Heritors on episcopal and burgh lands were also to enjoy their own teinds, subject to payment of one-fifth of the constant rent; the burghs, however, did not have to pay the royal annuity of 6 percent, unless there was a surplus left over after the expenses of the burgh's ministers, the schools, and the hospitals had been paid—an improbable contingency.[56] Episcopal lands were subject to the annuity, a reversal of a commissioners' decision of May 1627; it seems likely that this was done to forestall lay charges of favoritism, and possibly to punish the bishops for their foot-dragging. A deduction of one-fifth, the so-called "king's ease," was to be allowed on all tithes paid in kind, once the valuations were made—which meant that they too would be valued at 8 per cent of the annual value of the property—as a way of encouraging cooperation with the process.[57]

These principles were fair and equitable enough, but they were really no more than guidelines, ringed about with all sorts of exemptions, qualifications, and conditions. Charles optimistically wrote to the commissioners in October that, now that he had made his decisions, they could finish their work by the summer of 1630, when parliament was supposed to meet. This was quite unrealistic, however, and Charles soon realized it. In November 1629 he formally suspended a statute of 1617, due to go into effect in 1630, which would have prevented any legal challenge to any heritable rights which antedated 1577.[58] Since there were so many special cases, involving individual decisions, a great deal of work still lay before the commission and its subcommittees.

For the rest of Menteith's years of influence the commission soldiered on, doing its best to overcome the widespread aversion to subscribing the necessary submissions, and its own internal difficulties. Even those who, like the eccentric poet-traveller William Lithgow, genuinely favored restoring the teinds to the church, were skeptical about the methods employed. As the editor of the privy council register remarked, "Sub-commissioners and chief Commissioners alike took up their offices with a grudge and sought every opportunity of shirking the duties that pertained to them."[59] In March 1632 nine conveners of subcommittees were put to the horn for their failure to appear before the commissioners to make a progress report. But the commissioners themselves were no better. As before, the bishops were the worst offenders, but the burgess members were also slack. This could be remedied by the appointment of additional burgesses to the commission, which was done in December 1632; but there were only thirteen bishops. In November 1631 Charles found it necessary to create a special central subcommittee of the main commission, made up of members who had comparatively less work elsewhere, to sit every day and to make decisions even if the parties involved failed to appear.[60] And parties often did fail to appear. Even the prospect of being able to lead their own teinds was not enough to persuade some heritors to sign the submission and provide the necessary information; they feared that the commission would set a high figure on the teinds in order to benefit the titular to be bought out and to maximize the king's annuity. Titulars were equally unwilling for the opposite reason: they feared a low valuation, so that the heritor could buy them up cheaply and thus achieve his independence. Furthermore, since the commission in 1628 ordered the collection of the royal annuity on those teinds already valued, there was an obvious immediate advantage in delay. The result was, in some cases, a conspiracy of silence: neither party was willing to appear. Lord

Advocate Hope pointed out that the recalcitrant lords of erection could be pursued at law, but this was politically dangerous, and Hope found Lord President Skene anything but cooperative. At the convention of estates in July 1630 there was still contention over the principles that each heritor should have his own teinds and be able to buy them at nine years' purchase; Menteith had to intervene from the chair to get acceptance. The bishops, however, blocked an effort to end the rights of non-subscribers over other men's teinds. As a way out of this impasse, the commissioners declared in August 1630 that any non-subscriber who had appeared before the commission for any reason and who had not formally called attention to the fact of his non-subscription could be considered as having submitted; the estates were willing to accept this. Finally, in 1632, the commissioners were instructed to go ahead anyway, whether or not the parties had subscribed or appeared, and to be particularly careful not to undervalue the teinds in such cases.[61]

One of the commission's most vexing problems was that of clerical stipends, not because the commissioners were unwilling to raise substandard ones to the 800-merk level, but because they were unaware of the extent of their powers if they met resistance. In one case the commission ruled against a titular who argued that, since the minister's stipend had been raised in King James's time, he was not liable to pay a second augmentation; and in fact the commission made it clear that its own decisions on stipends were subject to future review and augmentation. It was probably for this reason that the purchase price of their teinds for the heritors was set so low, at nine years' purchase, below even the rate at which the government was willing to compensate the lords of erection for their lost superiorities: if there was a future adjustment of the minister's stipend, the heritors, if they had purchased their teinds from the titular or the tacksman, would have to pay it.[62] This may also explain why so many heritors were reluctant to buy up their teinds, though there was a statute of limitations of sorts operating here: in 1631 the commission ruled that once the teinds were valued, if a heritor refused the titular's offer to sell them, the titular was henceforth under no obligation to sell. In 1633 parliament gave the heritors a second opportunity. Heritors could buy their teinds, if they had been valued, until Martinmas 1635; for those not yet valued, they had two years from the date of valuation.[63] There is no evidence of any great rush to buy. Many heritors were already tacksmen of their own teinds, having leased them from the titular; they saw no reason to buy themselves out, so to speak. Another aspect of the problem which slowed down the commissioners' work was what was known as locality. Once the minister's stipend had been designated, the amount for which each of the heritors in the parish was responsible had to be determined. This was, in theory, the responsibility of the titular, but if he would not act, the commission would do so in his place, an unpleasant and time-consuming task.[64]

The evidence suggests that while the ministers benefited from the commission's work, the lay holders of teinds were not unduly hurt. In the parish of Scone, for instance, the minister's stipend was raised from £480 to £569, slightly over 850 merks. The teinds were worth about £1,400.[65] In accordance with Charles's wishes the commission avoided interference in most cases where a bishop was titular, and bishops appear to have been rather niggardly with their clerical subordinates.[66] But in one of those rare cases where a minister still collected his own teinds, and argued that he should be allowed to go on doing so in the old way, the commission ruled that, to protect the heritors, the teinds would have to be valued.[67]

Evaluating the teinds was not easy. On the surface the formula looked clear-cut enough. If teind payment was part of the rent, the teinds were assumed to be one-fifth of the constant rent, which was calculated at 40 percent of the annual value of the property. If the teinds were separate, they were valued at one-fourth of the rental, or, if paid separately in kind, the amount owed was calculated on the basis of what had been paid over the previous seven years. Valuation was easier if the teinds were separate.[68] Where they were mixed with the rent, those items which might be included in the rent but were not fruits of the land, such as mill-rents and profits from mining, had to be deducted before an accurate figure could be derived.[69] Titular and landholder might not agree as to the amount: the titular's figure as to teind owed from a particular property might vary widely from the landholder's calculation of one-fifth of the constant rent. The slowness of the teind commission's progress was frustrating two of the king's objectives, those of collecting his annuity and of allowing heritors to lead their own teinds. The decreets arbitral of September 1629 implied that the heritors were to have this right henceforth, whether or not the valuation had been accomplished. Sir Thomas Hope urged that this be done at once, with the heritors finding caution to pay according to the valuation once it was made, but the government chose to move cautiously. The rules it established had a presumption in favor of the titulars; in 1630, and again in 1631, it allowed only those heritors who had customarily done so, or who had permission from the commissioners, to lead their own teinds. Not until 1632 was the situation reversed, and all heritors allowed to lead their own teinds, except in those cases where the heritor rather than the titular was responsible for the delay. The titulars predictably disliked this, and Charles ultimately mollified them by agreeing to pay interest on any arrears owed to them when the valuation was made.[70] The commissioners were equally cautious about the king's annuity. Not until 1631 did they, on royal instructions, authorize its collection where the teind had not been valued, on the basis of one-fifth of the current rent. They also exempted payments made directly to ministers, including bishops, although the decreet of 1629 had authorized collection on bishops' tithes, an exemption confirmed in parliament in 1633, along with those paid to colleges and hospitals.[71] The commission's policy of taxing all teinds alike produced a protest from those titulars who held "by just and undoubted right," as they put it, rather than as lords of erection. They wanted no confusion of the two, and perhaps a lower rate for themselves, but in this they were disappointed.[72] The king wanted but could not get any kind of favorable response to his suggestion that a sum over and above the minister's stipend should be set aside from the tithe for poor relief and other social purposes. The proposal met with dead silence, and the king chose not to press it.[73] The poor remained dependent for relief on the kirk session, whose methods were frequently haphazard and whose income for this purpose came mostly from the fines it levied on the ungodly for their misbehavior. As one scholar put it, "Since fornication was always a major item of business it would be fair to say that the equilibrium of the godly parish was maintained by the lascivious regularly providing for the needy."[74]

The commission also had to deal with individual cases, often involving important people, like Sir David Lindsay of Balcarres, a titular, who complained that the valuation committee of the presbytery of St. Andrews listened only to the heritors and valued the teinds much too low, to his serious disadvantage, or Lord Balmerino, who argued unsuccessfully that a ministerial stipend for which he was responsible was already large enough—the commission ordered him to pay three more chalders of victual.[75] The king was not at all sympathetic to Balmerino,[76] nor, ultimately, to the earl of Rothes with respect to the complicated affairs of the abbey of Lindores, where Rothes had a tack of the feu duties,[77] which undoubtedly helps to account for their opposition to him after 1633, when Menteith's mediating presence was gone.

In June 1633 parliament ratified the policies contained in the decreets arbitral of 1629, with the modifications already noted. These favored the bishops, who did not pay the king's annuity on their teinds, and the titulars, who were not required to sell if the heritor made no offer to buy within two years of the valuation,[78] though the decision that the annuity was due as of 1628 on all teinds, both valued and unvalued, meant that many people owed arrears to the government.[79] The commission's work was not finished, of course, and parliament renewed its authority. It began to act more briskly, however, especially in the matter of augmenting clerical stipends,[80] and its policies changed to reflect the altered policy of the king after 1633.[81] But its work was far from complete when the troubles began in the summer of 1637.

Throughout these years the church's leadership continued to be both suspicious of and unhappy about the commission. The chief complaint, voiced in April 1630 by the synod of Fife and expressed in a formal statement on the part of the bishops in 1631, was that the valuation process was working against the church, by setting the value of the tithes too low (which also cut into the king's annuity, of course); they also charged the commission with corruption. Charles turned the matter over to Menteith, who extracted a promise of cooperation from Archbishop Spottiswoode, and Charles himself wrote to the commissioners instructing them to prevent any reduction in ministerial stipends, which, he heard, had occasionally resulted from the process of valuation.[82] But the church's fundamental grievance remained: the whole of the teinds was its rightful property, and of this it was being in large measure deprived. No honeyed words from king or commissioners could disguise that baleful fact.

Almost as bad, from the bishops' point of view, was their loss of influence with the king. In James's day Archbishop Spottiswoode had been the king's friend and confidant, his adviser on church matters and on much more besides. Charles respected the archbishop's office, as his grant of precedence in the council showed, and he welcomed Spottiswoode's and Bishop Lindsay of Ross's support of the royal prerogative. But he kept the bishops at arm's length and did not consult them on policy. He did not welcome their presence at Whitehall; like their English counterparts, they were under instructions to reside in their dioceses, though until 1634 Charles made an exception for the bishop of Caithness, who was also minister of Jedburgh and was of more use in his border parish than in his remote diocese, which was made very unsettled by the lawless behavior of its ruffianly and Popish earl.[83] A plan in 1628 to have Bishop Lindsay become "Commissioner *resident* at the Court of England" did not materialize.[84] The bishops' attitude toward the revocation annoyed Charles; he saw no reason to pay attention to their views. His only appointment to the bench in these years was that of his chaplain, John Leslie, a deracinated Scot who had spent most of his adult life abroad, to the bishopric of the Isles in 1628; Charles subsequently paid a good deal of attention to increasing the revenues of Leslie's dilapidated bishopric. Leslie turned out to be a poor choice. He proved both quarrelsome and neglectful; Charles translated him to Ireland in 1633.[85]

As for religious policy apart from the revocation, Charles at first continued that which he found in effect on his accession: non-enforcement of the five articles of Perth and leniency toward Catholics, coupled with an insistence that all new ministers accept the five articles and that the council see to it that the children of Catholic nobles were raised in the Protestant faith. Early in

1627, however, at the behest of the clergy, Charles authorized the court of High Commission to examine suspected Papists and priests on oath, a power it had not previously possessed, although with the restriction that evidence thus obtained could not be used in other courts.[86] In the following year a major anti-Popery campaign began, directed first against Nithsdale's dependents in the southwest, an indication of the waning of his influence even before the death of his patron Buckingham later in the year. Then the campaign shifted to the northeast, where Catholicism flourished on a wide scale owing to the patronage of Huntly and his Catholic official underlings in Aberdeenshire. The list of Papists there was so long that Spottiswoode advised Menteith not to allow it to become public, lest it encourage Catholics elsewhere. Force would be needed to implement the king's instructions there, opined the archbishop, because the important officials on the spot "are the maintainers of that Popish crew." In December 1628 the council launched a massive campaign there, and extended it to the rest of the country in 1629, at the same time asking the king to cooperate by excluding Papists from the court and council. The objective was to drive priests, especially Jesuits, and Catholic laity out of the country, with provision for an allowance of one-third of their income for those laymen who agreed to leave.[87]

These indications of the king's hardening attitude toward Catholics, and the continuing non-enforcement of the five articles of Perth, which by now had led to a good deal of backsliding on the part of the ministers who had originally conformed,[88] led some of the ministerial opponents of James's religious policy to hope that Charles might even officially condone nonconformity, allow the return of banished nonconformist ministers, and authorize a meeting of the General Assembly of the church.[89] They remembered, perhaps, that Menteith had voted against the Perth articles in parliament in 1621. They were to be grievously disappointed, however. That the king did not learn of their request for toleration and a meeting of the General Assembly can be deduced from his unruffled reaction to the list of proposals presented by the bishop of Ross, the messenger designated at the meeting at which these suggestions were formulated.[90] Furthermore, Charles was enraged when, in 1628, despite his express order to administer the sacrament in the prescribed way, two Edinburgh ministers had the effrontery to ask him to end the perennial argument over communion by authorizing people to receive it sitting, instead of kneeling as stipulated in the Perth articles.[91] He wrote Spottiswoode a stinging letter, ordering the punishment of those responsible and the enforcement of the communion article. "If we would believe daily information given unto us of the remissness of the bishops, we might justly blame them for the said disorder," he added.[92] In the following year the king issued instructions which amounted to a sort of Test Act. Communion was to be celebrated quarterly in the chapel royal at Holyrood; all councillors and other officials in Edinburgh had to attend at least once a year on pain of dismissal from their jobs. The same test was to apply in all other parishes in the country. Ministers were to keep lists of communicants; those whose names did not appear could not hold office.[93] There is no evidence that anyone ever lost his job as a consequence of this act.

Another disappointment to good Protestants, both conformist and nonconformist, was that the great drive against Popery turned out to be largely political. Its purpose was to force Huntly and his eldest son, Lord Gordon, to surrender their hereditary sheriffdoms of Aberdeen and Inverness. Once Huntly had done so, in June 1629, and received a promise of £5,000 sterling in compensation, the pressure on him was relaxed. The king, who never showed any interest in dragooning his Catholic subjects for religious reasons, ordered that Huntly be treated with consideration, provided he gave no scandal. Charles even permitted him to live at home and allowed the queen's physician, William Leslie, whom the council described as "a most seditious trafficking Papist" and had expelled from the country, to return to minister to him.[94] At the beginning of 1630 Lord Gordon, who was nominally Protestant, was entrusted with the task of enforcing the council's anti-Catholic decrees, which was rather like making an ex-*Mafioso* chief of police. He seems to have been diligent enough to win the bishops' approval, however—at least Charles said so, in a letter of congratulation written at the end of the year. The council continued to pursue Catholics, but the king, while paying lip service to these efforts, undercut them with his generosity in issuing licenses for those in exile to return. There were steady complaints, from the synod of Aberdeen among others, that this permissiveness confirmed Papists in their obstinacy, encouraged Jesuits to attempt to sneak back into the country, and discouraged the ministers, who found their efforts at conversion all for naught. The council forwarded these complaints to the king, but he did not change his policy. By 1633 the council had trimmed its sails to the wind from Whitehall, and informed the bishop of Aberdeen that it had decided against expelling a female Papist, lest Scotland get a bad name abroad as a country which persecuted for religion. In their reports to their superiors in Rome, the Jesuits continued to complain of the savagery of the clergy's treatment of Catholics, but in fact prosecutions for Popery were sporadic, and important Catholics—not only Huntly, but also people like Nithsdale, Angus, and Errol—were treated very gently.[95] The situation in England was very similar. Recusancy fines continued to be collected there, but the atmosphere at court became more and more sympathetic to Catholics with the waxing influence of Queen Henrietta Maria and her circle after the death of Buckingham.

At the beginning Menteith had encouraged the anti-Catholic campaign. He was particularly insistent that Huntly's wings be clipped, and in July 1629 he had chaired the council committee which produced the comprehensive nationwide program of action. But after Huntly's submission and the king's shift of attitude, Menteith shifted also. He was at court in the latter part of 1629 when Charles struck his bargain with Huntly. The king indicated his change in policy by a letter to the clergy instructing them to proceed with discretion against him and other Catholic grandees, and not to excommunicate the Popish wives of noblemen if their husbands guaranteed their good behavior, an order which allegedly led one bishop to comment that he had seen the day "when there was not a minister in Scotland durst for his hanging bring down such articles."[96] In Menteith's absence the council requested Charles to give him a commission against the Papists of the northeast. The earl had returned home when this request reached the king; his ally Alexander intervened to forestall it, and to leave the commission in the hands of Lord Gordon. Menteith did not complain of this, and, indeed, passed as being responsible for it: in December 1630 Louis XIII wrote to thank him for his benevolence to Scottish Catholics. King Louis's perception was not altogether accurate. Menteith did have Catholic kinfolk, including his brother-in-law, Lord Gray, but the Jesuits in Scotland regarded him as very hostile to Catholics, and described matters as going from bad to worse for members of the ancient faith during his years of power.[97] On the other hand, he had no wish to enhance the political position of the bishops by putting the machinery of the state at their disposal for this or any other purpose. Nor, at this juncture, did Charles, who for the moment was far more concerned to improve the lot of the ordinary ministers than he was to enhance the influence or authority of those ministers' episcopal superiors.

Contemporaries and modern historians alike have been highly critical of Charles's policy respecting the revocation. Sir James Balfour had nothing good to say of it; his comment on the parliamentary ratification of 1633 was that it "proved in the end a forcible rope to draw the affections of the subject from the Prince." Bishop Burnet, writing in the second half of the century, declared that the king's own officials were unreliable: Sir Thomas Hope's procedures were so snail-like as to amount to sabotage.[98] The evidence does not support this interpretation of Hope's behavior, though he, like his ally Menteith, had no enthusiasm for clerics in politics and no desire to enhance their position in the state.[99] Most modern historians follow the lead of Treasurer Depute Napier, who gave the king credit for good intentions, but also wrote: "that which his Majesty intended for the general good . . . (gave) general discontentment, through the ill carriage of the business." No one, said Napier, was satisfied: the clergy because all hope of recovering the teinds in their entirety was gone; the titulars and lords of erection because of their financial losses, both actual and anticipated, and the attack on their property rights; the heritors because they believed that their lands were overvalued, their own improvements not allowed for, and the price of the teinds set so high that they could not afford to buy them up. Even the king would not profit very much, after the ministers' stipends were raised, the maintenance of hospitals and schools provided for, and after "the titulars, either out of favour, or out of consideration for their loss . . . get satisfaction, which undoubtedly all will pretend, all demand, and most of them likely enough receive from so bountiful a disposition."[100] Furthermore the means employed "were most unfit to compass his [Charles's] ends, but fit enough to serve their turns that found their private prejudice to render the business intricate, longsome, and difficult, upon hope his Majesty would relinquish the same."[101]

Napier had an axe to grind in 1630, when this was written. He was embroiled in various financial scandals and would shortly be replaced in office by Traquair. He had no love for his fellow officials, especially Lord Treasurer Mar, and Mar's long-standing associate, Lord Advocate Hope, who was the leading saboteur, if sabotage there was. Undoubtedly Napier's purpose was to make his colleagues look bad. His analysis nevertheless is in many respects accurate. The evidence bears out what he says about the fears and complaints of the various groups involved, and also, by implication, his indirect criticism of Charles for making no effort to address those concerns. Modern scholars have stressed this latter point. "It is a measure of Charles's incompetence as a politician," writes David Stevenson, "that he received no gratitude for the revocation even from those who stood to benefit by it. . . . The king conjured up far more opposition and suspicion than was necessary, by failing to explain what he was trying to do or to reassure those who thought his actions high-handed."[102] It is also true, as Stevenson says, that Charles was financially unable to make very much practical use of the rights whose recognition he had extracted from his reluctant subjects. He did not have the money to buy up very many superiorities and hereditary rights, save occasionally, where it was politically convenient and not terribly expensive.[103] But he did make some progress toward his goal, and he wanted to make more. Anyone wanting a title or a promotion in the peerage, he wrote Menteith in November 1629, must be prepared to bargain for his hereditary office if he had one.[104] But Charles did resist the temptation to mortgage the future in order to acquire these offices. In 1626 the impecunious laird of Craigie Wallace offered to surrender the hereditary bailiary of Kyle in return for 4,000 merks a year paid from the customs duties. A group of councillors at Whitehall, which included Treasurer Depute Napier, advised Charles against this, and the policy of purchase by agreement on a lump sum became the normal procedure. Charles instructed Menteith that the proceeds of the tax of 1630 were to be used for this purpose, and the exchequer register indicates that this was done.[105] When money was scarce Charles, like his father, borrowed from his servants. In July 1632 he instructed Menteith to buy from the earl of Linlithgow his positions as hereditary keeper of the palace of Linlithgow and Blackness castle; he promised to reimburse Menteith at a convenient time. The ingenious Scotstarvet thought up a scheme which entailed the vassals of the lords of erection advancing the money to buy out their superiors in return for favors from the crown. Charles showed interest and asked the exchequer to look into it, but nothing seems to have come of it. By 1632 Charles had more than doubled the number of sheriffdoms in the crown's hands, and was contemplating the possibility of legal steps to recover the crown's right of appointment to the office of sheriff clerk in those places where a hereditary sheriff currently had this right.[106] All this was gain, but in a sense peripheral gain, in that the real basis of the great landholder's local power lay in his grant of regality, which gave him judicial authority over those who lived within it, and Charles did not have the financial resources to acquire these. Sell the sheriffdom of Sutherland to the king if you must, Sir Robert Gordon advised his nephew the earl; it will not matter much, as long as you can keep the regality.[107] And, in the view of historians, the psychological cost to the king's position was immense. The fear of what Charles would do, if he could, far outweighed his actual accomplishments, and it was certainly politically foolish of him to espouse such a disturbing policy without having the resources to carry it out.[108] The revocation, wrote Sir James Balfour in a phrase that is always quoted, was "the groundstone of all the mischief that followed after."[109]

It should be with some trepidation that one ventures to take issue with such unanimity of opinion, especially without great quantities of new evidence. Yet the existing evidence can, and perhaps should, be read another way. There is no doubt that, at the beginning, the revocation was profoundly disquieting, both because of its scope and because no one knew exactly what impact it would have upon him. The subsequent destruction of the power of the old king's councillors and the alteration of the court of session greatly increased the general apprehension. In the words of one authority, "Most of these actions lay in a grey area of law, or were openly outwith his powers." Furthermore, there was no way, short of forcible resistance, to challenge Charles's actions: "there was no single explicit source of law which could be made binding on the crown."[110] Following the appearance of some guidelines and the establishment of the commission at the beginning of 1627, however, the panic began to subside, due to the concentration on the teinds, the most complicated yet in most ways the least threatening element in Charles's program. The procedures that were developed for the evaluation and commutation of teinds and the provision of ministerial stipends were both beneficial and enduring—they lasted, with minor changes, until the 1920s.[111] "In its final shape," wrote S. R. Gardiner, "the arrangement thus made is worthy of memory as the one successful action of Charles's reign."[112] The sense of unease was reduced in 1627, then, but it did not vanish. There began a determined struggle for the king's ear, with various interest groups jockeying for position and the king apparently leaning in the direction of the heritors as opposed to the lords of erection, the other titulars, and the clergy, but insisting that all concerned sign submissions without indicating what use he planned to make of those submissions.

What made the difference was the ascendency of Menteith. In 1628 and thereafter royal pressure for rapid action did not exactly cease, but it became much weaker. The balance between the various interest groups was much more evenly held, as is indicated by Napier's comment that they were all to some degree discontented. Above all, the most important single group in Scotland, the great aristocratic landowners, felt comfortable with Menteith. He was one of them; through him they could make their feelings known to the king.[113] The royal program represented a very serious threat to them: loss of influence over their subordinates with the loss of superiorities, regalities, hereditary jurisdictions; loss of income from feu duties when the superiority was gone and from teinds if the heritor bought them up; increased payments to the crown. There were indications by the end of 1629 that the king was particularly interested in the reacquisition of monastic property, a policy he was to adopt in 1633 in order to reendow the bishoprics.[114] With Menteith having the king's ear, however, the threat to the magnates might be conjured away. At least the bishops would be kept at arm's length. The whole tone of Scottish political life changed in 1628: something like what might be called Jacobean normalcy returned. Not that the policy embodied in the revocation became popular; it did not, and fears were still being publicly expressed by the lairds at the convention of estates in 1630.[115] And certainly the criticisms levelled at Charles for his tactical blunders are justified. It is also true that Charles's employment of Menteith was fortuitous. The king was not looking for an agent to manage Scottish affairs for him; he was not aware that he needed one. He liked Menteith, and the bonds grew closer after the assassination of Buckingham.

Menteith's direct involvement in the implementation of the details of the revocation was sporadic, mostly concerned with mediating tricky individual cases, where he sometimes was, in Hope's words, "the chief and principal worker."[116] His contribution was twofold: to act as a messenger, conveying the king's wishes to Edinburgh officialdom and Scottish reaction back to Charles, and to create an atmosphere in which everybody's interests received consideration, and in which complaints against alleged unfairness could be heard. These were major contributions, and Menteith was very successful. The tensions which Charles's policy and tactics had created were defused. It is very difficult to supply the usual sort of "proof" of this sort of contribution. No one at the time sang Menteith's praises, save for the standard sort of sycophancy which it is customary to bestow on royal favorites; no one, save perhaps Charles, regretted him after he was gone. But the difference in atmosphere is unmistakable. By contrast with the universal jumpiness and uncertainty which ushered in the reign and the grim mood of approaching confrontation which followed Charles's disastrous visit to Scotland in 1633—a visit which coincided with Menteith's fall—the years of the earl's ascendancy were years of relative calm. Such a condition has got to be more than mere coincidence. Menteith and all he stood for represented Charles's best chance to create a viable regime in his ancient kingdom. Tragically for both men, the opportunity was to be wasted.

NOTES

1. Aug. 16, 1617, James to Mar, Sir William Fraser, *The Red Book of Menteith* (Edinburgh, 1880), I, 335. Mar was James's usual channel for such requests. The biographical information in this paragraph comes from Fraser's account, *ibid.,* pp. 331–94.

2. *Ibid.* I, 336–37, II, 320–23.

3. Dec. 22, 1626/Jan. 1, 1627, Contarini to the Doge and Senate, *CSP Venetian* XX, 78. William Forbes, *A Treatise of Church-lands and Tithes* (Edinburgh, 1705), pp. 261–62. *Stirling* I, 109. *RPCS* 2nd ser. I, 495–96.

4. Apr. 7, 1627, Loudoun to Morton, NLS Mss. 80, no. 27.

5. *Stirling* I, 117, 145. Sir John Connell, *A Treatise on the Law of Scotland Respecting Tithes,* 2nd ed. (Edinburgh, 1830), II, 80. The proclamation is in *RPCS* 2nd ser. I, 509–16.

6. *RPCS* 2nd ser. I, 513–14. On July 3, 1627, the commission's powers were extended indefinitely. *Stirling* I, 186.

7. July 13, 1627, Spottiswoode to Annandale, J. F. S. Gordon, *Ecclesiastical Chronicle for Scotland* I (London, 1875), 487–88.

8. See, e.g., Alexander's letter of Dec. 16, 1628, Fraser, *Menteith* II, 100–101, advising Menteith against claiming a reward for his service at a time when the treasury was unusually hard pressed. He had received a pension of £500 sterling seven months before. *Ibid.* I, 341. Menteith did not desist; in April 1629 Charles promised him £5,000 sterling when it became available, so that Menteith could float an anticipatory loan. *Ibid.* II, 12.

9. *Stirling* I, 119, 141, 151. *RPCS* 2nd ser. I, 583–84.

10. Apr. 12, 21, 1627, Hay to Morton, NLS Mss. 82, ff. 31, 27. *RPCS* 2nd ser. I, 525–26, 531–32, 609–10. *Stirling* I, 90, 232.

11. *CSPD 1627–1628,* p. 52. *RPCS* 2nd ser. II, 58–59. Sir William Fraser, *Memorials of the Earls of Haddington* II, 296. HMC, 14th Report, App., pt. III, p. 108.

12. *Stirling* I, 222–24. NLS Mss. 79, no. 68. Acheson had to give up his seat on the session. His replacement was Sir James Learmonth of Balcomie, one of the spokesmen for the lairds in the matter of the revocation.

13. In December 1628 Edinburgh recognized Menteith's new eminence by making him a burgess and a guild brother and by giving him a banquet. M. Wood, ed., *Extracts from the Records of the Burgh of Edinburgh, 1626–1641*, p. 51.

14. SRO, GD 22/3/590.

15. Fraser, *Menteith* II, 121–22.

16. Apr. 7, 16, 1629, Haddington to Menteith, Fraser, *Haddington* II, 165–66, 167–68.

17. Mar. 6, 1627, Melrose to Roxburgh, Fraser, *Haddington* II, 148.

18. Connell, *Tithes* II, 78.

19. See, e.g., Apr. 29, 1627, Charles to the commissioners, *Stirling* I, 167.

20. Connell, *Tithes* II, 79.

21. Fraser, *Haddington* II, 150–51. NLS Mss. 80, no. 71. For Hay's views see Mar. 18, 1627, Hay to Morton, NLS Mss. 82, f. 35.

22. Apr. 7, 1627, Loudoun to Morton, NLS Mss. 80, no. 27.

23. NLS, Wodrow Mss. LXVI, f. 17.

24. *Stirling* I, 171–72, 174, 175.

25. July 13, 1627, Spottiswoode to Annandale, Gordon, *Ecclesiastical Chronicle* I, 488.

26. Apr. 8, 1627, Hay to Morton, NLS Mss. 82, f. 37.

27. Apr. 11, 1627, Charles to Hay and to the commissioners, *Stirling* I, 157–58, 159.

28. June 5, 1627, Charles to the commissioners, *ibid.*, p. 181.

29. Apr. 21, 1627, Melrose to Morton, NLS Mss. 80, no. 63.

30. Mar. 29, 1627, Melrose to Roxburgh, Fraser, *Haddington* II, 151–52.

31. Apr. 7, 1627, Loudoun to Morton, NLS Mss. 80, no. 27. Loudoun urged Morton to try immediately to persuade Charles to ratify this vote before the clerical delegation, which was *en route*, arrived in London.

32. See, e.g., Mar. 16, 1627, Learmonth of Balcomie to Morton, NLS Mss. 83, no. 15.

33. Apr. 28, May 10, 1627, Melrose to Morton, NLS Mss. 80, nos. 70, 71.

34. Apr. 7, 1627, Melrose to Roxburgh, Fraser, *Haddington* II, 152–53.

35. Mar. 19, 1627, Mar to Charles, *M&K,* pp. 156–57. May 3, Charles to Mar, *Stirling* I, 168.

36. This paragraph is based on Hay's very interesting letter of Apr. 11, 1627, to Morton, NLS Mss. 82, f. 30.

37. Connell, *Tithes* II, 80–81. *M&K,* pp. 161–62. Mar, Roxburgh, and Lauderdale also sent formal letters of submission. *Ibid.,* pp. 159–61.

38. July 23, 1627, Traquair to Morton, NLS Mss. 81, nos. 69, 70. Aug. 5, Charles to Balmerino and Traquair, *Stirling* I, 194. Aug. 11, Dupplin to Hamilton, SRO, Hamilton Papers, c. 1, no. 78. Aug. 13, Traquair to Melrose, Fraser, *Haddington* II, 156–57. Traquair's assessment of the king's leanings is confirmed by Charles's letter to Hope on Aug. 17, instructing him to be sure that the titulars and tacksmen of teinds were not permitted to be unduly rigorous this year. *Stirling* I, 197.

39. See, e.g., *Stirling* I, 213, and Dupplin's praise of him to Morton, NLS Mss. 82, f. 41. This letter is undated; the context suggests that it was written in April 1628.

40. *RPCS* 2nd ser. II, 86–88.

41. Dec. 5, 1627, Sir Thomas Hope to Annandale, R. Paul, ed., "Letters of Sir Thomas Hope," *SHS Miscellany* I (Edinburgh, 1893), 102. Dec. 28, Charles to Dupplin; Dec. 29, Charles to Hope, *Stirling* I, 237–38, 241. In 1629 the commissioners ruled that any land feued prior to 1587 by a churchman to a layman with the tithe included in the feu duty, *cum decimis inclusis,* would be exempt from valuation. Connell, *Tithes* II, 82.

42. *RPCS* 2nd ser. II, 311, III, 192. Jan. 20, 1628, Dupplin to Morton, NLS Mss. 82, f. 47.

43. *RPCS* 2nd ser. I, 573, 602. The results of this survey have survived for forty-nine parishes and are printed in A. MacGregor, ed., *Reports on the State of Certain Parishes in Scotland,* Maitland Club (Edinburgh, 1835).

44. *Stirling* I, 170. July 14, 1627, Colin Campbell, younger, of Glenorchy to James Primrose, SRO, GD 112/39/406.

45. July 21, Nov. 15, 1628, Jan. 15, 1629, Charles to the commissioners, *Stirling* I, 300, 331, *M&K,* p. 170. Nov. 18, Dec. 26, 1628, Alexander to Menteith, Fraser, *Menteith* II, 96–97, 101–2. Dec. 31, the council to Charles, *RPCS* 2nd ser. II, 546. Connell,

Tithes I, 145–46. *RPCS* 2nd ser. III, 21–22, 52, 53–54, 70–74, 87–88, 105–6, 115–16, 151, 162, 165–66.

46. See, e.g., Mar. 15, 1628, Charles to Hope, *Stirling* I, 263–64.

47. *RPCS* 2nd ser. II, 368–71.

48. See, e.g., Oct. 23, 1628, Alexander to Menteith, Fraser, *Menteith* II, 94–95.

49. SRO, GD 22/3/582.

50. Connell, *Tithes* I, 338–39, II, 258.

51. Nov. 15, Nov. 18, 1628, Alexander to Menteith, Fraser, *Menteith* II, 95–97.

52. See, e.g., Mar. 13, 1628, July 28, 1629, Charles to Menteith, Dec. 2, 1628, Alexander to Menteith, *ibid.*, pp. 4–5, 16–18, 99–100.

53. The pattern for 1628 is typical. At the beginning of the year Menteith was at court; by February 21 he was in Edinburgh, carrying the king's instructions, dated February 11. Charles called him back to court at the end of April; he returned to Edinburgh late in July with another set of instructions, dated July 22. In December Charles summoned him to court again. See *ibid.*, pp. 3–8, *Stirling* I, 248, 270, 327.

54. *RPCS* 2nd ser. III, 293–313.

55. On this point see Connell, *Tithes* I, 181–83, II, 81.

56. Charles here was accepting what the convention of royal burghs had approved in July 1628; *RCRB* III, 266–68. Edinburgh had insisted on this from the beginning. Connell, *Tithes* II, 80.

57. *Ibid.* I, 179–80, II, 80. On the matter of favoritism see Apr. 7, 1627, Loudoun to Morton, NLS Mss. 80, no. 27.

58. Oct. 24, 1629, Charles to the commissioners, *Stirling* I, 387. *RPCS* 2nd ser. III, 538–41.

59. *RPCS* 2nd ser. III, intro., p. xi. For Lithgow see his poem, "Scotland's Welcome to Her Native Sonne and Soveraigne Lord, King Charles," in J. Maidment, ed., *The Poetical Remains of William Lithgow* (Edinburgh, 1863). This poem is not paginated.

60. *RPCS* 2nd ser. III, 401, 478–79, IV, 322–23, 398–99, 438. *Stirling* II, 560–61, 638. For the bishops see the council's stinging letter of Nov. 2, 1631, and Hope's letter to Menteith on Nov. 5, *RPCS* 2nd ser. IV, 348–49, Fraser, *Menteith* II, 123.

61. Connell, *Tithes* I, 146–47. SRO, GD 22/1/518, 22/3/584, 22/3/780, 22/3/781. *RPCS* 2nd ser. IV, 412–13. July 28, 1632, Hope to Charles, Aug. 15, Charles to the commissioners, Fraser, *Menteith* II, 145–47, 42.

62. On these points see Connell, *Tithes* I, 340–41, 343, 351, 387. In 1636 the minister of North Berwick received his second augmentation in three years; the decree contained a clause that this would not happen again. *Ibid.* I, 353, II, 287–91.

63. *Ibid.,* I, 305–7, II, 88. *APS* V, 34–35.

64. Connell, *Tithes* I, 466, II, 85, 87.

65. W. Makey, *The Church of the Covenant 1637–1651,* pp. 114–15.

66. This is Makey's opinion, *ibid.,* p. 113. See also Connell, *Tithes* II, 291.

67. Connell, *Tithes* I, 329.

68. On this point see Mar. 6, 1631, Charles to the commissioners, *Stirling* II, 502–3.

69. Connell, *Tithes* I, 159–64, 166–79, 195–97, II, 80.

70. *Ibid.,* I, 256–57, 261, II, 224–25. June 14, 1630, Mar. 6, 1631, Aug. 15, 1632, Charles to the commissioners, *Stirling* I, 450, II, 502–3, *RPCS* 2nd ser. IV, 7–8, 304. Hope's memorandum, Sept. 18, 1629, SRO, GD 22/3/781. For a case where the council had to intervene to protect the rights of both the titular and the minister against a heritor who tried to bend the rules to his advantage see *RPCS* 2nd ser. IV, 37–38.

71. *RPCS* 2nd ser. IV, 396. *APS* V, 32–33. See also Connell, *Tithes* I, 328–29; Mar. 6, 1631, Charles to the commissioners, *Stirling* I, 502–3; NLS Adv. Mss. 32.6.8, ff. 87–88.

72. HMC, 14th Report, app., pt. III (London, 1894), p. 236. The twenty-seven signatories included Huntly, Eglinton, Winton, Seaforth, and a large number of lairds.

73. June 7, 1629, instructions for Menteith; Dec. 28, Charles to the commissioners, *Stirling* I, 352–53, 408.

74. Christina Larner, *Enemies of God: The Witch-hunt in Scotland* (Baltimore, 1981), p. 56. For an example of the kirk's approach to poor relief see C. Baxter, ed., *Selections from the Minutes of the Synod of Fife, 1611–1687,* Abbotsford Club (Edinburgh, 1837), p. 115.

75. Connell, *Tithes* II, 236–37, 268–71.

76. See, e.g., July 19, 1632, Charles to Hope, *Stirling* II, 607.

77. NLS Adv. Mss. 32.6.8, ff. 86–87. Jan. 14, 1628, Charles to Mar and Napier, *Stirling* I, 243. Feb. 16, 1631, Lord Lindores to Morton, NLS Mss. 80, no. 39. SRO, GD 22/3/597.

78. On this point see July 13, 1633, William Maxwell to Sir John Maxwell, Sir William Fraser, *Memorials of the Maxwells of Pollok,* 2 vols. (Edinburgh, 1863), II, 243–45.

79. The legislation is in *APS* V, 23–39.

80. See Connell, *Tithes* I, 345, II, 279–80.

81. See below, chap. 5.

82. Baxter, *Synod of Fife,* p. 110. *Stirling* II, 543, 549–50, 551–52, 572, 628–29. Fraser, *Menteith* II, 38, 90–91.

83. *RPCS* 2nd ser. III, 248, 331. *Stirling* I, 377, II, 429, 622, 793–94.

84. Baxter, *Synod of Fife,* p. 107. Italics mine.

85. *RPCS* 2nd ser. I, 534–35, III, 519, IV, 89–90. *Stirling* I, 269, 318, 347–48, II, 443, 506–7, 562–63, 570, 840–42. Henry Guthry, bishop of Dunkeld, *Memoirs of Henry Guthry* (London, 1702), pp. 13–14, says that Leslie was Buckingham's candidate.

86. *Stirling* I, 126–27, 227, 242, 316. *RPCS* 2nd ser. I, 545–47, II, 536–37, 545, III, 20–21. Fraser, *Haddington* II, 158–62. G. I. R. McMahon, "The Scottish Courts of High Commission, 1610–38," *RSCHS* XV (1966), 206.

87. *RPCS* 2nd ser. II, 202–3, 222–25, 262–65, 285–86, 319–20, 358–61, 375–77, 494–96, 497–509, 535–36, 579–80, III, 24, 28–35, 78–80, 92–93, 102–4, 119–20, 146–47, 176–77, 182–86, 233–34, 237–46, 254–55, 326–31. *Stirling* I, 266, 331. L. Taylor, ed., *Aberdeen Council Letters* I, 289–90. Nov. 23, 1628, Spottiswoode to Menteith, Fraser, *Menteith* II, 77–78. Apr. 16, 1629, Haddington to Menteith, Fraser, *Haddington* II, 167–68.

88. On this point see the memorandum in Gordon, *Ecclesiastical Chronicle* I, 488–90.

89. *Row,* pp. 343–45. *Scot,* pp. 316–17. NLS, Wodrow Quarto XX, no. 25.

90. July 21, 1628, Charles to Hope, *Stirling* I, 302.

91. Nov. 27, 1628, Charles to the ministers of Edinburgh, *ibid.,* pp. 324–25, and to Menteith, Fraser, *Menteith* II, 10–11. *Row,* pp. 345–46. *Scot,* p. 320.

92. July 11, 1628, Charles to Spottiswoode, *Stirling* I, 296.

93. *RPCS* 2nd ser. III, 186–88, 361. *Stirling* II, 428.

94. *RPCS* 2nd ser. III, 275, 290–92, 317–19, 332–33, 363–64, 372–73, 417–18, 453–54, 552–53, 557–58, IV, 71, 514–16. *CSPD 1629–1631,* p. 48. John Spalding, *Memorialls of the Trubles in Scotland and in England, A.D. 1624–A.D. 1645,* ed. J. Stuart, I, 20–21. *Stirling* I, 367–68, 380, 381, II, 413, 541. Aug. 8, 1629, Charles to Spottiswoode, W. Forbes-Leith, *Memoirs of Scottish Catholics during the XVIIth and XVIIIth Centuries* (Edinburgh, 1909), I, 59–60.

95. *RPCS* 2nd ser. III, 373–76, 404–11, 438–39, IV, 184–85, 506, 508–10, 617–19, V, 50. *Stirling* I, 338, 370, 391. Dec. 17,

1630, Charles to Lord Gordon, *ibid.* II, 492. Forbes-Leith, *Memoirs* I, 86–91, 149–51.

96. NLS Mss. 3,926, pp. 360–61. *Row,* pp. 348–49.

97. Fraser, *Menteith* II, 36. Mar. 24, 1629, Haddington to Menteith, Jan. 12, 1630, Alexander to Menteith, *ibid.,* pp. 78–80, 107–8. *RPCS* 2nd ser. III, 233–34, 372–73. *Stirling* I, 391. Forbes-Leith, *Memoirs* I, 143, 154. In 1632 the Jesuits' annual summary of Scottish affairs accused Menteith and his fellow councillors of foot-dragging in the inquiry into the tragedy of the burning of Frendraught, for which see below, chap. 5, because the perpetrators were Protestant and the victims Catholic. *Ibid.,* pp. 134–35.

98. *Balfour* II, 200. Gilbert Burnet, *Bishop Burnet's History of His Own Time,* ed. M. J. Routh, I, 40.

99. See, for instance, his memorandum of Sept. 18, 1629, SRO, GD 22/3/781, and his letters to Menteith in December 1631, Fraser, *Menteith* II, 138–42.

100. Mark Napier, ed., *Memorials of Montrose and his Times* I, 65–69. The two quotations are on p. 67. The king's profit was indeed minimal; in 1642 he granted the annuity to James Livingston, a groom of the bedchamber, as security for a debt of £10,000 sterling. Connell, *Tithes* I, 270.

101. Napier, *Montrose* I, 24.

102. David Stevenson, *The Scottish Revolution 1637–1644,* p. 40.

103. On this point see C. A. Malcolm, "The Office of Sheriff in Scotland," *SHR* XX (1922–23), 305.

104. Fraser, *Menteith* II, 25–26.

105. *Ibid.,* pp. 31–32. BL Add. Mss. 23,110, p. 10. NLS Adv. Mss. 32.6.8, ff. 79a–80, 82–86. Craigie Wallace was among those paid at this time; he received £20,000 for his bailiary.

106. *Stirling* II, 439–40, 615, 624. NLS Adv. Mss. 32.6.8, f. 79a.

107. Sir William Fraser, *The Sutherland Book* II, 350.

108. See, e.g., Stevenson, *Scottish Revolution,* pp. 35–42.

109. *Balfour* II, 128.

110. R. Mitchison. *Lordship to Patronage: Scotland 1603–1745* (London, 1983), pp. 32, 46.

111. G. Donaldson, *Scotland: James V to James VII,* p. 298.

112. S. R. Gardiner, *History of England . . . 1603–1642,* new ed. (London, 1899), VII, 279.

113. See, e.g., Dec. 7, 1631, Hope to Menteith, Fraser, *Menteith* II, 138–39.

114. See, e.g., his letter of Dec. 10, 1629, to Dupplin, Mar, and

Hope regarding Inchaffray, *Stirling* I, 404. For his later policy see below, chap. 5.

115. *APS* V, 224–25. SRO, GD 22/1/518.

116. Hope used the phrase in connection with Menteith's role in the complicated and difficult business of Sir William Forbes of Craigievar, the earl of Rothes, and the temporalities of the abbey of Lindores. See SRO, GD 22/3/584, 22/3/597.

3

The Menteith Years:
War, Justice, and the Economy

For the first four years of his reign King Charles was at war, first with Spain and then with France as well. The country's war effort was laughably feeble; fortunately for Charles, his enemies were occupied elsewhere, and were willing enough to make peace when he abandoned his patently futile efforts. In strictly military terms the war cost Charles very little; its domestic repercussions, however, were substantial, in Scotland as well as in England.

The campaigning, such as it was, took place far from Scotland's shores. The government ordered wappenschawings, and occasionally displayed some interest in the creation of a warning system in case of invasion and some concern for coastal defense. Edinburgh eagerly took up one defense project, the fortification of Leith, as a means of obtaining permanent control over its port, but dropped the plan when the council refused to countenance the Good Town's transparent proposals.[1] Another abortive project was undertaken at Dumbarton castle, the condition of which gave particular cause for alarm. Its captain, Sir John Stewart of Methven, a bastard of the second duke of Lennox, had neglected the place. He was in serious trouble with the law on account of his mistreatment of his wife and had betaken himself to Ireland. Menteith headed a committee which reported that the castle was in deplorable shape. The council made Traquair interim keeper. He found the walls in ruins, the ordnance unmounted, a "garrison" of three men and a boy, and a few rusty muskets. By the time Traquair took matters in hand, however, the invasion scare was over, and the dowager duchess of Lennox, mindful of the interests of her young son the duke, the hereditary keeper, insisted, to Traquair's disappointment, that the castle be turned over to one of the family retainers, who did nothing. In 1634 the newly appointed captain, Sir John Maxwell of Pollok, declared that the walls "cannot hold out beasts, let be men."[2]

The principal Scottish contribution to Charles's war effort took the form of manpower. In 1626 and early 1627 the king commissioned various lords and gentlemen to raise troops to take service with Christian IV, Gustavus Adolphus, or the Dutch republic, and, since there was no hope of filling the ranks with volunteers, especially for the regiment of the unpopular and Catholic Nithsdale,[3] the government authorized the use of compulsion. Gypsies, sturdy beggars, and vagabonds, "masterless men and idle loiterers who . . . spends (*sic*) their time in ale houses and so are unprofitable burdens to the country" were to be pressed into service.[4] Officials and parish ministers in town and countryside were to cooperate by identifying and, if necessary, detaining suitable cannon-fodder, and by not permitting fraudulent "arrests" to avoid the press gang. Ship masters were not to allow potential soldiers to escape to Ireland. Pardons were dangled before criminals willing to enlist, save those guilty of murder or treason, and protection from prosecution was promised to debtors, of whom perhaps the most prominent was Nithsdale himself. Charles contemplated the possibility of dealing with highland and border chiefs to find soldiers amongst their kinsmen; the upshot was the recruiting of a troop of highland bowmen. Inevitably the recruiters overdid it—they made themselves hateful, said Melrose. They forced men into service who were not gypsies or the denizens of alehouses. A woman claimed that seven men broke into her house, kidnapped her husband, son, and servant, and sold them to a recruiter for £40 apiece. Among the other victims were students at the University of Edinburgh; parents were taking alarm and transferring their sons to Glasgow, St. Andrews, and Aberdeen. Students, proclaimed the council, were exempt from this sort of draft.[5]

In August 1627 there came a new request, for 2,000 men for the earl of Morton to lead to France, as part of Buckingham's ill-fated expedition to lift the siege of La Rochelle. These were to be "worthy persons and of good vigor and ability of body, not being of those who are in the common rolls for the service of the king of Denmark." The council was rightly doubtful of its ability to meet this request, given the demands already made on Scottish manpower. Within a month Charles was instructing the lord deputy of Ireland to assist in the rounding up of fugitive Scots idlers there to swell the ranks of Morton's army.[6] The fact is, that Scotsmen were unwilling to enlist in anybody's regiment. The war was unpopular, not merely because it was against France—as William Kerr of Ancrum pointed out to his father, the potential recruits were "only base people" who knew nothing of the ancient Scottish ties with France[7]—but because it meant hardship and expense. Local officials were uncooperative about producing lists of ne'er-do-wells who might be pressed into service, and some parishes reported that they had no shiftless and idle types living there. The soldiers' rate of pay was low, and their living allowances sometimes less than that of prisoners in the Edinburgh tolbooth.[8] Desertion was rampant, and apparently unaffected by threats of the death penalty. Soldiers deserted not only while awaiting transport overseas, which the government found difficult to arrange for financial reasons, but also while on the continent; they then made their way back to Scotland, where they spread slanderous stories about their commanders. Within four days of the grant of a commission to Sir Donald MacKay of Strathnaver to raise 1,000 men to serve the king of Denmark the council had to arrange to pursue fugitives from his regiment.[9] Morton's regiment was kept penned up on the Isle of Wight for almost a year, to keep the soldiers from deserting; predictably, they made themselves obnoxious to the inhabitants and allegedly fathered seventy bastards. "Since the Danish slavery never were these Islanders so oppressed," wrote Sir John Oglander, as "when the regiment of Scots ate and devoured the whole land." Buckingham's disaster at La Rochelle, which Sir James Balfour regarded as deliberate treachery, designed to bring ruin to the Huguenots, ended whatever willingness to accept Charles's policy might have existed in Scotland. In May 1628 the Venetian ambassador reported that the Scots were openly urging Charles to make peace with France.[10]

One reason for the unpopularity of the war was its devastating effect on Scottish commerce. Trade with France was prohibited. The lease of the customs duties could not be auctioned in 1627 because no one came to bid. The king even attempted to prevent the sale of the stocks of French wine already in Scotland, but the merchants' clamor was so great that he backed down. The merchants also complained bitterly about the general prohibition, arguing that it would simply throw all the carrying trade into the hands of the Dutch. What really galled them was their belief that English merchants were allowed to buy French wine in the Low Countries, while they were forbidden to do so.[11] But it was not merely the trade with France that suffered; all of Scotland's overseas commerce was imperiled, owing to the depredations of privateers, mostly out of Dunkirk. In April 1627 the council informed Charles that the privateers had so terrorized the Scottish merchants "that none of them dare adventure to put to sea;" the king's three ships, which he had sent to protect them, lay in harbor and did nothing.[12] They continued to do nothing, partly because the government was at its wits' end to find the money for their upkeep. In July 1627, while Charles was contemplating how best to raise a Scottish fighting force to accompany Buckingham to France, he authorized the sale of these ships because they were such a financial burden, and then instructed the council to deal with the new owners, whoever they might be, to transport Morton's troops to France. Under such conditions overseas trade continued to founder; an English traveler in Scotland in 1629 remarked that the great bulk of Scottish foreign trade was with England,[13] a trade which was itself hampered by the steadily lengthening list of English goods whose export to Scotland was prohibited. A dearth of cattle and sheep in 1627, which in turn meant a wool shortage, further damaged the economy. Small wonder that the Scots wanted peace with France; when, after the fall of La Rochelle late in 1628 Charles decided to cut his losses and make peace, he promptly authorized the reopening of the wine trade.[14]

The dislocation of overseas trade caused real financial crisis due to the decline in the crown's income from customs duties,[15] and made still harder the already difficult task of finding money to pay for the king's ships and soldiers. Morton, Nithsdale, and their fellow commanders had to be paid, as did the captains of the king's three ships. In theory the money for this was to come from the tax voted in 1625, but cash was scarce in spite of the best efforts of the new collector, Sir James Baillie of Lochend, who took over in February 1627 from the incompetent Nithsdale. Baillie had to borrow, especially to keep the ships supplied. By September he was in debt to the Edinburgh merchant William Dick in the amount of £178,000, and finally balked at assuming any more financial responsibility; in November Dupplin took over the job of tax collector. Early in the following year the council authorized Dick and a fellow merchant to recover part of their money by selling the cargo of a Lübeck ship which had been brought in as a prize, even though it was extremely doubtful that the seizure of the ship was legitimate. Under these circumstances the decision to sell the king's ships is hardly surprising.[16]

The government did what it could to add to its financial resources. It pursued officials who refused to turn over the tax money they had collected and delinquents who had not paid the taxes voted in 1621 and 1625, many of whom, interestingly enough, were clergymen. It persuaded a number of burghs to pay what they owed on the current tax in a lump sum instead of spreading the payments over four years, and, in addition, to make loans to the government, on the ground that the money would provide for naval defense against privateering. It experimented with new taxes—a two-shilling-per-ton export levy on coal and salt, for instance, to pay for fortifications on the Firth of Forth. Many of the owners of the coal mines and salt pans neglected to pay and were summoned to appear before the council to explain their behavior; by this time, however, the emergency had passed and so nothing was done.[17] The council remonstrated with the king for his practice of granting pensions specifically assigned to particular sources of revenue; this sometimes led the grantee to make a claim to the source of revenue itself instead of merely to its income, thus permanently depleting the crown's resources. It also protested against his decision to remit the collection of fines for certain offenses on the part of the inhabitants of the burghs; the burghs had pressed for this, in part on the ground that their trade was suffering. The council opined that the king's action would encourage future violations of statutes, especially those on usury, the export of specie, and the import of English beer at inflated prices, and would make it much more difficult to collect taxes—burgesses were especially skillful at devising ways of fraudulently avoiding payments of taxes on annualrents. The king recognized this, and in June 1630 authorized a commission to compound with those accused of tax evasion in connection with annualrents, in the interest of getting at least some of what was allegedly owed into the treasury.[18]

Among those who urged the king not to grant the remission the burgesses desired was the laird of Thornton, who in 1628 submitted a long memorandum detailing ways in which he could obtain more money out of the crown's regular revenues by more efficient administration. After considerable discussion the king granted him a commission to seek out those who had defrauded the crown on rents and casualties, with the right to keep half of what he turned up. Objections soon began to be heard. Mar protested that the wording was vague enough to be construed as including arrears of taxation; Dupplin, who at first had favored the plan, turned against it. Restrictions on Thornton's freedom of action did not quiet the critics. At the convention of estates in 1630 there was a vote overwhelmingly in favor of requesting the king to cancel the patent, in spite of Menteith's argument that it should be allowed to stand with further modifications. Treasurer Depute Napier, in his memoirs, attributed this vote to the machinations of Dupplin and Mar, who, he said, were annoyed because Thornton would not use his powers to go after Napier. There is no reason to believe that Thornton would behave in so uncharacteristically upright a fashion; moreover, Napier was concerned to blacken Dupplin and Mar. The members of the convention needed no urging to attack Thornton's patent, and shortly thereafter Thornton consented to its cancellation. The usual haggling over compensation followed, with Thornton settling eventually for £3,000 sterling.[19]

The war was not the only cause of unusual demands on the revenue in these years. There was also the question of the king's visit to his native land to receive his crown and hold a parliament, an event repeatedly planned and repeatedly postponed, which caused Charles's popularity to erode. Whenever such a visit was proposed the government made preparations, and such preparations entailed expense. Once, in 1628, it looked as though Charles really would come, on very short notice. There was no cash in the treasury, so the council tried vainly to borrow from Edinburgh, and had to write to the king, begging him to put off his visit till the following year.[20] Mar added a reminder that one reason for the treasury's condition was that he "was forced to obey your Majesty's other liberal grants"—in this respect Charles was more like his father than has sometimes been thought.[21] Charles agreed to postpone his visit; a dispute followed as to how to finance it when it did take place. The council wanted the king to summon the convention of estates and ask for a tax. Charles preferred to proceed by borrowing, and was encouraged by Treasurer Depute Napier, who offered to raise £10,000 sterling. No one else in the government favored this, and Napier's many enemies now combined to get rid of him, led by Dupplin, whom Napier had offended by taking over the lease of the Orkneys after Dupplin had been forced to surrender it, and Mar, who resented Napier's attempt to take charge of the preparations for the king's visit. Mar's mind, said Napier, had been poisoned by Baillie of Lochend, who, in Napier's words, "was basely born and had his education under a butcher" and was suited only to be "a clerk of a kitchen." Napier believed, with some justice, that Baillie was angling for his job, and in pursuit of that goal had convinced Mar that Napier wanted to replace him as treasurer.[22] Mar henceforth, said Napier, pursued him with implacable malice, actually undertaking a journey to court to this end, although he was so lame that he had to use crutches. Thornton, in the process of persuading Charles that there was money to be had through better administration of the crown's revenues, had accused Napier of misstating the accounts for wardships. The king was disturbed. Dupplin and Mar now had the further motive that Napier's incompetence (or worse) was to be the means of enriching Thornton, whom they both disliked, and they seized their chance. They accused Napier of taking kickbacks, both in the Orkneys, where he sublet to William Dick and took a 7,000-merk profit, and in a contract with the sergeant of the king's confectionary for the supplies of pastry for the intended visit. Napier's explanations were disingenuous. The king ordered the cancellation of both the lease and the contract, and reissued the Orkney lease direct to Dick; the 7,000 merks which had gone into Napier's pocket now went to the earl of Annandale, who seems to have had a hand in exposing Napier, as payment for his surrender of the hereditary stewartry of Annandale.[23] Napier was understandably reluctant to surrender the written evidence of his agreement on the pastry; once he did so, Charles finally agreed to his removal from office. The king's delays exasperated his officials. As Dupplin put it to Morton, "Can ever prince look to be faithfully served, except he either punish the offenders or calumniators?"[24] In May 1630, possibly at the insistence of his new lord treasurer, the earl of Morton, who replaced the ailing Mar in April, Charles instructed Menteith to find out what terms Napier would take to resign. Napier attempted to drive a hard bargain, thoroughly irritating Menteith, who called him "one willful fool."[25] The king rather liked Napier and had granted him a peerage in 1627, but Menteith kept him from changing his mind, and finally, in October 1630, Charles joined Traquair with Napier in the office, as he had once done with Alexander and Melrose. He also threatened Napier with a trial for malfeasance in office, and the latter finally, most reluctantly, resigned. In May 1631 Traquair received a grant of the office for life, an annual pension of £200 sterling, and instructions to see what could be done to increase the tack of the customs duties, which had been let at a low figure on account of the war: he was on his way to the real power he so much coveted. Napier by his own account was a solitary patriot surrounded by conniving rogues. About his only satisfaction was that his successor was Traquair and not the villainous Baillie, who, says Napier, lost his influence when Morton replaced Mar at the treasury. Iron-

ically, the preparations for the proposed—and again postponed—
royal visit had to be financed by borrowing, as Napier had
advocated.[26]

Borrowing was necessary because Morton inherited an empty
cupboard. In June 1629 the council had informed the king that
the normal pensions to the gentlemen of the privy chamber and
to the king's old nurse could not be paid. Things were no better
when Morton took over in the following April. "Never man entered to so bare a charge," Dupplin informed him, "and so over-
charged with debts which never can be paid except there be
taxations; still you can neither now promise payment of pension
nor precept, for there is nothing left to be taken up." A little later
Dupplin sent Morton copies of past exchequer commissions, call-
ing his attention to one issued "in a time much resembling this,
when King James of blessed memory and his crown here were
reduced to extreme penury." A further complication was a shortage of specie and the circulation of debased foreign coins, a situation which troubled the council, but about which it felt it could
do little until economic normalcy returned along with peace. Its
only positive step was to order the coinage of 500 stones of copper
in April 1629, to reduce the shortage of petty cash for the benefit
of the poor.[27]

The end of the war held out the hope of better times with the
restoration of normal channels of overseas trade. There were other
changes as well, among them the ending of the Nova Scotia venture in July 1631. There never had been any enthusiasm in Scotland for it; about the only time the council showed any initiative
was in protesting to Charles against his reported grant of lands in
the area to be held of the English crown. Attempts to persuade
people who wanted favors from the government to invest there
were unsuccessful, as was Alexander's plan to use various highland
chiefs as recruiters amongst their clansmen. The peace treaty with
France recognized the French claim to the area, which was important to France as a protection for the lifeline to the St. Law-
rence. There was a formal protest at the convention of estates in
1630 against the sacrifice of any territory to France, but that was
about all. The burghs had never shown any interest in the economic possibilities of Nova Scotia; there was no inducement,

economic or religious, for Scotsmen to emigrate there—religious refugees preferred the congenial theological climate of the Dutch republic, or, if Catholic, of France. From the beginning, the scheme had been artificial, the brainchild of Sir William Alexander and his associates; in the end, the colonial dream ws sacrificed to the more practical consideration of good relations with France.[28] The biggest loser was Alexander, who had invested heavily in the scheme and was financially ruined. The king's efforts to help him recover were to be politically very damaging.

One wartime activity which the peace treaties did not end was the recruitment of Scottish soldiers for service in foreign armies. Indeed, one new avenue opened up: in April 1630 Charles authorized Lord Gordon to raise 2,000 men for service with the French. A more important commission was that granted in September 1630 to the young marquis of Hamilton, Charles's close friend and Buckingham's successor as master of the horse, to lead 6,000 men into the service of Gustavus Adolphus. The king gave Hamilton a Garter, to raise his prestige, and, to help him finance his army, a gift of the income from the impost on wines, which amounted to 112,000 merks a year, for sixteen years.[29] Recruitment went slowly, however; before Hamilton could collect his 6,000 men, he was faced with an accusation which was launched first by Lord Reay, a professional soldier already in Swedish service, and which was then, rashly, taken to the king by Lord Ochiltree, that Hamilton intended to use his soldiers to make himself king of Scotland, and that he had enlisted Haddington, Roxburgh, and Buccleuch in this insane venture.

The origins of this story have never become clear. The Venetian ambassador speculated that it might have been floated first in Brussels, as a way of preventing Hamilton from bringing aid to the Swedes.[30] Charles refused to believe a word of it. He wrote to the council declaring his belief in everyone's innocence, and insisted that Hamilton share his bedroom for a night. Charles determined to make an example of Ochiltree, on the ground that Ochiltree, out of jealousy of Hamilton, had maliciously embroidered on a piece of soldiers' gossip. Why Ochiltree behaved as he did is hard to say. Perhaps he believed the story. Perhaps he thought he saw a chance to ruin the hereditary enemy of his house—he was the son of that Captain James Stewart who had dominated Scottish politics briefly in the 1580s while holding the Hamilton earldom. He certainly underestimated Charles's affection for and confidence in Hamilton, perhaps because it was well known at court that Hamilton and Menteith were at odds. At the end of 1631 Charles sent Ochiltree to Edinburgh to stand trial. At a preliminary hearing, however, Ochiltree defended himself with considerable skill, and it developed that the original source of the story, according to Reay, was the earl of Seaforth. Seaforth was never questioned, and the trial was repeatedly postponed. In July 1632 Charles wrote Menteith that it was clear, from Menteith's report, that a trial would not result in a heavy sentence. So there was to be no trial, but Ochiltree was not to come within fifty miles of court—a clear indication that his release was contemplated. It is a permissible deduction from the wording of this letter that Menteith was advocating such an action. But Ochiltree was not released, and in May 1633, after Menteith's fall, he was transferred to Blackness castle until further notice. He remained there for almost twenty years.[31]

Charles's commissions to Hamilton and others to raise regiments for Gustavus Adolphus were meant to provide some show of help for the unlucky Queen of Bohemia, whom Charles's own military efforts had been unable to succor. But there was another motive at work too. It was still believed, in spite of the recruiters' difficulties, that Scotland was full of idle vagabonds and sturdy beggars who would become still more of a nuisance than they already were if there was no way to siphon them off. The end of the war prompted the council in January 1630 to issue a proclamation recapitulating all the previous legislation against beggars and demanding its enforcement, not only against the beggars themselves but also against those who gave them alms, a demand repeated in a petition from the lairds at the convention of estates six months later. The council was particularly sensitive about the beggars' presence in Edinburgh, in view of the king's perpetually pending visit. The Irish were also a problem: "Great numbers of strong and sturdy Irish beggars are sent from Ireland in several companies toward this kingdom and they go in troops through the country." They were ordered to go home in fifteen days, in

November 1629 and again in September 1630.[32] After that, interestingly enough, there are no more proclamations. Either the council became discouraged, or, more probably, restortion of economic normalcy, after a decade of dislocation owing first to famine and then to war, made the problem less acute.

In Scotland as in England responsibility for seeing that the legislation against beggars was properly enforced lay with the justices of the peace. The administration of justice was a matter in which Charles took a personal interest in these years. In March 1627 the king indicated that he wanted a revival of the system of justice ayres in criminal cases.[33] Parliament had authorized these ayres in 1587, as part of James VI's program of making the system of justice less costly and time-consuming by making it unnecessary to have every case tried in Edinburgh. This effort failed, largely because James could not afford to let his handful of loyal and efficient government servants take the time to go on circuit; they were too necessary in the capital.[34] The system of ayres fell into disuse in the 1590s, and James made no further effort to revive it. Charles now resolved to do so. Personnel would be available: since members of the court of session were no longer privy councillors, they could go on circuit when the session was on vacation.

There was one administrative problem: the office of justice general was hereditary in the house of Argyll. Lord Lorne, the *de facto* head of the house in the absence of his Catholic father the earl, wanted the office renewed, but it was comprised in the terms of the revocation. Lorne agreed to surrender it, and did so in April 1628, in return for £4,000 sterling and a confirmation of his hereditary justiciarship in Argyll, Tarbert, and the islands (save Orkney and Shetland), as well as in his own property elsewhere in the highlands, in which areas the justice ayres would not operate. As further consolation Charles made him a privy councillor, and later let him succeed his father as master of the household.[35] Almost at once a dispute broke out between Lorne and the inhabitants of the western islands over the venue of his courts: could he hold them where he pleased, or was he bound to hold them in places specified in a statute of 1504? This dispute went on for over a year—Charles as a matter of course asked Menteith to look

War, Justice, and the Economy

into it—and was not definitively settled until 1632. The sites
Lorne preferred were those where the Lord of the Isles had once
held his courts;[36] Menteith would have done his master a service
if he had called the king's attention to this dangerous sign of the
ambitions of the future MacCailein Mór. There is no evidence
that he did so, and in the end Lorne prevailed, but the whole
business left him rather bitter. So too were the highlanders,
whose hope of weakening the influence of the predatory Campbells had been dashed.[37] Nor was this Lorne's only jurisdictional
problem. The king allowed the bishop of the Isles some criminal
jurisdiction in his diocese, which was within Lorne's justiciarship. Lorne had to stave off an effort by Seaforth, whose machinations and influence he feared, to end his justiciarship in the
northern Hebrides. The sheriff of Bute attempted to usurp his
jurisdiction; the marquis of Hamilton successfully evaded it, for
the isle of Arran. The council backed the earl of Sutherland when
he hanged some malefactors at Dornoch; Lorne argued that, as
residents of the western isles, the men came under his jurisdiction. These constant disputes were unlikely to content Lorne with
his bargain.

In addition to these jurisdictional disputes, Charles's government made a number of other mistakes, both of omission and
commission, in dealing with Lorne. It took no heed of the warning that he intended to follow the traditional expansionist policy
of his house, a message conveyed by his efficient crushing of the
rebellion of the MacIans of Ardnamurchan in 1624–25, a rebellion induced, in part at least, by Campbell goading. Lorne was
the most insular of Scottish aristocrats, never going abroad or to
court, and the government made no effort to cultivate him. He
was given no help about the question of his father's debts or his
effort to work out an arrangement with his half-brother, whom
he disliked, which would enable him to acquire Kintyre. The
government would not pay him what it owed him, and it interfered in the internal affairs of the clan. Lorne bitterly resented
this. His top political priority was always to hold the Campbells
together; he knew all about the awful days of his father's nonage,
when internecine rivalries, culminating in the assassination of
Campbell of Lochnell at his own fireside, had almost destroyed

the clan. Now, once more, the Campbells were pulling together, as they had in the last decade of James's reign in dealing with Lorne's father's extravagance and apostasy. Lorne intended that this should continue.

In short, Charles's government afflicted Lorne with pinpricks, but it made no serious effort to undermine his immense authority in his own area, as it had successfully done with Huntly, nor to weaken what might be called the Campbell network—the power of the successive heads of the house, both now and for the next hundred years and more, lay in their control of a kin group which was not limited to Argyll but was virtually nationwide. Perhaps action seemed unnecessary, since Lorne did not seem particularly politically minded—he played very little part in national affairs before the beginning of the troubles in 1637—and since, after all, Lorne was not yet head of the clan, and his father, the earl, lived in England. For whatever reason Charles did not diminish either Lorne's power or his resentment, and, like Charles, Lorne was a man who bore grudges, especially where the welfare of the Campbells was in question. The result is only too well known.[38]

Charles manifested his usual impatience in getting his experiment in revival of the justice ayres under way. His father's intentions and his, he wrote the council in August 1627, "do as yet sleep unperformed." When Lorne resigned as justice general, Charles appointed Menteith to the office.[39] The appointment took effect in July 1628; within a month the council had issued detailed instructions for the ayres. A total of eight justices were to go in pairs to two places for two weeks each, to hear a long list of criminal cases. Six of the eight were regular members of the court of session. The other two, both of whom were newly appointed extraordinary lords of session, were Menteith and the master of Jedburgh, a privy councillor and a member of the border commission whose specialized knowledge was thought to be necessary there. Their destinations covered the lowlands and borders; no circuit came closer than Perth and Aberdeen to Lorne's highland bailiwick. Menteith could determine which of the long list of crimes the justices should try; the punishment of those found guilty of a short list of particularly heinous offenses was to be left to the council. The king ordered that the justices should have proper robes and a pound sterling a day for up to forty days for expenses, and awaited what he hoped would be a favorable report on the outcome.[40]

Charles was to be disappointed. Even before the judges could set out there was complaint, from the lords of regality, who protested that their right to repledge—that is, to transfer to their own jurisdiction any tenant or inhabitant of the regality accused of a crime before another court, including the king's justice ayre—was being undermined. Charles hurriedly instructed Menteith to have lords of regality and their bailies join the circuit judges on the bench where appropriate: this was not a device to undercut their authority.[41] This disturbed Menteith. A memorandum of his on the circuit courts exists;[42] it is undated, and it is not clear whether it was written before or after the first year's experience. What is clear is that Menteith believed that lords of regality had the right to repledge only in cases of life and limb. If they could repledge in cases involving such laws as those against usury and the carrying of guns, a quarter of the king's subjects would in effect be exempt from these statutes, a state of affairs which Menteith regarded as unreasonable. Either the whole force of the government should be thrown into the effort at law enforcement, or the effort was not worthwhile. As soon as it became apparent that no all-out effort was in prospect, Menteith, who had never much liked the plan, backed off. In a memorandum written in 1629 he and Hope pointed out that the circuit courts were very unpopular, burdensome, and expensive. If Charles was indeed planning to come to Scotland in the following year, he should create some good will for himself by abandoning the vexatious device. Charles acquiesced. Grants of regality were included in the revocation, and eliminating them would have eliminated repledging; but, given that settling the question of the teinds had first call on the crown's limited financial resources, the king was not now in a position to attempt to get rid of heritable jurisdictions. So in November 1629, after the circuit of that year, he authorized the payment of £5,000 sterling to Menteith as reimbursement for his expenses in organizing the circuits, and in the council register for 1630 we read that "the Lords thinks (*sic*) fit that the holding of circuit courts for this year shall be forborne." They were not revived.[43]

Charles did not abandon his belief in the administrative possibilities of the justice ayres, as his use of the Book of Orders in England in the 1630s indicates, but in Scotland Menteith's counsels prevailed. All the evidence suggests that Menteith disliked judicial innovations. One consequence of his influence with the king was that the commission of grievances, inaugurated with such fanfare in 1626, was allowed to sink without a trace.[44] The circuit courts, combined with his new position as justice general, offered an opportunity, if fruitfully used, to strengthen the crown and increase his own personal power, as Menteith saw, but he did not advocate that they be so used, and when their unpopularity and the king's unwillingness to force the issue on repledging became apparent, he made his feelings known, and perhaps exaggerated them somewhat. Dupplin, who also disliked the circuit courts, wrote to Morton in April 1630 that "no man here doth speak so much [against them] as our Lord President (as he sayeth he hath done from the beginning to his Majesty)."[45] And certainly Menteith was right in believing that they caused more expense and political backlash than they were worth, unless the king intended to use them to break down the jurisdiction of the lords of regality. People were frightened of the courts, particularly of the fines they might levy;[46] they evoked no enthusiasm anywhere, least of all among the judges, who disliked the expense involved. Edinburgh also protested against them, though the capital's motives were hardly disinterested: successful circuits would cost Edinburgh legal business.[47] The reputation of the circuit judges was further diminished by the association of their work with that of Thornton and his unpopular patent for the seeking out of concealed money owed to the crown.[48] One rather unexpected result of the experiment with the justice ayres was that the lairds discovered the virtues of the office of justice of the peace: if there was judicial business to be done, better that they should do it than judges on circuit from Edinburgh. At the convention of estates in 1630 the lairds asked that more justices of the peace be appointed, and when the Covenanters were in power they did their best to revitalize the office, in the interest of better local justice.[49]

Among the crimes with which the circuit justices were instructed to concern themselves was witchcraft. There is no evidence that they paid special attention to witches, who were tried mostly by special commissions, as had been the case since 1597. Whether by coincidence or not, however, the years of the experiment with justice ayres saw an explosion in the number of prosecutions for witchcraft. For more than twenty years after the union of the crowns there had been very few such prosecutions, perhaps owing to the influence of Lord Chancellor Dunfermline, who was skeptical by nature and disliked clerical meddling in politics. After his death in 1622 there began a slow increase in the number of cases, an increase which was accelerated after the breaking of the power of his *quondam* colleagues on the council in the first year of Charles's reign. Then, from August 1628 through September 1630, over 300 cases were tried. This was one of the four great outbreaks of witchcraft mania in Scottish history, the others coming in the 1590s, in 1649–50, and in 1661–62. There is ample circumstantial explanation for the other three periods of intense persecution; what started this one is anything but clear. There is no indication that either Charles or Menteith and his colleagues on the council were much interested in pursuing witches, and Lord Advocate Hope, though he conducted a number of prosecutions, "made no mention of witchcraft at all in either his *Minor Practicks* or his *Major Practicks*."[50] Christina Larner has pointed to the build-up in the number of cases prior to August 1628, and to the privy council's stress on the necessity for law and order in instituting the ayres, as well as to the fact that these years saw the climax of the great persecutions on the continent as factors in the onset of the mania. It seems likely also that the council, in authorizing these prosecutions, may have hoped to focus the general discontent on something other than the revocation and the economic difficulties caused by the war and by soaring grain prices: from 1628 to 1630 the price of oatmeal in Fife equaled or exceeded that of the famine year of 1623. Ironically, if the poet William Lithgow is to be believed, the number of burnings added to the cost of living by causing a rise in the price of coal.[51] It was not, perhaps, coincidental that after the end of the war and the acceptance of the decreets arbitral of 1629 by the convention of estates in July 1630, the persecutions began to fall off: the 1630s saw only a handful of cases being tried each year.

Charles did not complement his temporary enthusiasm for circuit courts with much concern for other aspects of the careful administration of justice. In July 1628 he did appoint a committee to review current statutes, with an eye toward codification, but it accomplished no more than had previous commissions charged with the same task.[52] Not until July 1629 did Charles take steps to renew the commissions of the justices of the peace and fill the gaps in their ranks; this had not been done since James's death. The council must bear its share of the blame for this; Charles's letter of authorization indicates that this matter had just been called to his attention.[53] Another serious problem developed on the borders, where haphazard and inattentive administration led to a great deal of unnecessary difficulty.

One of the objectives of King James's administration had been to pacify what James liked to call the "middle shires," and it had succeeded very well, in part because of the creation of a bloody-minded patrol there. In 1621 James made the mistake of disbanding the patrol as an economy move, and trouble immediately began again. The upshot was not the revival of the patrol but the creation of a new commission headed by the earls of Annandale, Nithsdale, and Buccleuch. This worked fairly well thanks to the efforts of Buccleuch—Annandale was an absentee and Nithsdale's attempts to involve himself were firmly discouraged.[54] After James's death matters changed for the worse, owing to the increased influence of the incompetent Nithsdale, who characteristically blamed others for his shortcomings,[55] and the declining activity of Buccleuch. A meeting of the Scottish commissioners in February 1628 concluded that the root of the problem lay in the interruption of the activity of the old Anglo-Scottish joint commission, which made it easy for criminals sought in one jurisdiction to take refuge in the other, or in Ireland. This was certainly true: lawless men have always had a liking for ill-patrolled frontiers, and they tend to congregate there. The Scots commissioners asked Charles to renew the joint commission. Charles indicated that he was prepared to do so, and in July instructed Menteith to look into the matter. Nothing happened.

In July 1629 the council again recommended the revival of the commission, sending a draft and a list of suggested commissioners for the king's consideration.[56] Charles did not accept this advice. Instead, at the end of 1629 he ordered Menteith to hold a special justice court in Jedburgh and Dumfries in the spring of 1630. Menteith was to clean out the jails there, compel the lords of regality to sit with the court instead of permitting repledging, and accept a sworn dittay against the accused if no accuser appeared. Penalties were to be severe.[57] There is no record of the results of Menteith's visit to Jedburgh and Dumfries, but is noteworthy that complaints of lawlessness there dropped off. Talk of a guard, which these disturbances and those in the highlands had caused, ceased to be heard, and when in April 1631 the council ordered the enforcement of the legislation of 1567 and 1594 requiring landlords and bailies in the highlands to find caution to deliver any "tenants and servants and indwellers upon their lands" accused of crimes, it was not thought necessary to enforce these acts on the borders, though they applied there as well.[58] The calm was deceptive, however. The failure to renew the joint commission was a mistake. Once Menteith was gone the disorders broke out there once again.

In the highlands disorders never really ceased. From the beginning of Charles's reign the earl of Moray had been the king's lieutenant there; his highhandedness had caused frequent protests, especially on the part of the burgh of Inverness. In September 1629 the king decided, to Moray's annoyance, that such a grant of power was no longer necessary; by June 1630 the "insolences and oppressions daily committed within these northern parts" caused him to change his mind.[59] It was in the highlands that the consequences of Charles's destruction of the authority and prestige of the privy council had its most deleterious effects. As the government of James VI had realized, peace in the highlands depended on steady administrative attention and cooperation with the clan chiefs, or some of them at least, and it had achieved such good results that in 1622 Sir Rory MacLeod of Dunvegan could speak of "this delectable time of peace."[60] But now, in 1630, if one believes the council register, Menteith's own stewartry was swarming with "numbers of broken and lawless limmers

. . . who . . . were some few years bygone reduced to the obedience of law and justice . . . (and) now . . . go sorning . . . in troops."[61] Worse still, there was a revival of Roman Catholicism, especially in the western isles, thanks to the missionary work of a group of Irish Franciscans in the later 1620s. This added one more reason for reluctance to obey the central government and for dislike of the rapacious and mostly Protestant Campbells.[62] In July 1631 none of the highland chiefs showed up for their required annual appearance before the council, which later in the year in effect legitimated their recalcitrance by agreeing that any chief wishing not to appear should make a request to that effect in March: if there were no complaints outstanding, he could be excused.[63] The long-drawn-out tragedy of Frendraught, which involved the burning to death of one of Huntly's sons and the young laird of Rothiemay in Frendraught tower in October 1630, was never satisfactorily dealt with despite a long investigation, and caused endless turmoil.[64] The most notorious highland outlaw of the period was James Grant of Daltaleis. Late in 1630 Moray captured him, but his trial was repeatedly postponed, and in 1632 he escaped from Edinburgh castle. Lord Chancellor Dupplin had unsuccessfully urged the king to authorize a speedy trial, as an example to others; this business, he wrote, had vexed him more than gout or gravel.[65] And well it might have. It was very apparent to the clan chiefs, and to the likes of Lorne, Huntly, and Moray that the privy council had no independent authority, and could handle only trivia on its own responsibility. The king they would still obey, but what did the king know of James Grant or Rothiemay? And Menteith, constantly traveling, had no time. The circuits might have helped, but justice in the highlands was left in the hands of the feared and hated Campbells. It is not too much to say that it was in the highlands that the Jacobean system of government suffered its first permanent breakdown.

One other aspect of the judicial system concerned Charles: the salaries of the members of the court of session, which in 1629 he labeled "mean and small" but which, during the war, he could not afford to augment.[66] Want of money was indeed critical; as Dupplin pointed out to Morton, the new lord treasurer, in April 1630, a tax was essential if the exchequer was to meet its ordinary obligations. If Charles did not come to Scotland that year—and at that point it seemed likely that he would not, although the visit had not yet been officially postponed—Dupplin advised the summoning of a convention of estates rather than a parliament. Parliament would have a great deal of business to do in connection with the revocation; the passions the latter aroused might doom a tax bill to defeat. In a convention, on the other hand, a tax would be more likely to pass. "Many will be loath . . . to show themselves refractory, hoping when parliament shall be to receive either favor or hard dealing from his Majesty in their particulars according to their carriage in the convention." Charles, when he decided to postpone his visit yet again, took Dupplin's advice and authorized the meeting of a convention of estates, which began on July 28, 1630. It lasted for more than a week, but was by no means as harmonious as the chancellor had hoped.[67]

The king's formal agenda comprised four items: a tax, action on evaluation of tithes, the review of the laws, and the improvement of wool manufactures. His real agenda was somewhat different. The estates decided to begin with the tax, and voted for a renewal of that of 1625, brushing aside Dupplin's suggestion to vote it for more than four years in order to save themselves the trouble of having to renew it when it expired. This done, the estates ratified the king's controversial request for a pardon for all those convicted of violations of the penal statutes, with the exception of those on usury, tax fraud, and the carrying of guns. At this point Dupplin took to his bed with an attack of the gout;[68] Menteith was in the chair for the rest of the meeting. As has been said, it was he who pushed through, albeit with some difficulty and with some minor concessions, the ratification of the decreets arbitral in the matter of the revocation. He was less successful in defending Thornton's patent. By far his trickiest problem was to fend off an attack on the bishops by some of the lay patrons of benefices and a series of petitions from some members of the clergy which constituted an attack on the five articles of Perth. The ministers were worried. William Struthers of Edinburgh had written Menteith six months before, urging that there be no more innovations. The church was already "rent . . . grievously for ceremonies;" the bishops were odious already, and now there were rumors of "organs, liturgies, and such like."[69] Struthers was no radical—he wound up as dean of Edinburgh cathedral when Charles created the new bishopric there—and Menteith sympathized with much of what Struthers said; after all, he had voted against the five articles of Perth. He could not allow any debate on these matters, however, and with some effort he was able to stifle it. But he could not prevent Lord Balmerino, as spokesman for the lay patrons, from formally complaining that the bishops were imposing on candidates for benefices an oath other than the one sanctioned by parliament, and that they were depriving and suspending ministers without consulting the local presbytery, both of which impinged on the rights of patrons and congregations. Hope, when asked for a ruling on the legality of Balmerino's position, refused to give one without instructions from Charles, and there the matter rested.[70] Charles, who had ordered that nothing come before the convention save on written instructions from him or on Menteith's verbal orders, was well pleased with Menteith's handling of this, and indeed of all the rest of the convention's business, and rewarded him with a seat on the English privy council. Alexander received a peerage: he was now Viscount Stirling.[71] But Balmerino was a marked man.

By far the most surprising item on the king's agenda for the convention concerned economics. His proposal did not, as the agenda had indicated, have to do with textiles, in which he showed very little interest; his occasional gestures in the direction of improvement of wool manufacture were not followed up and came to nothing.[72] Instead he urged the establishment of an Anglo-Scottish fishery company, which became known as the Association for the Fishing. The king's letter went into considerable detail and asked for a response. The convention appointed a committee to consider the matter; after some wrangling a report emerged on the last day of the meeting. It found some difficulties with the king's plan; the burghs indicated that they wanted to make a counter-proposal; and the whole matter was put over until the first meeting of the council in November.

Prior to this time Charles had shown very little interest in Scottish economic development, and the destruction of the council's authority meant that that body was unable to take many initiatives. One long-standing problem was settled early in the reign when price levels were set for various types of grain. When the grain was selling below that figure, it could be exported; when above, export was prohibited and import allowed free of customs duties. Another long-standing issue continued, the dispute over Lord Erskine's tanning patent, which the burghs much resented. In spite of another conciliar pronouncement in Erskine's favor in 1629, the tanners still refused to comply with his rules and frequently suffered horning in consequence. There were also disputes from time to time over such issues as the export of coal, salt, cattle, and hides; normally the exporters were able to prevail over those who wanted to keep prices low at home. The war did bring some royal economic initiatives, in the form of a patent to a syndicate headed by that busy entrepreneur Nathaniel Udward to make iron ordnance and shot, and another to the earl of Linlithgow to make gunpowder. This latter, which gave Linlithgow very broad authority to dig for saltpetre on other people's property, caused a vehement outcry; after the war ended Linlithgow seems to have made no effort to implement the patent. The war also caused the king to concern himself with the state of the exchequer and produced the occasional gesture of retrenchment, such as the order to Lord Treasurer Mar in November 1629 not to fill vacant household offices which were no longer necessary in the absence of a resident court in Edinburgh and to cut back on excessive pensions and fees. These gestures continued after the war. Charles also wanted to be sure to collect all the money due him, so he continued to take an interest in schemes such as Thornton's, which involved increasing the amount of money obtained from regular sources of revenue or from taxation; there is no evidence that any of them worked. He occasionally asked for a balance sheet—in October 1632, for instance, he asked the clerk register for a statement of the crown's revenues and standing obligations in the form of pensions, etc., as they stood at his accession and at present. He could not understand why he was in such financial straits; he once asked Treasurer Depute Traquair "how it was that some kings of Scotland had made war on England, supplied France, and built fair buildings all at once, while he out of all the treasury of Scotland was not able to pay anything." He failed to see that he was a major contributor to this unfortunate state of affairs, on account of blunders such as the grant of the lease of the wine impost to Hamilton, which, as Traquair pointed out to him, deprived the treasury of its largest source of ready money. In this case Charles recognized his error. But in other ways he was less helpful: he continued to make grants of large sums of cash to his favorites, such as Hamilton, Menteith, and the bishop of Ross, and to officials like Mar, and to insist on the payment of the pensions of those around him.[73]

The plan for the fishery was the one economic proposal directly affecting Scotland which captured Charles's imagination. This plan arose in part from his dislike of the activities of the huge and well-organized Dutch fishing fleet, which operated in British waters with impunity and occasioned protests from Scots and English alike.[74] Repeated efforts to require the Dutch to pay a fee to fish in British waters had all foundered on Dutch intransigence, and had recently ended altogether because of the war. Many people in both England and Scotland shared Charles's distaste for Dutch behavior in this matter; the grievance was an old one. The chain of events which led to the proposal for the fishery company began with the controversy caused by the earl of Seaforth's plan to exploit the Mackenzies' newly acquired superiority in Lewis to organize a large-scale commercial operation there, including fishing. Seaforth's plan hinged on cooperation with the Dutch, who would supply the necessary shipping.[75] As a first step Seaforth petitioned Charles to implement the parliamentary enactment of 1597 and make Stornoway a royal burgh; there was none on the island. The convention of royal burghs at once objected, arguing that all sorts of unpleasant consequences would follow, including a virtual monopoly of the export business in fish, which would fall into the hands of the Dutch, who were, indeed, already fishing in the area, and very successfully. As an alternative the burghs proposed the creation of a company of Scottish adventurers which would purchase the island from Seaforth, establish a fishery there, and in the process spread the blessings of lowland language and civilization among the barbarous highlanders. The privy council supported the burghs' charge that Seaforth was behaving illegally in allowing Dutchmen into Lewis and exporting goods from there; this was a violation of the royal burghs' monopoly of the export trade. But it would not venture to make any decision on the policy question; it left that to the king. Charles, who had favored Seaforth's petition at first, and had made him a privy councillor, now changed his mind, perhaps at the prompting of Sir John Coke, the English secretary of state, who, in addition to economic considerations, was much alarmed at the prospect of the Dutch establishing themselves in Lewis. If they did so, Dutch ships would have available to them a route to the open sea other than the Channel, and the possibility of successful English pressure on the Dutch government would be correspondingly reduced. The king now declared that he had decided to launch a company of adventurers on a much grander scale, which would have a monopoly of all fishing in British waters and would thus be able successfully to challenge the Dutch.[76]

Charles's plan came as a nasty shock to the burghs, who, when they heard that the king had definitely decided against Seaforth, confidently expected the monopoly of the fishing for themselves. From the beginning they, and the privy council as well, regarded the Association for the Fishing as an English scheme to open up Scottish waters to English fishermen. The abortive treaty of union of 1604 had not gone as far as this proposal: in that document fishing up to fourteen miles from the coast had been reserved for the natives of each kingdom. Charles's plan was "very inconvenient," said the convention of estates, and from that opinion the Scots, especially the burghs, never wavered. If the Association was to come into being at all, it should be limited to those areas where the Dutch also fished. The Scots did not believe the inflated English predictions as to profits, and they knew that the plan to build 200 fishing vessels of between thirty and fifty tons was both impractical and far too costly. So, in an effort to block it, they dragged their feet, chiefly by means of endless argument over the areas to be reserved to the local fishermen and not subject to the operations of the Association. Paradoxically, one of the few Scots who was publicly anxious to be cooperative was Seaforth. In May 1633 an English fishing captain in Lewis said that the new earl of Seaforth—his brother and predecessor died early that year—was being most helpful, and was encouraging both Scots and highlanders(!) to take service with him.[77] Seaforth took this line partly because he stood to be compensated for whatever rights the king might take from him—and the council was urging the king to be generous—and partly because the Mackenzies well knew how to bide their time and eventually to profit from other people's inflated expectations of economic gain in Lewis.

For the better part of two years the haggling went on. The Scottish commissioners, headed by Morton and Menteith, who as usual served as the interpreter of king and Scottish officialdom to each other,[78] tried to keep the area reserved exclusively for Scots as large as possible. In the end they were able to salvage the areas between St. Abbs Head in Berwickshire and Red Head in Angus on the east coast and between the mulls of Kintyre and Galloway on the west, areas which comprised the firths of Forth, Tay, and Clyde. The king's enthusiasm persisted; he personally attended many of the commissioners' meetings, and at last, in September 1632, the Association formally came into being. From the beginning it was a disaster. The Dutch paid it no heed. The company's capital was too small, and its subscribers did not make their pledged payments; the contemplated fishing fleet was never built. And the natives were unfriendly. In the western isles the "islanders come in troops and companies out of the isles where they dwell to the isles and lochs where the fish are taken," declared the privy council in 1635, "and there violently spoils (*sic*) his Majesty's subjects of their fishes and sometimes of their victuals and other furniture and pursues (*sic*) them of their lives." Under such conditions it is not surprising that the undertakers were discouraged and profits non-existent. In 1635 they came to such straits that they petitioned for the right to admit foreigners, whose exclusion had been one of the *raisons d'être* of the organization. Charles did not respond directly to this, but in December 1636 he indicated his willingness to admit foreigners to the fishing if they paid a fee. Things had come full circle.[79]

The significance of the fishery company goes far beyond the sphere of economics. The Scots saw it as a symbol of the most galling side of Charles's regime: his "foreignness" and his disregard of their interests. It was not the only such example. While the discussions concerning the Association's charter were going on, Nathaniel Udward, who had a grant of the right to fish for whales in Greenland in order to supply his soap works, a grant which guaranteed him from molestation by any of Charles's subjects, was being harassed by the Muscovy Company, backed by the English privy council, to whom Udward appealed vainly for redress. The English government was allegedly improperly preventing Scottish merchants from doing business in Ireland. The English House of Lords in 1629 formally protested against giving precedence to a Scottish viscount over an English baron. There were no Scots in the household of the Prince of Wales, who was born in 1630. Proclamations involving Anglo-Scottish relations in such matters as the coinage all emanated from England. The result was a minor explosion which Charles would have done well to heed. In November 1630 the council, when it appointed the commission to negotiate the terms of the projected Association, instructed it to protest against the use of the term *Great Britain* in describing the king. There was no union yet, it pointed out, and the term was not used in England. The style it favored for Scottish documents was "King of Scotland, England, France, and Ireland." This was not a mere spasm of irritation. In March 1631 the council, in a letter to the magistrates of Berwick, showed open contempt for the ignorance of the English government respecting the situation there, and in May 1632 it authorized the use of its preferred styled until *King of Great Britain* was used in England too. There is no evidence that Charles took any notice, and in fact the style *King of Great Britain* continued to be used. "It probably did not occur to him," writes David Mathew, "that his northern subjects regarded England as a rich and ruthless country"—not only rich and ruthless, but dangerous as well. The union of the crowns, which in King James's time most Scots had regarded as a benefit, providing them with both opportunity and security, was now beginning to appear detrimental to both. It is significant that the first issue of coinage authorized after the troubles began, in 1642, dropped the style of *King of Great Britain,* etc., for that of *King of Scotland, England,* etc.[80]

Reform of the coinage was, in fact, much under discussion in these years, and the Scots regarded the king's proposals in this matter with the same sort of distaste as they did the projected fishing association. With respect to the coinage, everyone recognized that the principal problem was the circulation of too much debased foreign coin—dog dollars, they were called—which led to the export of Scottish coin and otherwise drove it out of circulation. The law against export was not enforced: "Let never your Majesty think," wrote John Acheson, the master of the mint, in 1630, "that your Highness can keep [Scottish] moneys within Scotland without severe and strait punishment." Acheson's solution was a recoinage. The burghs agreed in principle that a recoinage was necessary, but opposed Acheson's projected timetable on the ground that it would deplete the amount of money in circulation too extensively. Nothing was done. Late in 1632 the king sent Nicolas Briot, a Lorrainer who was the chief engraver of the English mint, to Edinburgh to investigate and make recommendations. He received a chilly reception, partly because he publicly charged the officials of the mint with laxity in permitting the circulation of the debased foreign coin and the merchants with profiteering from it. He too recommended a recoinage. In January 1633 the burghs, to the accompaniment of a good deal of personal abuse, heaped criticism on Briot's plan, partly because he stood to profit handsomely from it himself, partly because it would result in an issue different in weight and fineness from that of England: for all their irritation with the Southron, the merchants recognized the commercial value of an interchangeable currency. So once again nothing was done.[81] The council's only positive step in these years was to authorize the coinage of more copper in 1631, but this also was fraught with future difficulties, since the profits were assigned to Secretary Stirling to compensate him for his losses in Nova Scotia. Five years later people felt that there was too much copper in circulation. The merchants were officially blamed; unofficially, and deservedly, the odium fell on the king and particularly on Stirling, who, said the minister Robert Baillie, was "overwhelming us with his Black money." The country was being flooded with copper. Between 1613 and 1629 the coining of 1,400 stones had been authorized; between 1631 and 1634 Charles ordered the coining of the enormous quantity of 9,000 stones, and explicitly stated that he was acting to alleviate Stirling's financial distress—which was not, in fact, greatly alleviated. To make matters worse, there was also a good deal of counterfeit coin in circulation, enough to cause serious complaint on the part of the council in January 1635. Sir Robert Gordon of Gordonstoun's experience affords a good illustration of the unprofitability of the copper coinage. He had agreed to sell his rights in the abbey lands of Glenluce, which Charles wished to unite with the see of Galloway, for £2,000 sterling. In 1632 the king, with Stirling's consent, agreed that 25 pecent of the profits of the coinage should go to Gordon until he had gotten his money. He received so little that in 1635 the king settled with him by means of an exchange of property.[82]

Still another source of discontent for the Scottish merchant class involved the king's grants of monopolies, for such things as the manufacture of pins and needles and of silk, a new method of dyeing, and of salt-making (to the ubiquitous Udward and a courtier Scot, James Galloway, the master of requests). The burghs protested against the latter even though the inferiority of the existing processes required the Scots to import foreign salt. Charles even granted an Englishman a nineteen-year lease to search for metals in Scotland. The resentment these grants engendered was so great that in 1632 the convention of royal burghs proposed an addition to the burgess's oath: burgesses were to swear not to engage in a monopoly prejudicial to the burghs.[83]

Not everything Charles did was unpopular, of course. In March 1632 he issued a proclamation equalizing the customs payments charged any of his subjects in each of his three kingdoms. Four months later he issued a general ratification of the burghs' privileges, and at the end of the year elevated their principal spokesman, John Hay, the town clerk of Edinburgh, to the office of clerk register on the death of the incumbent. Charles was not deaf to protests. He abandoned a proposal to limit the export of Scottish salt when the coal owners declared that this would ruin their business, and another to prohibit salmon fishing on Sunday, in the face of complaint from both the burghs and prominent aristocrats with fishing rights.[84] It seems likely that, once the war had ended, none of his acts of commission or omission had much impact on the Scottish economy, save perhaps his failure to solve the problem of the coinage. But the impression Charles created was decidedly negative. The fishery and the continued heavy peacetime taxation, taken together—and they converged at the convention of estates in 1630—gave the impression of a regime which laid unprecedented burdens on Scotland and at the same time was not concerned for her interests, an impression which was reinforced by the repeated postponements of the king's projected visit.

Throughout these years, in all these questions, Menteith was Charles's principal agent. He dealt with the tithe commissioners and with preparations for the royal visit; he supervised the activity of the commission to revise the laws and the border commission; he inquired into the form of the new exchequer commission, the coinage, the export of salt, and what Napier's conditions for resigning his office were; he ran the justice ayres, the committee on Papists, and the convention of estates when it met.[85] The king had absolute confidence in him. He was a servant after Charles's own heart, obeying the king's instructions, seldom protesting, yet able to persuade the king to modify his goals or his tactics when necessary. How well he kept the king informed is not altogether clear. He knew of Charles's unwillingness to listen to information or opinion which ran counter to his views, and it seems likely that he frequently acted by indirection. His unique value to the king in this respect is underscored by the unperceptive comment of Secretary Stirling (who was present) after the convention of estates of 1630, with all its difficulties, that the Scots were well pleased with the king.[86] At the same time, because Menteith was who he was, his fellow landholders among the aristocracy and gentry had confidence that in him they had a pipeline to the king. It is worth pointing out that during Menteith's years of influence Charles initiated nothing which was contrary to the perceived economic interests of the landowning classes. Menteith was much at court, but unlike Charles's other Scottish intimates he was not deracinated; he was not a courtier.

Yet it is impossible, really, to speak of a Menteith "administration" in the same way that one can use that term in connection with the years of power of the earl of Dunbar in the reign of

James VI or the duke of Lauderdale under Charles II. Dunbar and Lauderdale were also much at court, more so than Menteith, but each had a very tight grip on the government in Edinburgh. Menteith did not—he did not try. He made no effort to restore the cohesiveness or morale of the council, which for the most part was reduced to handling trivia and carrying out the instructions he transmitted to it. The weekly digest of conciliar actions, which the king ordered sent to Secretary Stirling in 1632, cannot have been very illuminating.[87] Menteith was a haphazard administrator. The long-drawn-out saga of Napier's resignation is a case in point; Dunbar or Lauderdale would have been rid of him in a month. Menteith had to be reminded that Traquair, as Napier's successor, should be on the teind commission. He was capable of writing a memorandum to the king on a comparatively minor question like the extortionate behavior of the clerks of the court of session toward pleaders there; at the same time he admitted that he had not known about the laird of Thornton's patent until Thornton produced it at the council table, signed by the king, the lord chancellor, and seven other exchequer commissioners. Like his master, he was something of a loner. His two close allies were Secretary Stirling and Lord Advocate Hope. He did not get on very well with the triumvirate, who were naturally somewhat jealous. Dupplin thought that Hope manipulated Menteith but learned to speak fulsomely of him when necessary. Mar disliked many of the courtier Scots, including Stirling, and was difficult and irascible; his departure from the treasury, Stirling hoped, would make matters run more smoothly.[88] As for Haddington, in January 1631 he wrote a rather bitter letter to Annandale, his old colleague of Jacobean days, explaining that he could not be helpful in a matter pending before the court of session because he never saw any of the ordinary lords of session any more, and the extraordinary lords, like Menteith, were so busy that he could not talk to them "unless I would in the mornings and evenings climb up and creep down their stairs."[89] There were others as well with whom Menteith did not get along: Secretary Acheson, Scotstarvet, whose career as an extraordinary lord of session he promised to ask Charles to cut short,[90] the marquis of Hamilton—according to Reay's version of Hamilton's "plot," Menteith and his friends Stirling and Hope were marked for execution.[91] Stirling treated Menteith with some wariness, giving him advice on behavior, urging that he avoid quarrels, encouraging him with assurances of the king's goodwill.[92] Menteith had a careless and undiplomatic tongue, which made Stirling very nervous. It must have been trying sometimes for both the secretary and the advocate—Menteith did not exert himself very much, even for them. As has been pointed out, he was casual about Stirling's affairs; this was also true of his dealings with Hope. Late in 1631 Hope began to urge Menteith to use his influence to get an impending vacancy on the court of session for his son. His son was eminently qualified, in Hope's opinion, and the competition consisted of Spottiswoode's candidate, John Hay, the future clerk register, "a pest and a firebrand," and the hated Scotstarvet. "O what insupportable discredit, that one who justly may expect your wrath for his follies shall be preferred—an insult both upon your Lordship and me."[93] Hope's son received the appointment, but not until July 1632, and Scotstarvet got one too.

Menteith, in short, was not a politician. He admitted to being a bad correspondent, and rather prided himself on his lack of a courtier's tongue.[94] He had a few political friends, but he had no following, no network of kinfolk, no political faction built up through patronage, no residual goodwill. And he did have enemies, and lots of creditors. His position depended solely on the support of the king. If, for whatever reason, that support should be withdrawn, the earl's political career would be over. At the end of 1632, as he returned to Edinburgh from court to deal with Charles's instructions concerning his projected visit to Scotland, which this time really would take place, the storm which would engulf him had already burst.

NOTES

1. *RPCS* 2nd ser. II, 53–54, 88–90, 125–28, 133, 145–46, 159–61, 184–88. For one proposed warning system see *ibid.*, pp. 225, 244, 486.

War, Justice, and the Economy

2. *Ibid.* I, 337, 416–18, II, 52, 131, 133, 150–53, 156–58, 174–75, 252. Jan. 5, 1628, Traquair to Morton, NLS Mss. 81, no. 68. Apr. 9, 1634, Sir John Maxwell to Traquair, Sir William Fraser, *Memoirs of the Maxwells of Pollok*, II, 252–53. One reason for this, Maxwell added, was that the outward customs of the Clyde, formerly assigned to Lennox to finance Dumbarton's maintenance, had been acquired for the exchequer by Treasurer Depute Elibank in James's reign, thanks to Sir John Stewart's negligence.

3. Apr. 21, 1627, Hay to Morton, May 26, Lord Spynie to Morton, NLS Mss. 82, f. 27, Mss. 79, no. 29. Spynie, who, like Nithsdale, had a commission to raise 3,000 men to serve Christian IV, complained that the rumor that Nithsdale was to be in overall command discouraged recruiting.

4. The commission to Lord Spynie is typical. *RPCS* 2nd ser. I, 542–43.

5. *Ibid.*, pp. 552–53, 565–67, 580–81, 589, 603–5, 611, 613, II, 7–8, 36–37, 56, VIII, 431. *Stirling* I, 146, 195–96. May 20, 1627, Melrose to Morton, NLS Mss. 80, no. 72.

6. *RPCS* 2nd ser. II, 37–39, 63. *Stirling* I, 185, 193–94, 200–201, 206.

7. *A&L* I, 44–45. See also Sept. 3, 1627, Lord Lorne to Morton, NLS Mss. 79, no. 22.

8. *RPCS* 2nd ser. I, 634–36, 689–93, II, 93–94, 114–15, 168–71, III, 1–2, 4.

9. *Ibid.* II, 40, 113–14, 295–97, 303–4. Sailors also had to be pressed into service. *Ibid.*, pp. 71–72.

10. *Balfour* II, 158–59. *CSP Venetian* XXI, 107. For the Isle of Wight see L. Boynton, "Billeting: The Example of the Isle of Wight," *English Historical Review* LXXIV (1959), 23–40.

11. *RPCS* 2nd ser. I, 522–23, II, 242–43, 265–66, 284, 305–7, 567–68, 572–73, III, 24–25. T. Keith, *Commercial Relations of England and Scotland 1603–1707* (Cambridge, 1910), pp. 49–50.

12. *RPCS* 2nd ser. I, 571–72. See also *Balfour* II, 140–41.

13. HMC, *Lonsdale Manuscripts*, ed. J. J. Cartwright (London, 1893), p. 83.

14. *Stirling* I, 185, 189, 199–200. *RPCS* 2nd. ser. II, 12, 553–56, III, 44. Keith, *Commercial Relations*, p. 18. D. Evans, ed., *Acts of the Privy Council of England 1629, May–1630, May* (London, 1960), pp. 317, 328, 335.

15. On this point see J. Imrie and J. G. Dunbar, eds., *Accounts of*

the Masters of Works II (Edinburgh, 1982), intro., p. xxxiv, and the figures there cited. See also the council's letter to Charles in February 1628, *RPCS* 2nd. ser. II, 227–28.

16. *RPCS* 2nd ser. I, 550–52, 557, 603, II, 68, 76–77, 210, 222, 269–70, 279, 417–18, 574–75. *Stirling* I, 131, 232.

17. *RPCS* 2nd ser. I, 571, II, 72–73, 146–47, 426–27, 521–23, 582–83, III, 204–5. L. Taylor, ed., *Aberdeen Council Letters* I, 297–98. In November 1632 this tax was reimposed, to build and maintain a fort on Inchgarvie, by Queensferry. *RPCS* 2nd ser. IV, 570.

18. *RPCS* 2nd ser. I, 552, II, 137–38, 155–56, 182–83. For annualrents see *ibid.*, pp. 287–88, *Stirling* I, 444–45, 448.

19. SRO, GD 22/1/15, 22/1/518, 22/3/582, 22/3/777. *Stirling* I, 318, 342, 377, II, 457–58, 497. HMC, 9th Report, pt. II, p. 252. NLS Adv. Mss. 32.6.8, f. 81. Archibald, Lord Napier, *Memoirs of Archibald, First Lord Napier, written by Himself* (Edinburgh, 1793), pp. 31–33.

20. *RPCS* 2nd ser. II, 380–81, 383, 385–87. *Stirling* I, 291–93.

21. July 18, 1628, Mar to Charles, *M&K,* p. 168. On July 10, 1630, for instance, the exchequer register recorded warrants to pay Mar £10,000, Menteith and Hamilton £5,000, Hope £2,000 and Acheson £1,250, all sterling. NLS Adv. Mss. 32.6.8, f. 78.

22. *RPCS* 2nd ser. II, 413–16. Napier, *Memorials of Montrose* I, 33–35. Sept. 29, 1628, Mar to Charles, *M&K,* pp. 174–75, where the letter is wrongly dated 1630. Jan. 18, 1629, Traquair to Morton, NLS Mss. 81, no. 75.

23. Oct. 29, 1628, Baillie to Mar. *M&K Supp.,* pp. 246–47. Mar. 21, 1630, Dupplin to Morton, NLS Mss. 82, f. 69. *RPCS* 2nd ser. III, 126–27, 181–82, 199–200. *Stirling* I, 331, 351, 371, II, 812. Napier, *Memorials of Montrose* I, 38–42, 45–46.

24. Mar. 29, 1630, Dupplin to Morton, NLS Mss. 82, f. 71.

25. Mar. 20, 1630, Charles to Mar, *M&K,* p. 173. Mar. 21, 27, Dupplin to Morton, NLS Mss. 82, ff. 69, 79. May 25, Charles to Menteith, Sir William Fraser, *The Red Book of Menteith* II, 31. Sept. 5, Menteith to Morton, NLS Mss. 80, no. 75.

26. Aug. 12, 1630, Charles to Menteith, *Stirling* II, 472. Sept. 15, Oct. 14, Traquair to Morton, Oct. 6, Alexander to Morton, NLS Mss. 81, nos. 103, 84, 40. Imrie and Dunbar, *Masters of Works* II, intro., pp. xxxix–xl. See also *Stirling* II, 486–89, 517, 523, 525. Dupplin urged Morton to retain Baillie. Mar. 29, 1630, Dupplin to Morton, NLS Mss. 82, f. 71. Napier's own account of his troubles is in his

Memoirs, pp. 24–95. In one case, at least, his suspicions were unfair. Alexander, whom he accused of all sorts of chicanery, was hopeful that he could save himself as late as January 1630. Jan. 1, 1630, Alexander to Menteith, Fraser, *Menteith* II, 105–6.

27. *RPCS* 2nd ser. III, 130–32, 171–72. Mar. 29, Apr. 8, 1630, Dupplin to Morton, NLS Mss. 82, ff. 71, 25.

28. *RPCS* 2nd ser. II, 489. *Stirling* I, 352–53, 386, II, 544. Oct. 17, 1629, Charles to Menteith, Fraser, *Menteith* II, 22. *APS* V, 219–20. For a discussion of the Nova Scotia venture see G. P. Insh, *Scottish Colonial Schemes 1620–1686* (Glasgow, 1920), esp. pp. 16–26, 36–39, 57, 85.

29. *Stirling* II, 432–33. 473, 499–500, *RPCS* 2nd ser. V, 306. Oct. 15/25, 1630, Soranzo to the Doge and Senate, *CSP Venetian* XXII, 432.

30. July 8/18, 1631, Soranzo to the Doge and Senate, *ibid.,* pp. 526–27.

31. *RPCS* 2nd ser. IV, 263. *Stirling* II, 603–4. Sept. 18, Dec. 26, 1630, Traquair to Morton, NLS Mss. 81, nos. 80, 85. Dec. 2, 1631, John Maxwell to Sir John Maxwell of Pollok, Fraser, *Pollok* II, 215–17. NLS Mss. 1,945, pp. 93–96. July 17, 1632. Charles to Menteith, Fraser, *Menteith* II, 41. S. A. Gillon, ed., *Selected Justiciary Cases 1624–1650* I, Stair Society (Edinburgh, 1953), 176–97. Thomas B. Howell, ed., *Cobbett's Complete Collection of State Trials* III (London, 1809), 425–520. There is an account of this affair in H. Rubinstein, *Captain Luckless* (Edinburgh, 1975), chap. 3.

32. *RPCS* 2nd ser. III, 65–68, 354, 411–15, IV, 22–23. *APS* V, 219–20.

33. *RPCS* 2nd ser. I, 563.

34. M. Lee, Jr., *John Maitland of Thirlestane,* pp. 123–25, 157–58, 180, 278.

35. May 31, 1627, Feb. 12, 1628, Charles to Hope, Feb. 17, 1628, Charles to the exchequer commission, *Stirling* I, 178, 252–53, 258. *APS* V, 77. *RPCS* 2nd ser. II, 331–32, 420–21, V, 49–50. The government's proceeds from the ayres were to be used to pay Lorne. *Stirling* I, 321.

36. I owe this point to E. J. Cowan.

37. *RPCS* 2nd ser. II, 363, 535, 632–34, III, 164, 171, 272–73, 631, IV, 459, 574. *Stirling* I, 352–53, 366. E. J. Cowan, *Montrose for Covenant and King* (London, 1977), pp. 52–53, argues that the clans' support for Montrose in the civil war was owing in some measure to

Charles's attempt to abolish hereditary jurisdictions. It seems to me that it was precisely because Argyll's jurisdiction over them had *not* been abolished that they were so eager to attack the Campbells.

38. *RPCS* 2nd ser. III, 266–68, IV, 425–26, V, 224–25, 420–21. *Stirling* I, 378. NLS Mss. 79, no. 24, Mss. 81, no. 28. SRO, GD 112/39/459. John Willcock, *The Great Marquess* (Edinburgh, 1903), pp. 19–23. Sir William Fraser, *The Sutherland Book* I, 222. N.d. and Feb. 27, 1629, Lorne to Morton, Willcock, *Great Marquess,* pp. 362, 361. See also May 31, 1627, Feb. 11, 1628, Charles to Lorne, July 11, 1628, Charles to Napier, *Stirling* I, 178, 247–48, 299. D. Gregory, *The History of the Western Highlands and Isles of Scotland,* 2nd ed. (London, 1881), pp. 405–12. For an example of Lorne's vengefulness see E. J. Cowan, "The Angus Campbells and the Origin of the Campbell-Ogilvie Feud," *Scottish Studies* XXV (1981), 36–37.

39. *Stirling* I, 199. *RPCS* 2nd ser. II, 364. The appointment was for one year, and was renewed annually until Menteith's fall.

40. *RPCS* 2nd ser. II, 345–47, 434–39. *Stirling* I, 273, 295–96, 382.

41. Oct. 20, 1628, Charles to Menteith, *Stirling* I, 314. For re-pledging see J. Irvine Smith, "Criminal Procedure," in Stair Society, *An Introduction to Scottish Legal History* (Edinburgh, 1958), pp. 430–32.

42. SRO, GD 22/3/787.

43. SRO, GD 22/3/582. *Stirling* I, 398. *RPCS* 2nd ser. IV, 12.

44. The last mention of the commission of grievances in the council register comes in July 1627. *RPCS* 2nd ser. II, 5–6.

45. NLS Mss. 82, f. 25.

46. So said Haddington. Apr. 1, 1629, Haddington to Menteith, Sir William Fraser, *Memorials of the Earls of Haddington* II, 164–65.

47. R. K. Hannay, "The Office of the Justice Clerk," *Juridical Review* 47 (1935), 324–25. M. Wood, ed., *Extracts from the Records of the Burgh of Edinburgh 1626–1641,* intro., p. 48. The fear that they might be revived persisted; Edinburgh protested against them again in 1633. *Ibid.,* p. 317.

48. SRO, GD 22/3/579. *Stirling* I, 377.

49. *APS* V, 224–25. D. Stevenson, "The Covenanters and the Court of Session, 1637–1650," *Juridical Review* n.s. 17 (1972), 243.

50. Christina Larner, *Enemies of God: The Witch-hunt in Scotland,* p. 186. This paragraph depends heavily on Larner's excellent book.

51. R. Mitchison, "The Movements of Scottish Corn Prices in the Seventeenth and Eighteenth Centuries," *Economic History Review* 2nd ser. XVIII (1965), 283. W. Lithgow, "Scotland's Welcome to Her Na-

tive Sonne and Soveraigne Lord, King Charles," in James Maidment, ed., *The Poetical Remains of William Lithgow*. This poem, which is not paginated, was written in 1629, at the height of the persecutions, in anticipation of the king's proposed visit.

52. *RPCS* 2nd ser. II, 365–67, 424. See also *ibid.* IV, 116, 137–39, 149–50. *Stirling* II, 592, 639–40.

53. *RPCS* 2nd ser. II, 466, 472–73, III, 223–24.

54. For the border in James's last years see M. Lee, Jr., *Government by Pen: Scotland under James VI and I*, pp. 207–9.

55. See his letter to Menteith in Sir William Fraser, *The Book of Caerlaverock* II, 108–10. The letter is undated; the context suggests that it was written in 1628.

56. *RPCS* 2nd ser. II, 222–25, 254, III, 265. *Stirling* I, 304.

57. Dec. 30, 1629, Feb. 9, Mar. 8, Apr. 20, 1630, Charles to Menteith, *Stirling* I, 410, II, 424–25, 433–34, Fraser, *Menteith* II, 27–29.

58. Mar. 21, 1630, Dupplin to Morton, NLS Mss. 82, f. 69. *RPCS* 2nd ser. IV, 198–99.

59. *Stirling* I, 375, II, 459. Mar. 1, 1630, Moray to Morton, NLS Mss. 80, no. 82. For Inverness's complaints see *RPCS* 2nd ser. II, 5–6, VIII, 376–77, 380–81, *RCRB* III, 270, 316. Moray's commission did expire in October 1632. *Stirling* II, 628.

60. Lee, *Government by Pen,* p. 145.

61. *RPCS* 2nd ser. IV, 100.

62. On this point see David Stevenson, *Alexander MacColla and the Highland Problem in the Seventeenth Century* (Edinburgh, 1980), pp. 53–54.

63. *RPCS* 2nd ser. IV, 280, 676.

64. For the Frendraught affair see below, chap. 5.

65. NLS Mss. 82, f. 73.

66. *Stirling* I, 335. Hannay, "Office of the Justice Clerk" pp. 324–25. In 1631 Charles asked the justices to work out a proposal for increased fees for themselves. *Stirling* II, 529.

67. Apr. 8, 1630, Dupplin to Morton, NLS Mss. 82, f. 25. *RPCS* 2nd ser. III, 575–76. The record of the convention is in *APS* V, 208–28. There is also a set of notes on the discussions in SRO, GD 22/1/518.

68. Aug. 4, 1630, Captain Mason to Secretary Coke, *CSPD 1629–1631,* p. 322.

69. *Balfour* II, 181–84.

70. The discussion on the church is not in the formal record. See

SRO, GD 22/1/518, NLS Mss. 3,926, *Row,* pp. 350–51, and *Scot,* pp. 326–29.

71. June 2, 1630, Charles's instructions for Menteith, Fraser, *Menteith* II, 31–32. Sept. 5, Menteith to Morton, Traquair to Morton, NLS Mss. 80, no. 75, Mss. 81, no. 73. P. A. Penfold, ed., *Acts of the Privy Council of England 1630, June–1631, June* (London, 1964), p. 75. *RPCS* 2nd ser. IV, 269.

72. For these gestures see *Stirling* II, 610–11, 756.

73. *RPCS* 2nd ser. I, lxxxv, 277–78, II, 64, 333–34, 338–39, 425–26, 439–40, III, 107–9, 133–35, 151–52. *RCRB* III, 195–96, 212, 279–80. *Stirling* I, 154–55, 249, 313, 347, 397, 399–400, II, 520, 521, 626–27. N.d. but after 1630, Traquair to Morton, NLS Mss. 81, no. 98. Gilbert Burnet, *The Memoirs of the Lives and Actions of James and William, Dukes of Hamilton* (London, 1673), pp. 25–26.

74. See, e.g., *RPCS* 2nd ser. I, 147–48.

75. This is clear from the Seaforth muniments, SRO, GD 46/18/138–42.

76. *RPCS* 2nd ser. II, 336–37, 353–54, III, 42, 94–96, 260, 479–80, 491, 495–96. *RCRB* III, 257–62, 279–80, 291–94. *Stirling* I, 358–59. *CSPD 1629–1631,* p. 109. Dorothea Coke, *The Last Elizabethan: Sir John Coke 1563–1644* (London, 1937), pp. 213–14. *APS* IV, 139. It should be noted that the burghs were not unanimous in their opposition to Seaforth. Aberdeen did not feel threatened, and flatly refused to participate in any company of adventurers. Taylor, *Aberdeen Council Letters* I, 286–89, 309–10, 313–15.

77. *CSPD 1633–1634,* p. 71.

78. See, e.g., July 31, 1631, Charles to Menteith, and his instructions of Aug. 15, 1632, *Stirling* II, 550, 617–18.

79. *RCRB* III, 318–19. *APS* V, 226. *RPCS* 2nd ser. IV, 106–7, VI, 96, 346. *CSPD 1635,* p. 90. The fullest accounts of the fishery are in T. W. Fulton, *The Sovereignty of the Sea* (Edinburgh, 1911), chap. 6, and J. R. Elder, *The Royal Fishery Companies of the Seventeenth Century* (Glasgow, 1912), chaps. 2–5. See also W. R. Scott, *The Constitution and Finance of English, Scottish, and Irish Joint-Stock Companies to 1720* (Cambridge, 1912), II, 363–70; Keith, *Commercial Relations,* pp. 30–31; W. C. Mackenzie, *History of the Outer Hebrides* (Paisley, 1903), pp. 290–326.

80. SRO, PS 1/99. ff. 76–77. *RPCS* 2nd ser. III, 354–56, IV, 56–57, 157–58, 487. Penfold, *Acts of the Privy Council 1630, June–1631, June,* pp. 327–28, 332–33, 341–42. *CSPD 1629–1631,* pp. 240,

513, 542. Taylor, *Aberdeen Council Letters* II, 3–7. C. Russell, *Parliaments and English Politics 1621–1629,* p. 408. SRO, GD 22/3/785. S. T. Bindoff, "The Stuarts and their Style," *English Historical Review* LX (1945), 213–14. D. Mathew, *Scotland under Charles I,* p. 34. R. W. Cochran-Patrick, *Records of the Coinage of Scotland* (Edinburgh, 1876), II, plate 13.

81. *RPCS* 2nd ser. IV, 63–64, 564, 580–82, V, 20. Cochran-Patrick, *Coinage* I, intro., pp. clxxii–clxxvi. There was a silver shortage in England also in these years. B. E. Supple, *Commercial Crisis and Change in England 1600–1642* (Cambridge, 1959), pp. 164–78.

82. *RPCS* 2nd ser. V, 436–38, 476. Sir William Fraser, *The Sutherland Book* I, 200–201, II, 14–16. For the copper coinage see R. B. K. Stevenson, "The 'Stirling' Turners of Charles I, 1632–1639," *British Numismatic Journal* XXIX (1958–59), 128–51. The quotation from Baillie is on p. 136.

83. *RPCS* 2nd ser. IV, 28–31, 41, 209–14. *Stirling* II, 454, 506, 610–11, 647. *RCRB* IV, 531. Wood, *Extracts,* intro., p. xxxi. It should be added that in 1632 Charles terminated a monopoly, that of pearl fishing. *RPCS* 2nd ser. IV, 548.

84. *RPCS* 2nd ser. IV, 255–56, 458–59, V, 28–29. *Stirling* II, 550, 586, 609. Taylor, *Aberdeen Council Letters* I, 334–37, 384–86.

85. The king's written instructions, and supplemental letters when Menteith was in Edinburgh, are for the most part printed in Fraser, *Menteith* II, 3–48. They begin in February 1628 and end in December 1632.

86. Aug. 22, 1630, Stirling to Carleton, *CSPD 1629–1631,* p. 332.

87. *Stirling* II, 584.

88. Apr. 3, 1630, Stirling to Menteith, Dec. 7, 1631, Hope to Menteith, Fraser, *Menteith* II, 113–14, 138–39. SRO, GD 22/3/582, 22/3/788. Apr. 8, 1630, Feb. 2, 1631, Dupplin to Morton, NLS Mss. 82, ff. 25, 61. Nov. 28, 1630, Mar to Haddington, Fraser, *Haddington* II, 169.

89. *Laing,* p. 189.

90. Feb. 3, 1629, Traquair to Morton, NLS Mss. 81, no. 106. Menteith was not very successful; Scotstarvet remained an extraordinary lord until October 1630, when Charles replaced them all except Menteith himself. *Stirling* II, 480.

91. Howell, *Cobbett's State Trials* III, 428.

92. See, e.g., Stirling's letters to Menteith on Nov. 18, 1628, Dec.

2, 1628, Dec. 2, 1629, Jan. 12, 1630, Oct. 29, 1630, Mar. 27, 1631, Fraser, *Menteith* II, 96–97, 99–100, 104–5, 107–8, 115–16, 118–19.

93. Nov. 10, 11, 1631, Hope to Menteith, *ibid.,* pp. 125–29.

94. See his letter to Morton on Sept. 18, 1630, in Sir Harris Nicolas, *History of the Earldoms of Strathearn, Menteith, and Airth* (London, 1842), App., p. lxxvii.

King Charles I, by Daniel Mytens. In a private Scottish collection

Sir James Balfour, Lord Lyon King of Arms, by an unknown artist.
Scottish National Portrait Gallery

Sir Archibald Napier, Treasurer Depute, 1622–31, by George Jamesone. Scottish National Portrait Gallery

James Hamilton, Marquis, later Duke, of Hamilton, by Daniel Mytens. In the Collection of the Duke of Hamilton

Archibald Campbell, Lord Lorne; later Marquis of Argyll, by David Scougall. Scottish National Portrait Gallery

John Spottiswoode, Archbishop of St. Andrews, by an unknown artist.
In the collection of the Faculty of Advocates, Edinburgh, Scotland

Sir Thomas Hope, Lord Advocate, by George Jamesone. Scottish National Portrait Gallery

John Stewart, Earl of Traquair, Lord Treasurer 1636–41, by an unknown artist. In the collection of Peter Maxwell Stewart of Traquair House, Innerleithen, Peeblesshire

William Alexander, Earl of Stirling, Secretary of State, by an unknown artist. On loan to the Scottish National Portrait Gallery

William Douglas, Earl of Morton, Lord Treasurer, 1620–36, by an unknown artist. Scottish National Portrait Gallery

William Graham, Earl of Menteith, by George Jamesone. Scottish
National Portrait Gallery

4

The Royal Visit

W ILLIAM GRAHAM was seventh earl of Menteith, the lineal descendant of the first earl, Malise Graham, who had received the title from James I. Malise was the eldest son of Sir Patrick Graham and Countess Euphemia Stewart, only child of David, earl of Strathearn, the eldest son of King Robert II, who reigned from 1371 to 1390, by his wife Euphemia Ross. Robert II's marital affairs were extremely messy. His first wife, from whom the Stewart dynasty descended, was Elizabeth Mure. They had lived together for years before their marriage, and their children, including Robert II's successor, had been born out of wedlock. In addition Elizabeth had been precontracted as a child, and one of Robert's other mistresses was her relative within the prohibited degrees. There were, of course, papal dispensations, which legitimated their many children, but there remained considerable doubt whether the pope could dispense with all the obstacles to this technically incestuous union, and even if he could, it was far from clear that legitimation carried with it the right of succession to the throne. After Elizabeth's death Robert married Euphemia Ross; their two sons, David and Walter, were unquestionably legitimate.

Shortly after his accession Robert II took pains to clarify the succession by parliamentary act, leaving the throne to his three surviving sons by Elizabeth Mure, and then to those by Euphemia Ross, and their heirs male; if the direct male line should die out, the throne would then pass to heirs general. He also created his son David earl of Strathearn, an earldom he had himself received from his predecessor, David II. The grant was made to David and his heirs of line. James I, on the pretext that this was not the case and that Strathearn was in fact a male fee, took it from Malise, who had inherited through his mother, and gave him the much inferior earldom of Menteith instead. James then conferred Strathearn in liferent on his uncle Walter, earl of Atholl, the other son of Robert II by Euphemia Ross. Atholl was one of the principals in the conspiracy to murder James I; the conspirators persuaded Atholl that he was the rightful king of Scotland, on the ground that the descendants of Elizabeth Mure were illegitimate and could not succeed to the throne. After Atholl's execution for treason the earldom of Strathearn reverted to the crown.

This genealogical excursion is necessary in order to explain the fate that overtook Menteith—a fate which, it must be said, he brought on himself. From his youth he had been fond of rummaging in his charter chest and pursuing genealogical research into his ancestors and their possessions, a taste he shared with many of his contemporaries on both sides of the Tweed. It took little research to demonstrate that Malise had been wrongfully deprived of the earldom of Strathearn. In 1629 Menteith, secure in the king's favor and mindful of the fact that in 1630 the statute of limitations on claims antedating 1577 would go into effect, decided to do something about it. He carefully explained to the king that he wanted none of the lands or rights of the earldom now annexed to the crown, and would make whatever renunciation was deemed necessary. Charles was perfectly agreeable to this, and ordered his officials to cooperate with Menteith.[1] The earl and his friend Lord Advocate Hope then set to work to draw up the necessary documents. An inquest jury was empaneled and found for Menteith, and he was retoured heir to David, earl of Strathearn. He made the necessary renunciations, excepting only the barony of Kilbryde, which was once part of the earldom of Strathearn but had been part of that of Menteith since Malise's days, and any other lands, outside Strathearn, that he might claim as Earl David's heir. In July 1631 Charles signified his approval of all this and created him earl of Strathearn.[2]

It is difficult to see anything more in all this than an antiquarian ego trip. Menteith showed no interest in making anything out of his position as earl of Strathearn. In 1631 and 1632 he concentrated on raising the money to buy two pieces of property that had no connection with the earldom, the baronies of Drummond and Airth, from the earls of Perth and Linlithgow respectively; he went heavily into debt in the process.[3] But he had unwittingly given his enemies a weapon against him, which they now used with devastating effect. Scotstarvet was, by his own account,[4] the chief agent of Menteith's ruin. He had been responsible for the earl's rise to greatness, said Scotstarvet, and now Menteith had ungratefully turned on him and threatened to break his neck.[5] But Scotstarvet had plenty of help, not only from jealous colleagues like Acheson and Haddington, but also from a number of major landholders like the earls of Seaforth and Tullibardine, who feared that Menteith, either in his capacity as earl of Strathearn or as heir to the other possessions of Earl David, might be in a position to make some demands on them. Menteith's favor with Charles, combined with the legal skills of his ally the lord advocate, made them understandably nervous, at a time when no landed property right seemed totally secure. Behind them stood the marquis of Hamilton, who did not get on well with Menteith, and who never forgot his own family's place in the succession to the throne.[6] The accusation they made was startling: Menteith had not renounced his rights as a blood descendant of Earl David, and, furthermore, Earl David was described as the eldest son of Robert II's *first* marriage. Why, then, should not Menteith declare himself to be the heir of Robert II— i.e., claim the crown of Scotland?[7] Scotstarvet's legal friends' opinion on this was accompanied by the report that Menteith had boasted of having the reddest blood in Scotland, and by a screed from the poet William Drummond of Hawthornden, Scotstarvet's brother-in-law, painting in lurid colors the troubles that afflicted countries where the identity of the rightful ruler was in doubt, and suggesting that Charles might well solve the problem by extirpating Menteith and all his kin.[8]

Charles was shocked and incredulous—and sad. "Mr. Maxwell," wrote Scotstarvet, "is said to have heard his majesty say it was a sore matter that he could not love a man but they pulled him out of his arms."[9] After four years the memory of Buckingham was still green. The king wanted a way out, and the ingenuity of Sir Thomas Hope provided it for him. Hope supplied Menteith with a document indicating that the earl's motive in having himself served heir to Earl David was to make his renunciation binding—i.e., to tighten the king's grip on the annexed lands of the earldom.[10] None of the documents in fact described David as the son of Robert II's first marriage. Only the version of Stewart family history that Scotstarvet presented to the king did that, though this was a currently held view, to be found in the pages of historians like Hector Boece and George Buchanan, who said that Robert II's children by Elizabeth Mure were born before his marriage to Euphemia Ross, and that he married Elizabeth after Euphemia's death.[11] There is no indication that Menteith ever claimed to be the descendent of Robert II's first wife, whatever he may have believed. Morton and Dupplin intervened on his behalf, because, Scotstarvet says, Menteith promised to get Morton the Garter.[12] Menteith came to court in December 1632, begged forgiveness for any error he might have made, and Charles happily forgave him. But the grant of the earldom of Strathearn was to be invalidated and Charles himself declared to be Earl David's heir. The justification for this was to be that there was no proof that Earl David's daughter *was* his daughter, or that Malise Graham was her son, a fiction which nobody, including the king, believed.[13] To preclude any possible future revival of Menteith's claim, he was to give up not only Strathearn but also the title of Menteith—but not the property. From now on he would be earl of Airth, a title derived from his newly acquired estate. But the lands of the earldom of Menteith were annexed to it, and he would retain the precedence accorded the Menteith earldom. His patent as earl of Airth was drawn up on January 21, 1633. Charles wrote him a friendly letter, promising him that if the reduction of his claim to the earldom of Strathearn cost him his ancestral barony of Kilbryde, he would get it right back. The crisis was apparently over.[14]

This was not what Menteith's enemies had in mind at all. They wanted to ruin him completely, and they thought they saw the line to take. It was the job of the court of session finally to pronounce on the reduction of Menteith's claim to the earldom of Strathearn, and to declare Charles nearest in blood to Earl David, and the court, in Charles's view, was taking too much time to act.[15] The king was evidently nervous about the implications of Menteith's claim. The proceedings before the court also produced a gain for Menteith's enemies, in the form of a quarrel between the earl and Lord Advocate Hope, who said that he had seen charter evidence that would destroy the flimsy pretext on which the reduction was based—that Euphemia was not Earl David's daughter, and so on. Hope was undoubtedly concerned for his professional reputation, since he had acted as Menteith's legal adviser from the beginning. Menteith wanted no delays, however; he was aware of Charles's sensitivity on this subject.[16] The quarrel led Menteith to make a terrible mistake: in place of Hope, he now began to confide in Treasurer Depute Traquair.

Menteith certainly had not read Traquair's character aright— perhaps, at this time, no one in Scotland had. The treasurer depute was a man of considerable ability, who paid attention to detail; he was a skillful negotiator and conciliator; and he was on good terms with Lord Treasurer Morton, who had been so helpful to Menteith in getting him out of his difficulty. All this Menteith knew, which no doubt explains his decision. What he did not understand was that Traquair did not like him, was boundlessly ambitious, saw himself as, potentially, Charles's manager for Scottish affairs, and therefore regarded Menteith as an obstacle in his path.

On March 22, 1633, the court of session formally declared that Charles was the heir of David, earl of Strathearn. The king promptly ordered that all evidence that Menteith had been served heir to the earldom be expunged from the registers; Traquair commented to Morton that the only way to make absolutely sure of the king's position was to destroy "all writs that may concern this business that can be found either in the registers or elsewhere."[17] Almost at once Scotstarvet and his allies resumed their attack. Sir James Skene, president of the court, who was allegedly provoked because Menteith had criticized him to the king, charged that Menteith had said that he should rightfully be king of Scotland, and that he had a better, or at least an equal, right to the crown.[18] Scotstarvet alleges that Morton and Dupplin turned against Menteith when Morton learned that Menteith not only was not going to help him get a Garter, but was angling for one for himself, and that they went to Henrietta Maria and urged her to get Charles to investigate Skene's charges.[19] There is no evidence for most of this, though a phrase in one of Charles's letters to Menteith, about a promised favor, may refer to a Garter, and there were rumors going round that he would receive one, and a marquisate as well.[20] It is unlikely that Menteith, in his present straits, would have treated Morton so shabbily. Nor is it clear that Morton was hostile to him—on May 18, 1633, Archibald Campbell of Glencarradale wrote to Sir Colin Campbell of Glenorchy that Morton was prepared to work through Menteith to get Glenorchy a peerage if Menteith remained in favor[21]—but in view of Charles's nervousness over the implications of Menteith's claim, it would be folly for Morton or anyone else to appear too friendly with Menteith now. On May 1 the king appointed a committee to investigate Menteith's alleged speeches; it included Dupplin, Morton, Haddington, Spottiswoode, and Traquair, among others. At the same time Charles instructed Traquair to tell the earl's creditors to be patient; he was sure, he said, that Menteith would clear himself. A week later he gave Menteith "permission" to retire to one of his houses for the duration of the hearing.[22]

It is likely that this enforced sequestration was fatal to Menteith. When he first heard of Skene's charges, he was indignant; he wrote to Charles that he had done nothing save by Hope's advice, and that his enemies, Scotstarvet, Skene, and the others, were acting out of spleen. The charges, when examined, turned out to be mostly hearsay. Only one of those questioned, the earl of Wigtown, ever admitted hearing Menteith say what he was alleged to have said, and Wigtown said that he could not remember the words exactly. One of the witnesses, Lord Fleming, named as his source the dowager Lady Hamilton; when she told Menteith he was talking foolishness, said Fleming, Menteith allegedly rejoined that he had said as much to the king himself![23] The improbability of this sort of thing is clear enough. Menteith continued vehemently to deny that he ever made any such remarks. But now pressure was put on him, particularly by Traquair, to submit to the king's will and ask for mercy. His isolation began to tell on him. He wavered. Nothing was proven, he said. If he had said anything foolish "in madness or drunkenness," he was sorry. But this would not do: he must either confess, or deny and stand trial.[24] By this time Charles had been in Scotland for some weeks; as his visit drew to a close the earl at last caved in. On July 15 he signed a submission whose text was worked out in collaboration with Traquair. He could not remember ever saying any of the things Skene alleged, he said, but since "persons of quality" said that he did, he submitted to the king's will. For good measure he also submitted for all his dealings in the earldom of Strathearn.[25]

The gamble failed. Traquair forwarded the submission to Charles with the insidious suggestion that the king consider what sentence to pass on Menteith. His enemies succeeded in keeping him from the king; Charles left Scotland without seeing Menteith and without making any decision. The most he would promise was that the earl's life, lands, and title were safe; "but," wrote William Maxwell, "it is surmised that his creditors will kill him." Menteith tried sending his wife after Charles to plead for him; Charles forbade her to come to court.[26] Finally, in October, Charles made his decision. Menteith was guilty as charged, and had admitted it; he was to lose his offices and his pension, and remain on his estates. The earl appeared personally before the council in November 1633, once again admitted his errors, and surrendered his offices.[27] Politically his career was over. Even after this the king continued to brood over the question of Strathearn; for a believer in divine right the nagging doubt must have been terribly acute, especially if he believed Boece's and Buchanan's version of Robert II's marital career.[28] Charles was not personally vengeful, though, and did what he could to help Menteith stave off his creditors, who were upset at what they regarded as Charles's unjustified attempts to prevent them from getting their money. If the earl's complaints over the next few years can be taken at face value, however, he was in dire straits. He even appealed to his old foe the marquis of Hamilton for help, evidently with some success.[29] Not until December 1637 did Charles release him from house arrest; early in 1638 he was restored to favor, after a fashion, because he was not a Covenanter.[30]

But he played no role in the troubles, though his eldest son died fighting for the king. He lived to see the restoration, and died in 1661.

The fall of Menteith completely changed the character of Scottish politics. Charles thereby lost his principal link with the Scottish aristocracy, whom he did not know and made no effort to cultivate. He also lost his most important source of accurate information: English officialdom knew far less about Scotland in the 1630s than they had in the days of Queen Elizabeth, whose diplomatic agents and spies kept her and her ministers abreast of Scottish affairs. Furthermore, Menteith's removal left a vacuum at the center, rather like that which developed in England in James's time after the deaths of Salisbury and Northampton. None of the great officers of state was capable of taking Menteith's place. Dupplin and Haddington, the relics of the last reign, were too old. Stirling was also elderly, and was preoccupied with the losses, both personal and financial, that the Nova Scotia disaster had inflicted on him. Morton was an amiable nonentity. Hope, the best brain of the lot, had too many enemies, was too involved in the details of the work of the teind commission, and had been singed by what he called the "fire of Strathearn."[31] Of the aristocracy the only one whom Charles knew and trusted was the marquis of Hamilton, a courtier who was still in his twenties and who showed no inclination to undertake the work Menteith had been doing. That left Traquair, who was both able and willing— but not yet in the king's confidence. It took him almost three years to work his way up to the position of Charles's principal agent in Scotland. Unfortunately the methods he employed destroyed his reputation, and by the time he achieved power he was unable, and disastrously unwilling, to make any effort to alter the king's policy. Counterfactual history is by its very nature not altogether convincing, but it is certainly possible to argue that had Menteith retained his influence, he might have averted the catastrophe which was to overtake his master.

The first stage in the drama of the destruction of the Stewart monarchy took place during the king's long-expected visit to

Scotland in the summer of 1633. Menteith took no part; the king's stay coincided with the hearings on Skene's allegations. Preparing for the visit involved a lot of labor and expense, and the council must have had a sense of *déjà vu*—they had done this so many times before. The most crucial matters were repairs to the roads the king would travel and the palaces in which he would stay, and the provision of vehicles, lodging, food, and drink for the men and beasts in his retinue. Then there was the question of the site of the coronation: St. Giles, or Holyrood kirk? At first the decision had gone in favor of St. Giles, since Holyrood kirk was in bad shape, both inside and out. It lay along a heavily traveled route between Edinburgh and Musselburgh and other towns to the east, and those who used the road habitually defiled the kirkyard "with filth and other ways especially at the very side of the kirk and direct under the windows of his Majesty's gallery of Holyroodhouse."[32] But the road was blocked off, the church-yard cleaned up and the church and palace renovated, at a cost of over £17,000, and the king decided in favor of Holyrood. Edin-burgh had to be got ready also. A suitable provost was to be chosen, beggars were to be removed from the streets and the heads of malefactors from the West Port. The council authorized the bailies of the Canongate to assess those who would not give voluntarily to raise money to do something for the poor. Edin-burgh proposed the building of a house of correction for idle beggars, masterless men, disobedient servants and children, and "lewd livers, common scolds and incorrigible harlots, not amend-ing by the ordinary discipline of the church." Charles did nothing about this for the moment, but after his visit he gave permission to build such houses to Edinburgh and all other royal burghs that wished to do so. There were proclamations against forestalling and regrating, and no one (except privy councillors) was to eat flesh in Lent, so that there would be plenty for the king's table.[33] The king himself undertook to write to William Dick, who loaned £360,000, Baillie of Lochend, and other Edinburgh bur-gesses, soliciting loans to meet the expenses of the visit, and promising them that they would not be the losers thereby.[34] The precedents of James VI's visit in 1617, which had gone very smoothly, were a great help. And so, when the great day came, government and people were ready to receive their master. Logistically the visit was a success. The failures lay elsewhere.

On Wednesday, June 12, 1633, King Charles entered the land of his birth, which he had left almost thirty years before as a little boy of three. It was sixteen years since Scotland had last seen her king; in the next two decades she would see a reigning sovereign twice more, and then not again for almost two centuries. Despite all the meticulous preparations there was worry. "I pray God that his Majesty resolve well what businesses to prosecute and set afoot in his parliament," wrote Dupplin to Morton, "and that these (*sic*) upon whom the great burden will lie may know them, and their advice had what is to be done and how, and that I never see my gracious master return from this as his father did, being set on to attempt things neither the advisers did well understand how to go about nor had credit (to) further him in."[35] This letter was written in 1630, but Dupplin's forebodings applied equally well in 1633. Charles had given no indication of his intentions. The law provided that before each parliament there were to be meetings of committees of each estate to consider grievances and prepare a list of proposals for consideration by the lords of the articles. This time, however, no such meetings were held; instead, Charles ordered that anyone with business for parliament should submit it to the clerk register by June 1. A group of antiepiscopal clerics did so, and, since Clerk Register Hay was, in Balfour's words, "a sworn enemy to religion and honesty and a slave to the bishops and court," they took the precaution of having their action notarized. The petition was a compilation of the grievances of the presbyterian party, lamenting most of the changes that had come about in the last forty years, especially the usurped authority of the bishops, the five articles of Perth, and the withering away of the General Assembly of the church. Since its authors believed that Hay would bury it, Thomas Hogge, a minister who had been expelled from his benefice for nonconformity, contrived to present a supplication to Charles while he was at Dalkeith, on his way to Edinburgh, asking him to respond favorably to the petition. Whether or not Charles read the supplication is unclear—William Scot says he did, John Row says not. In either case it made no impression on him. "I wish," said Lord Treasurer Morton, the king's host at Dalkeith, to Hogge, "you had chosen another place than this house for the presenting of your supplication."[36]

The scene at Dalkeith struck the first jarring note of Charles's visit; the coronation ceremony provided the second—or perhaps a whole choirful. It went off with great splendor, a complete contrast to the shabby and improvised service that ushered in the reign of Charles's father and the still more irregular goings-on that inaugurated that of Charles II, the last coronation of a king of Scotland. John Spalding, the clerk of the bishop of Aberdeen's consistorial court, and therefore no presbyterian, remarked that the bishops who took part in the coronation wore white rochets and sleeves, that there was "a four newked (cornered) table [in the] manner of an altar" in the church, with candles on it, and a tapestry behind it "wherein the crucifix was curiously wrought," before which the bishops genuflected as they passed, "which, with their habit, was noted, and bred great fear of inbringing of popery."[37]

Just before the ceremony there was an incident that showed the way Charles's mind was running. He sent Sir James Balfour, the Lord Lyon, to Lord Chancellor Dupplin, whose protégé Balfour was, to ask him to yield precedence to Archbishop Spottiswoode on this one occasion. Dupplin had received an earldom the day before—he was now earl of Kinnoul—and Charles might reasonably have expected a show of gratitude. He received a flat refusal. Kinnoul replied that he was willing to resign, but as long as he was chancellor he would uphold the dignity of the office. "Well, Lyon," said the king, "let's go to business. I will not meddle further with that old cankered goutish man, at whose hands there is nothing to be gained but sour words." During the ceremony the participating bishops wore surplices—including Spottiswoode, who donned for King Charles's anointing what he had refused to wear at the old king's funeral eight years before. The frequently repeated story that Bishop Laud thrust the archbishop of Glasgow aside for not wearing a surplice is an invention, however: he marched in the procession. The wearing of surplices, at the ceremony and at subsequent services Charles attended while in Scotland, notably one in St. Giles on June 23 where the bishop of Moray preached in a rochet and the English prayer book was used, created additional unease. Such a costume, said Spalding, had not been seen in Scotland since the Reformation. The introduction of Anglican ritual, wrote a Scottish Jesuit to his superior, "mortified and exasperated the Puritan preachers and their adherents." The odor of Popery was becoming stronger.[38]

It became apparent during Charles's visit that one of his purposes, perhaps his chief purpose, in coming to Scotland was to complete the work his father had begun: to assimilate the church of Scotland to the English church. To most Scots this came as a surprise and something of a shock, because hitherto Charles had been distinctly cool toward the Scottish bishops and had shown no interest in the project of the unification of the two kingdoms which had so concerned King James. Charles never did show any interest in such a project. His motive was religious: he believed in the polity and ritual of the church of England as expounded by Bishop Laud, and he intended to extend them to Scotland—in Gilbert Burnet's words, "what his father begun (*sic*) out of policy, was prosecuted by him out of conscience." Laud, says Clarendon, accompanied the king to Scotland expressly for that purpose.[39] Just when the king came to this decision is not clear. In 1629 the draft revision of the liturgy prepared in King James's time was brought to Whitehall by John Maxwell, one of the Edinburgh clergy, on Charles's instructions. In discussions with Laud, who wanted to impose the English liturgy on Scotland without change, Maxwell pointed out that the Scots would prefer to draw up their own.[40] Nothing was done at that time: perhaps Laud concluded that he needed more support among the Scottish bishops, or possibly Menteith, having received Maxwell's colleague William Struthers's anguished letter and having experienced the difficulty of blocking off discussion of religion at the convention of estates in 1630, managed to prevent it. All this is speculative; but the death of the archbishop of Glasgow at the end of 1632 enabled Charles in 1633 to translate that enthusiast for the prerogative, Bishop Lindsay of Ross, to the archbishopric and elevate Maxwell to the vacated see, moves which reflect Laud's influence. The campaign could now begin.

Laud's conversations with the Scottish bishops during the king's visit were inconclusive. Most of the latter wanted no change, but if there was to be change, they felt that the English prayer book should not be imposed. It contained a number of serious defects and the Scots would resent it because it was English. According to Clarendon, Laud wanted to pay no heed to these objections, but Charles decided to postpone any decision for the time being.[41] But in preparation for the day when the decision would be made, parliament was to be asked to give Charles a free hand to impose whatever religious settlement he wished.

The king had made a considerable effort to assure a manageable parliament. Since the first summons to a parliament in 1628, in preparation for Charles's projected visit in that year, there had been constant governmental interference to bring about the election of suitable representatives of the shires. As late as May 15, 1633, the sheriff of Perth was instructed to summon the electors of Perthshire and have them elect someone other than the lord chancellor's son: "upon good considerations it is not thought fit that he shall supply that charge at this time."[42] It was too late to hold an election, though Dupplin's son did not sit; consequently, Perthshire had only one representative at parliament.

If there was to be effective opposition to the king's program at parliament, it would have to emerge in the committee of the articles, which drew up the legislation upon which parliament would vote, and the aristocracy would have to take the lead. The government assured itself of a docile committee by having bishops and nobility elect each other's representatives, a device for choosing the committee occasionally used under James VI. The bishops could be depended upon to support the crown, and to choose nobles who would do likewise.[43] So it turned out; none of the nobles elected was apt to make difficulties. The list was headed by two permanent courtiers, Lennox and Hamilton, and contained two Catholics, Angus, newly raised to the rank of marquis (of Douglas) and Winton. There is no evidence of dissension in the committee, most of whose meetings Charles attended. It had a very brief time to work, and therefore very little opportunity for debate on the king's proposals: parliament convened on

June 18 and ended on June 28. The king also decreed that there was to be no debate at the final session of parliament. If he had hoped totally to prevent the expression of opposition in this way, however, he was disappointed.

The king's legislative program was his own, worked out with the aid of Menteith's old allies, Stirling and Hope.[44] It is possible to see in it the first fruits of Menteith's fall; had the earl remained in favor, it is likely that both the program and the king's tactics would have been less abrasive. The religious legislation Charles wanted was deceptively simple in appearance: one act ratified previous parliamentary legislation concerning religion—the five articles of Perth, among other things—and a second combined an act of 1606 recognizing the royal prerogative and one of 1609 authorizing the king to determine clerical dress. The purpose of combining these two was to minimize opposition to the act on clerical dress by making any negative vote on this question also a vote against the royal prerogative. The ploy failed. In the plenary session on June 28 Rothes, the spokeman for the opposition, knowing that he could not debate, made his position clear by raising procedural questions. He asked that the two acts in the second measure be separated; he also asked whether the five articles of Perth, which he had opposed in 1621, might be excluded from the ratification of the previous religious legislation. Both requests were denied; both measures received a number of negative votes, in spite of Charles's attempt to intimidate opposition by ostentatiously keeping a tally of those who voted no. The vote on the measure on dress and the prerogative was very close. The clerk register announced that it was carried, "whereof some that were present doubt much to this hour," wrote William Scot; one observer declared that it was carried by proxies.[45] The king's behavior was much resented. No one had any doubt about his ultimate objective: "By means of the statute," wrote the Jesuit John Leslie to his superior in Rome in September, "the King proposes to introduce the whole of the English ecclesiastical ritual into Scotland." "This unseemly act of his majesty's," wrote Balfour, "bred a great heartburning in many against his majesty's proceedings and government."[46] Charles's anger at those who opposed him did not vanish. The patents for earldoms for lords Lindsay and Loudoun were withdrawn, and not granted until Charles, in very different circumstances in 1641, felt it necessary to buy their support. Nor was his retaliation limited to aristocrats. In 1634 he ordered the removal of Patrick Leslie as provost of Aberdeen for having, as he put it, "wronged your trust"—i.e., voted with the opposition.[47]

The other major actions of the parliament were to ratify the controverted revocation and the acts that followed from it, and to vote a tax—a much larger tax than before. The tax of 1630 was reenacted, but for six years this time instead of four, and annualrents were taxed at the rate of 6¼ percent instead of 5 percent. In addition it was enacted that, as had happened in England in 1624, the maximum charge for interest was to drop from 10 percent to 8 percent. The lower rate would not go into effect for three years; in the meantime the extra 2 percent—what became known as the two-in-ten—was to go to the crown. Taken together, these two enactments hit creditors and lenders—that is, the moneyed classes, particularly in the burghs—very hard. The rate they could charge for loans was reduced by 20 percent, and the tax on their return on investment raised by 25 percent. In addition parliament approved a special levy of ten shillings in the poundland of Old Extent, designed to bring in 200,000 merks, to be converted into an annual income to support the court of session.[48] Both these taxes met with opposition, and in order to get the two-in-ten accepted, Charles had to promise never to levy it again. There were other proposals which were also going to cost money, notably Spynie's charges as muster-master general, which would have amounted to a poll tax of sixteen shillings on all ablebodied men between sixteen and sixty. This issue caused considerable controversy; the government only staved off defeat by agreeing to defer a decision and refer the matter to the council. The gentry and the burghs believed that the measure had been voted down altogether; there was a request for a second vote, apparently from Loudoun. The lord chancellor refused, saying that anyone who challenged the report of the vote did so at his own risk, and Charles backed him, threatening to "take order" if Loudoun could not make his charge stick. Loudoun prudently fell silent.[49]

After parliament ended, Charles spent about two weeks on a brief progress, mostly in Fife, returned briefly to Edinburgh, and then set out for home. His stay in Scotland lasted for slightly more than a month. The Venetian ambassador, who to his great delight was not required to accompany the king, had predicted that Charles's stay in Scotland would be short; during and after the visit he forwarded reports that Charles was well pleased with his reception, the coronation, the way parliament went, everything.[50] If this was indeed the case—and Charles never gave any indication that it was not—his reaction is another striking example of his lack of political sensitivity. Opposition to his religious policy had broken into the open, and he had had ample warning that this would happen.[51] His tax policy was equally resented, although when he left Scotland Charles may not have been aware of the depth of the hostility it had caused: a memorial complaining about the two-in-ten and the heavy taxation of annualrents, which, the memorial said, had been originally accepted in 1621 on the understanding that it was a one-time emergency measure, had been drawn up before the end of parliament but apparently not presented to him. Furthermore, wrote Balfour, he "was made believe by his parasites that such fleeces might be so easily shorn off his poor subjects with no more labor and expense, than the cunning bestowing of some court cream on the commons, and some preferments and money amongst the great ones"—there were a number of creations and promotions of peers at the coronation. The heavy burden of taxation was unprecendented—Edinburgh's tax bill was more than doubled—and collecting it involved methods which people found galling in the extreme. The tax on annualrents, said the abortive memorial, entailed "an inquisition in men's estates, as is not practised in any other nation in Christendom."[52]

What had happened was that in the eight years of Charles's rule the government had succeeded in transforming what had been a measure reserved for emergencies into an annual levy, and now at a heavier rate than ever before. The tax was felt by everyone in Scotland who dealt in money, not merely the traditional taxpaying groups on the land and in the royal burghs—the Canongate, for instance, a burgh of regality, compounded for £400.

And who was benefiting from this? Not the Scottish exchequer. In return for his surrender of the income from the lease of the impost on wines, the marquis of Hamilton became collector of all three of the new taxes. His first responsibility was to pay the king's debts, amounting to over £700,000, including what he himself was owed for his expenses on his unsuccessful military expedition, which came to almost half a million pounds. Hamilton's reputation for financial responsibility was not good. As master of the horse he claimed the right to Edinburgh's gift to the king on his official entry, a purse of 20,000 merks; "and at two throws only of the dice Pembroke and Holland I saw win the same, and so all Edinburgh (their offer) at two throws."[53] It is possible to argue that Scotland was not, in fact, heavily taxed, but the perception of heavy taxation was felt by many. Rulers, wrote Drummond of Hawthornden, no enemy of the government, should not "gall and perpetually afflict a people by a terrible Exchequer."[54] That the money should go to benefit the king's favorite was bound to be resented. Nor was it wise to complain publicly. Charges of peculation brought by Secretary Acheson's clerk, George Nicoll, against the leading officers of state were hushed up and the unfortunate Nicoll sentenced by the council—i.e., by those whom he accused—to be pilloried, whipped, and banished for life. "The Parliament's end is the beginning of our country's trouble," wrote Sir James Douglas to the earl of Buccleuch. The taxation, said Douglas, was the cause, especially the two-in-ten, which "has moved a great resentment and outcry."[55]

Taxation and religion were the obvious foci of complaint; resentment by no means ended there, however, though perhaps outcry did. None of the burghs' requests on such matters as monopolies, Erskine's tanning patent, and English restrictions on Scottish trade were met; parliament referred them all to the privy council for future action. And in ratifying the convention of estates's general pardon for violations of the penal statutes, parliament added to the short list of exceptions the statute prohibiting the export of specie.[56] And the burghs, like the lairds, resented the taxation and the fiscal implications of Spynie's appointment as muster-master.[57] But worse still was the general sense among

Scots that their king was a stranger to them, Anglicized and deracinated, as well as chilly, standoffish, and pettily resentful of those who opposed him. It was apparent that Charles bore grudges. During the latter part of his stay he persistently snubbed those who had voted against him in parliament, and, as a Venetian ambassador was to observe a few years later, "anyone whom he has once detested may be sure that he will never recover his favor."[58] The indications of his foreignness were ubiquitous, from his appointment of a large number of Englishmen, including Bishop Laud, to the privy council to his insistence on the use of the Anglican liturgy and modes of clerical dress when he attended church. The most deeply alienated class was the nobility, the men who regarded themselves as, by right, the companions and advisers of the king. What had already been apparent to those who, since the destruction of the Jacobean system of government, had had to make the costly trip to London to catch the royal ear was now apparent to all. The magnates were annoyed at the expense to which the visit had put them, and bitter at the diminution of their power and influence, and, wrote Clarendon with rueful hindsight, they "watched only for an opportunity to inflame the people."[59] As early as the beginning of the reign a few nobles, like Rothes, whose hostility to James's religious policy had made him sensitive on the point, were bemoaning the aristocracy's lack of influence;[60] now, with Menteith in disgrace, there were no more links between aristocracy and court. "It evidently appeared," wrote Clarendon, "that they of that nation who shined most in the Court of England had the least influence in their own country." Clarendon did make an exception for Hamilton, but this was because he later came to distrust Hamilton, and so believed that he was even then in touch with the king's enemies. Burnet was nearer the truth with his comment that, apart from the matter of the wine impost and the tax collection, Hamilton played no active part in Scottish affairs until 1638.[61] Menteith had been the king's link to the people who counted in Scotland; the deracinated Hamilton could not take his place, nor did he try. His appointment as collector was resented because he was an absentee almost as Anglicized as his master. The timing of Charles's visit, coinciding as it did with the shock of Menteith's ruin, was unfortunate; it made the king's alienness all the more apparent. In short, the royal visit was a disaster; it would have been far better for Charles if he had never come at all. The Scots now knew, from firsthand experience, that they had an Englishman for their king. They were not going to forget it.

This Anglicized king and his religious mentor, who in August 1633 became archbishop of Canterbury, gave up the policy of simply imposing the English liturgy on Scotland with considerable reluctance. They delayed the decision to proceed with a separate Scottish liturgy until they could discover whether the Scots might accept the English prayer book after all, if they became accustomed to its use. A Scottish edition of the book appeared, and in October 1633 Charles ordered that it be used in the bishops' oratories and in the chapel royal. In a very firm letter of instructions to Archbishop Spottiswoode the king commanded its use in services at St. Salvator's college, St. Andrews, which the university community was to attend. Students were not to attend services in town, nor were townspeople to be admitted to St. Salvator's. The emphatic tone of the king's letter indicated that he was less than convinced of the archbishop's zeal for the cause. At the same time the king ordered both archbishops to exert themselves to recover the crown's rights of patronage, especially in the lordships of erection, and issued his instructions on clerical dress, which were inserted in the parliamentary record. Ministers might preach in a black gown, but they were to wear surplices while reading divine service, christening, burying, and administering communion, and bishops were to wear a rochet and sleeves. Councillors and judges were to set an example by taking communion at the chapel royal at least once a year; communion services were to be held there monthly, and the dean was always to preach in his whites.[62] In 1634 Charles ordered councillors and judges to communicate twice a year and laid down the rules for church attendance for students at Glasgow and Aberdeen. He also decreed that everyone must take annual communion in his or her own parish, and not wander afield in search of a more agreeable—i.e., nonconformist—minister. The Scots saw these orders as the work of William Laud, whom Row characterized as "a Popish-Arminian-Protestant bishop." Laud was accused of referring to the Scottish reformation as "Deformation," and the numbers in his name added up to 666, the number of the beast.[63]

Another unpopular royal decision that Row attributed to Laud was the creation of a new bishopric. Henceforth there was to be a bishop of Edinburgh. Charles made the decision public in a letter of October 11, 1633, ordering the demolition of the east and west walls within St. Giles, so that the church would be grand enough to serve as a bishop's cathedral.[64] From the point of view of orderly episcopal administration the king's decision made excellent sense. Edinburgh was part of the diocese of St. Andrews, by far the most populous and administratively complex of all the Scottish sees. The order nevertheless caused intense exasperation in Edinburgh, as much for the expense involved as for the creation of the office, and helped to bring about a notable worsening of relations between the king and his capital.

Save for the flare-up over ministerial salaries in the first year of the reign, these relations had been quite good prior to the royal visit. This was in part owing to the negotiating skill of John Hay, the town clerk, who was the capital's—and, on occasion, the convention of royal burghs'—envoy to the king when an envoy was required. Hay persuaded Edinburgh officialdom to make a comparatively prompt formal submission on the matter of the revocation, which pleased the king. He also made himself useful to the teind commission and in the matter of the fisheries, and in addition was impeccably conformist in religion. Charles came to like him, and in 1632 rewarded him with a knighthood and the office of clerk register. For the capital, Hay's great service was to keep Charles on Edinburgh's side in its continuing effort to get control of Leith. At issue was the ratification of Edinburgh's privileges, including the charter granted by King James in 1603. Charles issued the ratification early in 1627, but then ordered it held up because, he said, he understood that James's charter infringed the privileges of some members of the aristocracy. The constable and admiral had some questions also. Edinburgh officialdom reacted tetchily, refusing to allow any inspection of the burgh's records, and so the struggle over ratification began.[65].

Relations between the privy council and the town government were frequently difficult, owing mostly to the council's effort to prevent Edinburgh from unfairly restricting the merchants and craftsmen of Leith and the Canongate. The town much preferred, if it could, to have its cases go before the court of session, dominated as it was by the Edinburgh legal fraternity, rather than the council, and customarily petitioned to that end whenever its privileges were in question.[66] In 1632, for example, the coffinmakers in the Canongate complained that four coffins made for Edinburgh citizens had been wrongfully seized. The Edinburgh government replied that the coffins had to be to some degree "made" in Edinburgh, since the corpses had to be measured there, and demanded that the case go to the court of session. The council denied the motion, on the ground that it had jurisdiction, since the seizure of the coffins was an act of violence. It then ruled that the wrights of the Canongate had the right to sell coffins in Edinburgh, as long as they did so on market days only.[67]

With respect to Leith the Edinburgh government in October 1629 obtained a letter from the king ordering that the jurisdictional disputes between them be tried in the session, as Edinburgh wished, and, incidentally, ordering the council to prevent the inhabitants of Leith from committing violence against the magistrates of the Good Town. Early in 1630 the court of session ruled in Edinburgh's favor; the council immediately ordered the decision suspended until the complainants against it could be heard. The session's decision added one more to the long list of complaints Leith had against Edinburgh, a list which at first contained seventeen items and which ultimately swelled to eighty-four.[68] One issue on this long list attracted more attention than any other, and became the touchstone for all concerned: could grain be stored for export in Leith without the permission of Edinburgh officialdom? Charles was concerned to be fair to Leith, and wanted to see justice done; he had not acquiesced in the capital's attempt to take advantage of the war by offering to build fortifications at Leith in return for recognition of its superiority over the port. But he did not care for the council's action in suspending the court of session's decree in Edinburgh's favor, and he could not help but remember—and, indeed, Edinburgh officials kept reminding him—that the burgh of Edinburgh was the largest single taxpayer in the kingdom, and was always accommodating about anticipating tax payments and making them in a lump sum when they were voted.[69] Furthermore, Edinburgh proved very conciliatory on matters of less importance. With a flourish the capital declared in January 1630 that in accordance with the act of revocation it would renounce any rights of regality contained in the charter of 1603, as well as whatever other "strange clauses which are not competent to a subject" the king found in that charter. It was prepared to work out agreements with the neighboring landowners which would meet the latter's complaints that the charter encroached on their legal jurisdiction—a wise move in view of the importance of some of those involved, the earls of Morton and Winton, for instance. It was conciliatory respecting the rights of the lord admiral, the duke of Lennox, who happened to be the king's cousin; it was less obliging, though, with regard to the rights of the constable, the earl of Errol, a man with much less political influence. And so it won on the main point. The council, to save face, insisted on holding hearings before lifting its order suspending the session's decree, and Edinburgh made one key concession: it agreed to allow aristocratic landowners to store *their* grain in Leith. And so, in June 1631, a "compromise" was announced: the citizens of Leith were prohibited from storing grain in their own town without permission from Edinburgh. Seven months later the king wrote to the council confirming his ratifications of the capital's rights and privileges, and instructing them to implement these privileges in future cases.[70]

This was not all. Edinburgh's domination of Leith, and of the Canongate too, was to be sealed by its acquisition of the king's and the earl of Roxburgh's rights in the barony and regality of Broughton, thanks to its position under the will of the goldsmith George Heriot, who earmarked the bulk of his estate for the building of Heriot's Hospital; Edinburgh received these rights in payment of Charles's and Roxburgh's debts to Heriot. Broughton was a lordship of erection, carved out of the property of the abbey of Holyroodhouse, granted to the then justice clerk, Sir Lewis Bellenden, in 1587, and acquired from his grandson William by the earl of Roxburgh in 1627. Roxburgh was William's uncle, and his cautioner for a debt he owed to Heriot; it was in consequence of the debt that Roxburgh acquired Broughton. What Edinburgh obtained was the superiority of Leith and the Canongate, which had been excepted from the general surrender of such superiorities to the king. The capital also obtained indirect control of the rest of the barony, which went to Heriot's Hospital: the provost, bailies, council, and ministers of Edinburgh were the governors of the hospital under Heriot's will. Throughout this process, which began in 1631 and ended five years later, Charles was very helpful to the capital.[71]

The king also served Edinburgh's interests in other ways. For example, he rapidly abandoned the experiment with justice ayres, which had made Edinburgh very uneasy, since it would have cost the capital legal business, and dropped a proposal to shorten the term of the court of session when Edinburgh protested.[72] So, in March 1632, a month after Charles's letter to the council confirming Edinburgh's rights and privileges, the city fathers made a generous gesture which they soon had cause to regret. They announced to the council that Edinburgh was prepared to build a new parliament house, as well as a new house for the council and the court of session. The king was delighted,[73] and apparently took this gesture, and the town's willingness to borrow money (in anticipation of receiving Heriot's legacy) in order to buy land, as evidence that Edinburgh could bear a good deal more expense as well. The tax voted in parliament in 1633 more than doubled what Edinburgh had to pay, as has been said. Charles revived the issue of ministerial stipends and insisted that the town now pay its senior ministers 2,000 merks annually, and the others 1,300, instead of the 1,200 they had all previously received, plus 200 merks' house rent apiece; in return parliament provided that Edinburgh, if she wished to do so, could raise an annual tax of 12,000 merks for this purpose. The tax would far more than make up for the increment in salaries, and therefore would relieve a bit of the pressure on the town's treasury. But whatever relief there might be for the treasury, there would be none for the citizens who had to pay the tax, and they somewhat illogically blamed the ministers for their additional burden, especially after Charles's decision to establish the new bishopric of Edinburgh became known.[74] This entailed not only the remodeling of St. Giles but also the building of two new parish churches to replace those lost in that remodeling. For good measure the king also ordered the building of a new charter house to store the government's records, which had outgrown their current repository in the castle.[75]

Thus Edinburgh all at once found itself committed to an enormous program of building and remodeling of churches and public buildings. In addition she had to pay the heavy taxes voted in parliament in 1633, the special tax for ministers' salaries, and the expenses entailed in the royal visit. The king's casual consignment of the town's entry gift to the marquis of Hamilton struck a jarring note, as did his use of the English prayer book and his insistence that the clergy wear dress which many people regarded as Popish. So it is not surprising that the city fathers dragged their feet over finding the money for the ministers' salaries and the buildings the king had ordered built. Charles applied pressure: in 1634 he specified whom the town was to elect as its officials, paid no attention to the ensuing protests, and two years later suggested the creation of a "constant council" to make annual elections unnecessary. A royal order in October 1634 to those officials to stop procrastinating and deal with a committee of the council on ministerial salaries produced no results.[76] So in 1635 Charles went further and threatened to enforce the statute which prohibited the export of specie, a statute which the Edinburgh merchant community habitually and extensively violated. In 1634 Charles had granted Edinburgh an exemption from the statute on account of its "great charge and trouble of late"; the threat to prosecute brought the town to heel. In May 1635 Edinburgh agreed to implement the statute raising money for ministers' salaries, and to build the churches, as well as the parliament house, of course, and Charles therefore continued the town's exemption from the statute regarding export of specie. Only one church, the Tron Church, was ever built. A site was obtained for a second, and some work begun, but with the abolition of episcopacy in 1638 the town government abandoned it and promptly repartitioned St. Giles.[77]

The consequence of all this for Edinburgh was a very heavy financial burden, which had to be met by borrowing. This marked a substantial acceleration of a trend that had been going on since the beginning of the reign. Only once in the reign of James VI had the capital's annual expenditure exceeded £51,000; only once in Charles's reign was it as low as £52,000, and in 1635–36 it reached over £147,000. Between 1625 and 1637 there were deficits every year but two; in 1636 alone the deficit increased by about £50,000, and by November 1638 it stood at £151,000. In 1636 the king attempted to help the town meet its expenses by granting it the proceeds of a special customs duty on all imports into Leith and Newhaven and on goods imported anywhere in Scotland by Edinburgh merchants, but this was not helpful; this duty was difficult to administer and had the effect of scaring off some foreign merchants. The levying of the tax for the payment of ministers' salaries was postponed on account of a dispute over the legal profession's long-standing claim to exemption from such obligations; the question was not settled until July 11, 1637, twelve days before the great riot.[78]

Edinburgh was by no means impoverished as a consequence of its heavy expenditures, but it was resentful. It was being compelled to spend money, to go heavily into debt, borrowing even from its new-made bishop, for purposes of which the citizenry did not approve.[79] Edinburgh did not want a bishop in the first place, and certainly not the ones it got: first, William Forbes of Aberdeen, who was learned and pious but who, while serving as minister in Edinburgh ten years previously, had been the center of a considerable controversy because of his alleged softness on Popery; and then, after his death, David Lindsay, translated from Brechin, one of the principal supporters of the five articles of Perth, a man whom only Charles's intervention saved from a trial before the court of session for tax evasion.[80] Its ministers, mostly eager conformists—Charles insisted on this—pleased the citizens no better.[81] As might have been expected, the burgesses' gratitude for Charles's support on other matters was all but forgotten in their resentment of a policy which simultaneously afflicted their pocketbooks and their consciences. A measure of their disenchantment was their hostility to Charles's imposition on them of their former town clerk, John Hay, as provost in September 1637; Hay was identified with Charles's religious policy.[82] The king's alienation of his capital was to have serious consequences.

NOTES

1. Sept. 29, 1629, Charles to Menteith, Nov. 9, Charles to the clerk register, Sir William Fraser, *The Red Book of Menteith* II, 21–22, 24–25. Sept. 29, Charles to Hope, *Stirling* I, 382.

2. Fraser, *Menteith* I, 342–45. Between 1631 and 1633 Menteith should properly be called Strathearn, and after 1633, earl of Airth. For convenience's sake he will continue to be Menteith.

3. *Ibid.*, pp. 347–48. See also Hope's letters to him on Nov. 10 and 11, 1631, *ibid.* II, 125–29. *RMS 1620–1633,* pp. 633–34, 669–70.

4. Scotstarvet's "Trew Relation" on this subject is printed in *SHR* XI (1914), 284–96, 395–403.

5. *Ibid.*, p. 285.

6. Laud's biographer, Peter Heylyn, *Cyprianus Anglicus* (London, 1671), pp. 347–51, accused Hamilton of contriving Menteith's ruin. Heylyn detested Hamilton and overstated the case, but there is contemporary evidence of people's belief in Hamilton's hostility to Menteith. See May 3, 1633, James Baird to George Baird, W. W. Fraser, ed., *Genealogical Collections Concerning the Sir-Name of Baird* (London, 1870), p. 74.

7. *SHR* XI, 290–91.

8. *Ibid.*, pp. 292–94.

9. *Ibid.*, p. 294. It is worth noting, perhaps, that if King James had said this, historians would have fastened upon it as evidence of James's sexual proclivities.

10. Fraser, *Menteith* I, 356–58.

11. Hector Boece, *The Chronicles of Scotland,* ed. E. C. Batho and H. W. Husbands, Scottish Text Society (Edinburgh, 1941), II, 336–38. George Buchanan, *The History of Scotland,* ed. J. Aikman, (Glasgow, 1827), II, 41–42.

12. *SHR* XI, 294.

13. On this point see D. Laing, ed., *A Diary of the Public Correspondence of Sir Thomas Hope,* Bannatyne Club (Edinburgh, 1843), p. 13.

14. Fraser, *Menteith* I, 358–62. Jan. 21, 1633, Charles to Menteith, *ibid.* II, 49. *RMS 1620–1633,* p. 719.

15. See his letter of Feb. 4, 1633, to Hope, *Stirling* II, 649.

16. See Mar. 16, 1633, Traquair to Morton, Fraser, *Menteith* I, 365–66.

17. *Ibid.*, pp. 363, 365–66. *Stirling* II, 662.

18. Fraser, *Menteith* I, 367. Apr. 27, 1633, Clerk Register Hay to

Morton, NLS Mss. 82. no. 72. June 21, Sir James Douglas to Buccleuch, Sir William Fraser, *The Scotts of Buccleuch* (Edinburgh, 1878) II, 351–52.

19. *SHR* XI, 401–2.

20. May 3, 1633, James Baird to George Baird, Fraser, *Genealogical Collections*, p. 74. May 7, Charles to Menteith, Fraser, *Menteith* II, 53.

21. SRO, GD 112/39/494.

22. Fraser, *Menteith* I, 370, II, 50–53.

23. *Ibid.* I, 368–73.

24. July 10, 13, 1633, William Maxwell to Sir John Maxwell, Sir William Fraser, *Memoirs of the Maxwells of Pollok* I, 440, II, 243–45. July 13, Sir James Douglas to Buccleuch, Fraser, *Buccleuch* II, 352–53.

25. Fraser, *Menteith* I, 375–76, II, 152–53.

26. July 22, 1633, William Maxwell to Sir John Maxwell, Fraser, *Pollok* II, 246–47. Aug. 15, Charles to Traquair, *Stirling* II, 674.

27. *Stirling* II, 680–81. Fraser, *Menteith* I, 377–78. *RPCS* 2nd ser. V, 139–41.

28. Oct. 8, 1633, Charles to Lord Chancellor Hay (now earl of Kinnoul), *Stirling* II, 686. Fraser, *Menteith* I, 379.

29. See, e.g., Feb. 3, 1634, Menteith to Hamilton, SRO, Hamilton Papers, c. 1, no. 281. In August 1636 he wrote Hamilton to thank him for his kindness. *Ibid.*, no. 342. Mar. 3, 1634, Menteith to Charles, Fraser, *Menteith* II, 154–55; May 2, Nov. 5, Charles to the court of session, July 14, Charles to Morton and Traquair, *Stirling* II, 734, 772, 803–4. Jan. 31, Mar. 13, 1635, Loudoun to Hamilton, SRO, Hamilton Papers, c. 1, nos. 302, 305.

30. Fraser, *Menteith* I, 383.

31. Laing, *Hope's Diary*, p. 13.

32. *RPCS* 2nd ser. III, 74.

33. Aug. 15, 1632, Charles to Menteith, Fraser, *Menteith* II, 43. *RPCS* 2nd ser. V, 39–41, 47–49, 67–69. NLS Adv. Mss. 31.3.70, f. 93. J. Imrie and J. G. Dunbar, eds., *Accounts of the Masters of Works* II, intro., p. lxxviii.

34. *Stirling* II, 643–44. Imrie and Dunbar, *Masters of Works* II, intro., p. xl.

35. NLS Mss. 82, f. 69.

36. *RPCS* 2nd ser. V, 81–82. *Balfour* II, 206. *Row*, p. 362. *Scot*, pp. 329–35, prints the petition, as do *Row* and *Balfour;* Morton's comment is in *Scot*, p. 335.

37. John Spalding, *Memorialls of the Trubles in Scotland and in En-*

gland, A.D. 1624–A.D. 1645, I, 36. The coronation service is printed in *Balfour* IV, 383–404.

38. *Balfour* II, 141–42, IV, 387. John Rushworth, *Historical Collections* (London, 1659–1701), II, 182. Spalding, *Memorialls* I, 39. W. Forbes-Leith, *Memoirs of Scottish Catholics during the XVIIth and XVIIIth Centuries* I, 157.

39. G. Burnet, *The Memoires of the Lives and Actions of James and William, Dukes of Hamilton,* p. 29. Edward, Earl of Clarendon, *The History of the Rebellion and Civil Wars in England,* ed. W. Dunn Macray (Oxford, 1888), I, 111.

40. G. Donaldson, *The Making of the Scottish Prayer Book of 1637* (Edinburgh, 1954), pp. 41–42.

41. *Ibid.,* p. 42. Clarendon, *History* I, 111–14. Clarendon opined that if Charles had proposed his liturgical changes at this point, the Scots might have acquiesced.

42. *RPCS* 2nd ser. V, 100.

43. For the committee of the articles see R. S. Rait, *The Parliaments of Scotland* (Glasgow, 1924), pp. 371–74.

44. Feb. 2, 1633, Charles to Hope, *Stirling* II, 648.

45. *Scot,* pp. 338–39. June 28, 1633, John Maxwell to Sir John Maxwell, Fraser, *Pollok* II, 235–40.

46. Forbes-Leith, *Memoirs* I, 165. *Balfour* II, 200.

47. John Stuart, ed., *Extracts from the Council Register of the Burgh of Aberdeen, 1625–1642* (Edinburgh, 1871), pp. 70–72.

48. A poundland of Old Extent, by decree of the lords auditors of the exchequer in 1586, equaled approximately fifty-two acres. Two such poundlands, or forty shillings of Old Extent, was the basis of the franchise for those holding land directly of the king. See J. D. Mackie, ed., *Thomas Thomson's Memorial on Old Extent,* Stair Society (Edinburgh, 1946), esp. pp. 314–20.

49. For this episode see June 28, 1633, John Maxwell to Sir John Maxwell, June 29, William Maxwell to Sir John Maxwell, Fraser, *Pollok* II, 235–41; these two letters constitute the fullest contemporary account of the final session of parliament. It was probably this episode which led Gilbert Burnet, writing in the next generation, to attribute the challenge of the vote to Rothes, over the act on prerogative and clerical apparel, in which version the story has been repeated by some modern historians. No contemporary account mentions Rothes in connection with a challenge to a vote. Gilbert Burnet, *Bishop Burnet's History of His Own Time,* ed. M. J. Routh, I, 38. The acts of this parliament are in *APS,* V, 10–161. The tax roll for the taxation of

1633 is printed in Sir William Purves, *Revenue of the Scottish Crown, 1681,* ed. D. M. Rose (Edinburgh, 1897), pp. 185–200. The Aberdeenshire figures for the two-in-ten are printed in J. Stuart, ed., *The Miscellany of the Spalding Club* III (Aberdeen, 1846), 71–139. The yearly total for Aberdeenshire came to somewhere over 15,500 merks.

50. See his letters during June and July, 1633, *CSP Venetian* XXIII, 117 ff.

51. *Row,* pp. 362–63.

52. *Balfour* II, 180–81. The memorial is in *Row,* pp. 364–66. For Edinburgh see R. K. Hannay and G. P. H. Watson, "The Building of the Parliament House," *Book of the Old Edinburgh Club* XIII (1934), 16.

53. June 28, 1633, John Maxwell to Sir John Maxwell, Fraser, *Pollok* II, 235–40. Kinnoul, Morton, and Haddington objected to the form in which Hamilton's original patent for the taxation was drawn, and the necessarily complex financial arrangements were not completed until July 1634. July 22, 1633, Kinnoul to Morton, NLS Mss. 82, f. 85. July 22, William Maxwell to Sir John Maxwell, Fraser, *Pollok* II, 246–47. *RPCS* 2nd ser. V, 305–16. For a good brief summary of the king's finances see D. Stevenson, "The King's Scottish Revenues and the Covenanters, 1625–51," *Historical Journal* XVII (1974), 17–41, esp. pp. 17–26.

54. Quoted in I. M. Smart, "Monarchy and Toleration in Drummond of Hawthornden's Works," *Scotia* IV (1980), 45.

55. July 13, 1633, Douglas to Buccleuch, Fraser, *Buccleuch* II, 352–53. For Nicoll see S. A. Gillon, ed., *Selected Justiciary Cases, 1624–1650* I, 218–22; *RPCS* 2nd ser. V, 8, 37–39; *Stirling* II, 651.

56. *APS* V, 43, 48–49. For an example of the kinds of things the burghs wanted, see Taylor, *Aberdeen Council Letters* I, 384–86.

57. June 28, 1633, John Maxwell to Sir John Maxwell, Fraser, *Pollok* II, 235–40.

58. Rushworth, *Historical Collections* II, 183–84. Burnet, *Hamilton,* p. 30. *CSP Venetian* XXIV, 297.

59. Clarendon, *History* I, 108, 137.

60. See his letter of Apr. 14, 1625, to Sir Robert Kerr, *A&L* I, 35–38.

61. Clarendon, *History* I, 108. Burnet, *Hamilton,* p. 26.

62. Donaldson, *Prayer Book,* pp. 42–43. *Stirling* II, 677–81, 693. *APS* V, 21. Rushworth, *Historical Collections* II, 205–6.

63. *Row,* p. 369. *Stirling* II, 743, 745–47. *RPCS* 2nd ser. V, 275, 421–22. Laud's remark was taken out of context; he was referring crit-

ically to the post-Reformation remodeling of the interior of a Gothic church.

64. *Row,* pp. 369–70. *RPCS* 2nd ser. V, 136–37. *Stirling* II, 684.

65. Apr. 2, 1627, Charles to Mar, *Stirling* I, 154. Apr. 28, the council to Charles, *RPCS* 2nd ser. I, 589–91.

66. See, e.g., *RPCS* 2nd ser. II, 451–55.

67. *Ibid.* IV, xxxi–xxxiii, 460–63.

68. *Ibid.* III, 349–50, 506–8, 633–65.

69. Oct. 12, 1630, Charles to the council, *Stirling* II, 482. *RPCS* 2nd ser. III, 433–34.

70. For the course of the dispute between Edinburgh and Leith see *RPCS* 2nd ser. III, intro., pp. xxvii–xxix, IV, intro., pp. xxix–xxxi, and the relevant entries in the register, esp. III, 215–20, 260–61, 349–50, 422–23, 433–34, 440, 443, 454, 501–3, IV, 80, 82–83, 248–51, 432, 598–607, V, 298–300, 611–12, 620, 625–26. See also *Stirling* I, 409, II, 415, 458–59, 466, 482, 533; NLS, Mss. 79, no. 73, Mss. 80, nos. 42, 70; M. Wood, ed., *Extracts from the Records of the Burgh of Edinburgh, 1626 to 1641,* pp. xxv–xxix.

71. Wood, *Extracts,* pp. xlvi–xlvii, 328–34. July 31, 1631, Charles to Menteith, Fraser, *Menteith* II, 58. Oct. 26, 1633, Charles to Morton and Traquair, HMC, 9th Report, App. II, 245.

72. Wood, *Extracts,* pp. x–xi, 48, 317.

73. *RPCS* 2nd ser. IV, 448–49. *Stirling* II, 611.

74. Hannay and Watson, "Parliament House," pp. 29, 38. Wood, *Extracts,* pp. 156, 161.

75. Hannay and Watson, "Parliament House," p. 38. Oct. 6, 1633, May 14, 1634, Charles to the government of Edinburgh, *Stirling* II, 685, 753.

76. Wood, *Extracts,* p. 179. *Stirling* II, 750, 786. The fact that the committee had an episcopal majority may have affected Edinburgh's attitude.

77. *Stirling* II, 744. Hannay and Watson, "Parliament House," pp. 37–44. Wood, *Extracts,* pp. vii–xvii, xlviii.

78. On these points see Taylor, *Aberdeen Council Letters* II, 44–45; Hannay and Watson, "Parliament House," pp. 43–44, 51–52; *RPCS* 2nd ser. VI, 478; *Stirling* I, 170, 173, 219; Wood, *Extracts,* pp. xlii–xliv; W. Makey, *The Church of the Covenant, 1637–1651,* p. 119. The legal profession made good its claim to exemption, and then agreed to make a voluntary contribution.

79. For Edinburgh's financial situation see Hannay and Watson, "Parliament House," pp. 34–49; Wood, *Extracts,* pp. vii–xvii, xlii–

xlviii, 164. See also *Stirling* II, 684; *RPCS* 2nd ser. V, 209, 232, 234–36, VI, 165.

80. Apr. 3, 1634, Charles to Kinnoul, *Stirling* II, 728–29.

81. See, e.g., Oct. 20, 1634, Charles to the bishop of Edinburgh, *Stirling* II, 800. Of the eight parish ministers in office in 1637, one, James Fairlie, became bishop of Argyll that year and four others were subsequently ousted for their support of the service book. Only one, William Arthur of St. Cuthbert's, subscribed the Covenant.

82. J. Inglis, "Sir John Hay, the 'Incendiary'," *SHR* XV (1917–18), 135–37.

5

The Rise of Traquair

Whatever other people, including Charles himself, may have felt about his visit to Scotland, one man had every reason to be satisfied: Treasurer Depute Traquair. He was now an earl; the king thought well of him, and so did the king's close confidant Bishop Laud. Traquair was well aware of the importance of cultivating Laud, and was so successful at it, according to Clarendon, that he became the only Scottish layman Laud trusted.[1] Traquair had taken advantage of Menteith's mistakes to clear him out of the way, and had managed so adroitly that the fallen earl still looked on him as a friend.[2] With Menteith gone, there was now no one to act as the conduit between Whitehall and Edinburgh. Traquair took it upon himself to do so, and again met with success: by February 1634 Charles was using him as the bearer of his instructions.[3] Traquair's pattern of travel began to resemble that of Menteith. He went to court on an average of twice a year, usually in late winter and again in late summer, staying from six to ten weeks each time.

Traquair was not Menteith, however; he could not play Menteith's role, and could not hope to do so. He had no natural constituency, as Menteith had, nor did he possess the king's affection. To Charles he was a useful agent, who had already done one piece of good service in persuading him and the marquis of Hamilton that it was unwise to turn over the impost on wines, the largest single source of regular income, to the latter to pay for his expedition to Germany;[4] Charles hoped and expected that he might do more. Money was much on the king's mind in 1633 and 1634, in connection not only with Edinburgh but also with the state of his revenues generally. In February 1634, for example, Charles with his usual impatience ordered Traquair "betwixt this and Easter" to give him an account of all intromissions with the crown's rents and casualties and of the audits of the taxations of 1625 and 1630.[5] The financial situation was not good, in spite of the heavy taxation, which was earmarked to pay off the crown's creditors, starting with Hamilton, its collector, and could not be of help in other directions. Here was Traquair's opportunity to prove himself useful to his master: if he could not be Menteith, perhaps he could do still better and become another Dunbar, the lord treasurer who ruled Scotland with an iron hand for King James, and was so successful that at his death he was at the height of his power.

Becoming another Dunbar turned out to be very difficult, however. The financial problems were extraordinarily intractable. Charles, and everyone else, was concerned about the extensive circulation of foreign coins; the king wanted their importation stopped.[6] This proved to be impossible. Dollars were brought to Scotland by foreign purchasers of coal and salt, mostly Dutch; an attempt in January 1634 to require such purchasers to use Scottish coin or certain stipulated gold and silver pieces rapidly collapsed. The coal owners pointed out that the buyers would simply take their dollars elsewhere, probably to Newcastle, and thus ruin the Scots' export business. The council agreed, suspended its order, and the dollars continued to flow in.[7] The king made matters no better by his generous authorization to Sir William Alexander, now earl of Stirling, to coin copper to recoup his losses in Nova Scotia; the result was a flood of "black money," some of it counterfeit, as has been said. Dollars were counterfeited too. Unless something was done, lamented the council in April 1635, "in short time this country will be filled with this foul and filthy dross."[8] Traquair kept urging the king to act, but nothing useful was done. The only result was still another proclamation prohibiting the importation of dollars, issued in August 1635. It proved as futile as its predecessors.[9]

In other directions matters went little better. On Charles's orders Traquair and his colleagues did their best to prevent tax fraud and to pursue delinquents who had not paid what they owed on their earlier taxes, as far back as 1621. Neither was easy to do, in part because neither Charles nor any other monarch of the time had at his disposal a bureaucratic machine capable of carrying out his wishes. The government nevertheless did what it could. Hamilton and his subordinates squeezed the burghs as hard as they could in the negotiations for compounding their payments for the taxes voted in 1633; Aberdeen, for example, wound up paying 5,000 merks more than the limit it had authorized its agent to pay.[10] The king instructed the court of session that the unpopular new tax, the two-in-ten, was to be collected in full: no one was to be allowed to plead successfully for a defalcation. Unfortunately the tax lent itself to various ingenious schemes to avoid payment, such as fraudulent backdating to make it appear that a loan had been made at 8 percent before the parliamentary enactment, in which case it was tax-exempt, or fraudulent attempts to make loans appear to be rental payments, which were not subject to the tax.[11] To raise cash Charles authorized the teind commission to sell to those who had to pay the king's annuity the crown's rights therein, including arrears, for fifteen years' purchase, after scolding the commissioners for their sloppiness in valuing tithes without stipulating the annuity. Charles's complaint was apparently justified; the only recorded sales of tithes for early 1634 do not mention the annuity.[12]

Charles knew that he could expect little ready cash from the new taxes; so in May 1634 he appointed a commission to make recommendations as to administrative reform and ways in which the king's ordinary revenues could be increased.[13] The committee reported in August; its picture of the king's financial situation was gloomy in the extreme. The king's debts amounted to almost a million pounds; interest payment on the debt, plus pensions, fees, allowances, etc., involved an annual expenditure of over £330,000. The most striking of the remedies it suggested derived from the act of revocation: Charles might legally seize the feu maills of all lords of erection who had not signed the general submission. He could also eliminate pensions, cut fees, abolish unnecessary offices, reform the coinage, and collect his annuity on the teinds retroactively to 1628. In November Charles accepted most of this, although his approval said nothing specific about the elimination of pensions, which in fact the king continued to grant;[14] but implementing these remedies would take time, and some of them were politically impossible. He could not simply seize the feu duties of the lords of erection. Nor could he simply abolish pensions, especially without compensation; too many landed families were dependent on them for ready cash. But some things could be done, especially with feudal tenures, which were to be restored to tenure by ward and relief from tenure by taxt or blench ward. The king ordered that a start be made with the estate of the recently deceased earl of Buccleuch. He assigned the wardship of Buccleuch's heir, still a minor, to Secretary Stirling, and completed the process of restoring the heir of the long-dead earl of Bothwell to a portion of the earl's estates which Buccleuch had held, in violation of a promise made to the old earl, a process which cost the new earl some £50,000. It is not surprising that Buccleuch became a staunch Covenanter.[15]

Traquair took a leading part in the work of the commission. In another direction he was equally busy. In October 1634, reverting to a matter about which he had expressed concern before, Charles wrote to Lord Advocate Hope, expressing his dissatisfaction at the length and annual rate of return of the existing customs tack, which had been let for fifteen years in 1628 for £54,000 a year. On Traquair's advice the lease was nullified on the ground that a tack of more than five years was illegal; in January 1635 a new tack was let to the invaluable William Dick for £60,000 a year, plus a 2,000-merk grassum. Charles wrote to express his approval—and included in his letter a complaint from a member of the previous syndicate, offering more and grumbling about Traquair's behavior. Charles ordered his exchequer commission to investigate this offer.[16]

This letter may well have disquieted Traquair. He had worked very hard for a year and a half on the king's finances, and did not have anything in the way of enhanced influence to show for it. Or, indeed, anything in the way of results: in July 1635 Charles was to write him and Morton that the master of the wardrobe had complained that he and his staff had not been paid for four years, and that his subordinates were threatening to sell the wardrobe's possessions to compensate themselves.[17] Furthermore the odium of the king's unpopular exactions was falling on him, among others—in 1635 Drummond of Hawthornden, no political radical, was writing pointedly of "the avarice of the officers and favourites of the prince, who are brought foolishly to believe that by tearing off the skins of the flock they shall turn the shepherd rich."[18] In fact there was no indication that Traquair had any influence with the king at all outside of the financial area, and even here he had a rival: it was Clerk Register Hay, not Traquair, whom Charles in July 1634 ordered to come to court as soon as the auditing of the accounts of the collectors of the taxes of 1621, 1625, and 1630 which Charles had ordered was done.[19] Traquair's candidate to succeed Sir James Skene as president of the court of session was bypassed in favor of Sir Robert Spottiswoode, the archbishop's son—and Traquair, unlike Clerk Register Hay, was not keen on clerical influence in politics. Charles followed Spottiswoode's elevation by making the clerk register a regular member of the court, thereby violating his rule that officers of state and members of the privy council were not to hold such appointments. He rather lamely declared that this did not really represent a change of policy: his rule applied, he said, only to nobles—an argument apparently concocted by Stirling.[20]

The crowning blow came in December 1634. In that month Charles gratified Archbishop Spottiswoode's lifelong ambition by announcing his intention to appoint the archbishop lord chancellor of Scotland, in succession to the recently deceased earl of Kinnoul.[21] It was an alarming appointment in all sorts of ways, and not only to Traquair. Spottiswoode was the first clerical lord chancellor since Cardinal Beaton almost a century before. His appointment was one more example of the growing political influence of the clergy in both kingdoms—and not merely of the clergy, but of a breed of cleric that was particularly obnoxious to all those people in Scotland, both clerical and lay, who were unhappy with the current condition of the church. That Laud should become archbishop of Canterbury in succession to George Abbot was no more than a formalization of his position as Charles's principal ecclesiastical adviser. But the Scots regretted Abbot's passing; he was, wrote John Row, "not violent against honest ministers and professors in his time, and was a great friend to

Scotland."[22] Spottiswoode himself was no Laudian, but he was old and no longer very energetic. Those few Scottish clerics who thought like Laud were the ones who received promotion, notably John Maxwell and Thomas Sydserf, both of whom had had stormy careers as ministers in Edinburgh—Row called Sydserf "a violent, virulent man."[23] By the end of 1634 both were bishops. By that time, too, eight bishops out of fourteen were members of the privy council, and, more significantly perhaps, were being appointed, along with large numbers of parish ministers, as justices of the peace, following Charles's order to that effect in March 1634. Traquair knew all about this; he was instrumental in making the appointments, and in April received a warm letter of thanks from Laud for his services. By the end of the year the job was done.[24]

Traquair and everybody else could see what all this portended. Charles had completely altered the attitude toward the clergy he had displayed in the Menteith years; the political influence of churchmen was waxing, as was their involvement in government. The king followed the same policy in England too, where Bishop Juxon became lord treasurer in 1636. For all of his concern about the income of the crown Charles repeatedly intervened to do financial favors for individual bishops: tax exemption for the bishop of Dunblane; arrears of pension for the bishop of Brechin; legal assistance for the bishop of Ross, to help him recover his rents; the purchase of the town house of the fallen Menteith as a residence for the bishop of Edinburgh; requests for contributions to rebuild Dornoch cathedral; a gift of £5,000 sterling to the archbishop of Glasgow.[25] In addition, Charles was planning a massive reendowment of the bishoprics, beginning with St. Andrews, which would receive the property of the priory of St. Andrews, a lordship of erection in the hands of the duke of Lennox. In October 1634 Charles obtained Lennox's agreement to the transfer.[26]

Mere financial skill, then, would not suffice to make Traquair the king's chief agent in Scotland, any more than it had for Dunbar. But Traquair could never have what Dunbar had had: long years of intimacy with the king as one of his favorite courtiers. No Scot had ever had such a position with Charles, not Menteith, not even Hamilton. Nor, indeed, did any Englishman, now that Buckingham was gone. King James had had many intimate friends; King Charles never had but one. So Traquair, if he was to become Charles's Dunbar, had to persuade the king that he could be more useful than any of those bishops who, by virtue of their office, stood so well with Charles and his new archbishop of Canterbury. Fortunately for Traquair, the possibility of fishing in drumlie waters was there. The existing administration had very little cohesion. The old men were dead, save for Spottiswoode and Haddington; Mar as well as Lord Chancellor Kinnoul died in 1634. There were continuing jars with the incorrigible Scotstarvet over his administrative practices and fees. Lord Advocate Hope got on with few of his colleagues, clerical or lay, and was a constant source of friction. Traquair and he were at odds over a number of matters, including money and a piece of property Hope held of the priory of St. Andrews which he was trying to except out of the general surrender which Lennox was preparing to make preliminary to its annexation to the archbishopric of St. Andrews. Hope succeeded in hanging on to the property in spite of the opposition of both Traquair and the bishop of Ross—one of the few matters on which the latter two agreed.[27] The jangling was such that Stirling wrote worriedly to Morton in March 1634, urging cooperation; there are those, he said, who would like to see all the incumbents swept out of office.[28]

As potential political rivals to Traquair the members of the Scottish episcopal bench were not individually very formidable. The new lord chancellor might have been, but it was the great misfortune of Spottiswoode's political life that he obtained his coveted office too late. He was in his seventieth year, lacking vigor, and, indeed, lacking sympathy with Laud, and therefore without influence at court, even in the question of appointments to vacant bishoprics. He was in fact a cipher now, and, like his predecessor, would do as he was bid. Of the other bishops there was only one who looked potentially dangerous: John Maxwell, newly elevated to the see of Ross. Maxwell was well connected; his cousin, James Maxwell of Innerwick, was one of the king's gentlemen of the bedchamber. He had been involved in political matters for a long time before he became a bishop; he was Menteith's replacement as an extraordinary lord of session in 1633, was appointed to the exchequer commission in 1634, and, according to John Row, he was ambitious to be lord treasurer, as Bishop Juxon was about to become south of the Tweed.[29] Maxwell was dangerous. But Maxwell could be forestalled, if Traquair acted promptly and spectacularly. And so he did, and made a serious mistake which was to be very damaging to his master: he voted for the conviction of Lord Balmerino.

John Elphinstone, second Lord Balmerino, lived his life under the shadow of, and bitterly remembering, the fate of his father. The first Lord Balmerino had been a major figure in the government of James VI; he had been secretary of state for over a decade, and then, in 1609, had been ruined. James had needed a scapegoat because one of his clandestine approaches to the pope had come to light at an embarrassing juncture, and Balmerino had been the obvious person to victimize.[30] He did not survive his disgrace for long; after his death James restored his forfeited estates and titles to his son, in part, perhaps, because the latter was contracted to the sister of James's then favorite, Robert Kerr. Balmerino believed that his father had been most unjustly treated, that the king had cozened him into making a confession by promising lenient treatment and then had gone back on his word, and he turned into a chronic opponent of the government. He voted against the five articles of Perth. In 1630 at the convention of estates he publicly aired the grievances of the lay patrons of church benefices. He argued unsuccessfully with the teind commission over the stipend of the minister of Restalrig—he was patron of the parish and tacksman of its teinds—and in doing so he attracted the king's unfavorable attention.[31] He voted against the king in parliament in 1633. So, when in 1634 Charles learned that Balmerino had in his possession, and apparently was circulating, a seditious libel, it is not surprising that he ordered that Balmerino be put on trial.[32]

The circumstances were these. After the parliament of 1633, but while Charles was still in Scotland, those who had voted against him thought it would be wise to draw up a statement explaining their views, since no debate had been allowed at the parliament. William Haig of Bemersyde, a prominent lawyer and the king's solicitor, drew up a draft in which he argued, in respectful but pointed language, that the government had broken faith by renewing the tax on annualrents and was placing an intolerable burden on the king's good subjects with "so huge taxations"; that another promise was broken when parliament failed to consider the grievances expressed at the convention of estates in 1625 and 1630; that the committee of the articles was rigged because the bishops elected lords who were "known either to be popishly affected or . . . of small knowledge of the estate or laws of the country"; that the king's religious policy was disquieting and the religious legislation adopted at the parliament unnecessary; and that Charles's behavior in refusing to allow debate and in noting the names of dissenters was unprecedented. For good measure the document pointed out that the five articles of Perth had "occasioned innumerable evils and distractions" and that "reports of an allowance given in England for printing of books full of Popery and Arminianism in this country without censure" occasioned great apprehension. The conflation of the legislation respecting apparel and prerogative led people to "suspect a snare"; blessed King James would never have done such a thing.[33]

This document was, to say the least, tactless; it was not difficult to imagine how Charles would receive it. Its sponsors nevertheless made an attempt to show it to him. Rothes, their spokesman, was extremely cautious: would the king receive a petition? If it was suitable, said Charles; if not, you present it at your peril. Rothes tried again. He had an unsuitable petition with him, which he had accordingly suppressed: would the king like to see it? No, said Charles, he had no time for it. Rothes returned it to Balmerino, saying that it was too hot to handle. Rothes was right. Balmerino nevertheless kept his copy, and one day made the mistake of showing it to one of his men of business, John Dunmure, who surreptitiously made a copy of it. Eventually the document reached the hands of Archbishop Spottiswoode, who took it to the king, apparently because he believed that copies of it were being circulated in Fife, an allegation made by the archbishop's informant and spread in England but which was never proved. Charles immediately ordered an investigation, and that

Balmerino be warded in Edinburgh castle pending the outcome.[34] The king's intention was clear enough: to strike a blow at the opponents of his religious policy by the prosecution of one of their leaders, and thus cow them into acquiescence.

It became apparent almost at once that unless Balmerino confessed and threw himself on the king's mercy the government would have trouble convicting him. Haig promptly fled the country, and from his refuge in the Dutch republic wrote to the council acknowledging the authorship of the supplication; so the charge that Balmerino was "art and part of the penning and setting down of a scandalous libel" could hardly be made to stick. Balmerino in fact refused to submit; instead, in November 1634, after he had been warded for some five months, he asked for copies of various documents and the appointment of legal counsel to prepare his defense.[35] Charles appointed the earl of Errol to act as justice general for the trial, with three members of the court of session, all zealous supporters of episcopacy, to sit with him as assessors: Archbishop Spottiswoode's son, Clerk Register Hay, and James Learmonth of Balcomie, whose brother was about to receive the abbey of Lindores.[36] Popular opinion held the bishops responsible for Balmerino's troubles; he was imprisoned, wrote Balfour, on account of "the over-ruling power of the bishops, and their wicked and corrupt court adherents."[37] The preliminary hearing was held in December 1634; it took almost two weeks of wrangling before the decision to send Balmerino to an assize was taken. The signs that matters were not going well for the government were multiplying. It was not surprising that the countess of Haddington should write indignantly about "this unjust trouble that is befallen my good lord of Balmerinoch"; he was, after all, her brother-in-law.[38] More telltale was Sir Thomas Hope's noting in his diary "the plot for laying the blame on me if it [the trial] miscarry," and speaking of the "calumnies laid on me" in connection with it.[39] The king had fair warning of what might happen if he persisted. There were demonstrations in the streets during the preliminary hearing.[40] The earl of Lauderdale, who was to be one of the fifteen-man jury, wrote frankly to the marquis of Hamilton that he was no friend of Balmerino and had always been the king's faithful servant, but that, on the basis of what he now knew, he could not vote to convict.[41] The government paused. But, since Balmerino still refused to submit, the king decided to go ahead, though by this time he himself may have feared the worst. He instructed Errol to keep Balmerino in prison until further orders in the event of an acquittal.[42]

The trial, held in March 1635, was a fiasco for the king; it was, in its way, Charles's Scottish ship money case. Balmerino spoke eloquently in his defense and won a good deal of sympathy for himself by his complaint that neither minister nor physician had been allowed access to him though his health suffered in prison. He argued that he had no reason to suppose that the supplication was seditious until the judges said so, which they had done only in the course of the trial, and that the statute under which he had been charged, that of leasing-making—i.e., lying, either to the king and government about the people, or to the people about the king and government—for his failure to reveal the existence of this allegedly seditious document had never been used before. He was, indeed, convicted, but only of knowing about the document and failing to reveal that Haig was its author, and only by one vote: Traquair's. He was acquitted of writing the supplication, of instigating it, of spreading it, of failing to try to arrest Haig. In short, he was found guilty merely of doing nothing.

Traquair was the chancellor of the assize. In its deliberations he argued that the supplication clearly was libelous, and so Balmerino was guilty of leasing-making, since he admittedly knew about the document and failed to reveal it. Lauderdale replied, repeating Balmerino's arguments and contending that the death penalty was too severe for such an offense; this was one of those laws designed to terrify rather than to be implemented. The assizemen divided, 7–7; Traquair's casting vote gave the king his victory. Balmerino was indeed sentenced to death, and, if one believes John Row, the bishops clamored for his blood. But cooler heads prevailed; Balmerino was remanded to his prison while Traquair went to consult the king.[43]

Traquair had argued vigorously for Balmerino's conviction, and had been responsible for it: this was what the king wanted, and this would enable him to prove to Charles that he was more useful than the bishops. But he must have cast that decisive vote with a good deal of misgiving. The only result more displeasing to the king than a one-vote victory would have been an acquittal, and that in the long run might have been less damaging to the government—though not, in the short run, to Traquair's chances for promotion. Traquair could hardly have been unaware of the public reaction to the trial. Even so staunch a supporter of the government as William Drummond of Hawthornden, Scotstarvet's brother-in-law and Stirling's friend and fellow poet, was outraged, and wrote scathingly, not only of the unfairness of the prosecution, but also of its stupidity. "If these papers," he wrote, "were, for the King's honour, not to be seen or read . . . . is this the way to suppress and hide them—to imprison, arraign, banish, and execute the persons near whom they are found? Or is it not rather to turn them in[to] a piece of the story of the time to make such a noise about them, and, by seeking to avoid the smoke, to fall into the fire?"[44] Furthermore, the king's victory was useless—and, as Lord Deputy Wentworth later commented to Laud about another show trial that backfired, that of William Prynne and his associates, "a prince that loseth the force and example of his punishments, loseth withal the greatest part of his dominion."[45] Charles could not possibly make an example of Balmerino after such a conviction, and on such a charge. The verdict was extremely unpopular. Those who voted to convict were heavily criticized,[46] and there were rumors that there would be violence if there was any effort to carry out the sentence. Both Traquair and Laud urged the king not to try.[47] So, in June 1635, Charles indicated that Balmerino was to be spared. He was released from the castle and ordered to remove to his house and stay within a six-mile radius; the council rather tactlessly authorized Traquair to convoy him there. A little more than a year later Charles granted Balmerino a full pardon, "to the bishops' great displeasure and discontent," wrote the anti-episcopal Balfour.[48] Balmerino, not surprisingly, did not change his views as to the nature of Charles's government; he eventually became a vehement and enthusiastic Covenanter.

The prosecution of Balmerino was a disaster, both for the king's personal prestige and for that of his government. To all appearances Charles had engaged in a vicious and petty act of persecution against a perfectly respectable member of the aristocracy at the behest of the bishops, who, said Balfour, packed the court, prevented Balmerino from explaining himself to the king, and howled for his blood. Balmerino himself had excepted against nine members of his jury as either having expressed the opinion that he was guilty or as having been "solicited by prayer and request to find . . . [him] guilty." One admitted the charge and was replaced.[49] Six of the remaining eight voted "guilty." And the verdict went for naught after all: the intended victim could not even be punished. Yet those who pursued him received their rewards. In the midst of the prosecution Archbishop Spottiswoode became chancellor and a year later Traquair became treasurer—rewards for behavior that alienated every aristocrat in Scotland without terrifying any of them. Given Charles's obstinate character, his readiness to agree not to punish Balmerino suggests that he could have been prevented from prosecuting him at all if he had received sound advice. Once again, and not for the last time, the absence of Menteith had proved enormously costly to the king. Bishop Burnet, writing in the next generation, and, perhaps, echoing the views of Lauderdale, opined that the "conspiracy" against the government dated from Balmerino's trial.[50] This is going rather far; it would be difficult to prove that any conspiracy existed in 1635. But it is certainly true that, more than any other single action he took, not excepting even the revocation, which had turned out to be more threatening in prospect than in fact, Charles's decision to prosecute Balmerino alienated the Scottish ruling class and turned it against him and his government. This was a government in which the aristocracy now had no spokesman and no place; a government which, in addition to this petty persecution of one of their number, was apparently going to keep another, Lord Ochiltree, in prison without trial; a government dominated by an ambitious bureaucrat and a superannuated archbishop who took his orders from his counterpart in London, and whose appointment as chancellor the aristocracy bitterly resented; a government which treated complaint as a capital offense. The fears to which Charles's visit had given rise had been amply confirmed.

Charles's behavior in other matters also offered the aristocracy little solace. That the king bore grudges was made patent once again in his order of May 1634, almost a year after his visit, that the unissued patents for earldoms for Lindsay and Loudoun be called in and destroyed.[51] Even when he did act in behalf of an individual nobleman, he usually did so in a way that nullified whatever feelings of gratitude that individual might have had. His treatment of Lord Lorne is a good case in point. At the beginning of 1634, at Stirling's behest, he made Lorne an extraordinary lord of session; at the end of the year he forced Lorne to submit unconditionally to his decision in a jurisdictional dispute with the bishop of Argyll. In 1635 the privy council, at Lorne's request, intervened to prevent his half-brother from disposing of his property in Kintyre to the earl of Antrim and his son, on the ground that such an action might pave the way for the revival of the clan Donald, whose power in Kintyre and the western isles had been broken twenty years before. Charles, who had previously endorsed the sale, reversed himself, which doubtless gratified Lorne, and then appointed a commission to look into the crown's rights in Kintyre. Lorne's reaction to this has not been recorded, but can be imagined. Traquair evidently did not see the need for conciliation; it was at his suggestion that Charles began this investigation.[52]

The new direction Charles imposed on the teind commission increased the aristocracy's unease. Now that parliament had granted the necessary statutory authority, Charles urged the commission, newly constituted in July 1633, to get on with its work, to concentrate on the kirks in the lordships of erection, and to work longer hours, including Mondays, which King James had always treated as a day off for his administrators. Now that the lords of erection were bereft of Menteith's mediating presence, Charles openly treated them as obstructionists. He informed the commissioners that the lords were attempting to coerce their vassals into surrendering their feus, and that they must be stopped. It also became apparent that the king now had a different set of priorities. Under Laud's influence Charles now became deeply concerned with the income of the clergy, and particularly of the bishops, to whose interests he had not been notably sympathetic prior to 1633.[53] The act of parliament establishing the principle that heritors were to lead their own teinds made an exception for those churchmen who still had the right to collect their own teinds, Charles reminded the commission. He instructed the commissioners that they were to make no arrangements that would diminish episcopal incomes, including arrangements that involved increasing ministerial stipends where the bishops were the recipients of the tithes. Where a bishop was titular of teinds, he had had priority over heritors in purchasing them from tacksmen; Charles encouraged the bishops to do this, and ordered the tithe commission to give them time to do so. He also ordered an investigation into the patronage rights of crown and bishops dating back to 1541, instructed Hope to initiate legal actions against laymen who had acquired such rights, informed the archbishops that he intended to exercise the patronage rights to all churches now in the hands of lords of erection, and ordered the return to the bishops of their *quondam* patronage the crown had acquired in consequence of the Act of Annexation of 1587. He observed to Archbishop Spottiswoode that in England, when a man was elevated to a bishopric from a parish, the crown had the right to fill the vacated parish; in his view this ought to be the case in Scotland as well. It was clearly his intention to expand the patronage of crown and bishops and reduce that of laymen—mostly aristocrats—as far as he legally could. This could be very far indeed, in view of the fact that over 80 percent of Scottish benefices had been appropriated, particularly to monasteries, prior to the Reformation.[54] Charles appointed the son of the episcopally minded Clerk Register Hay as secretary of the teind commission. He repeated his concern that there be no collusion between titular and heritors in the evaluation process, to the detriment of the king's annuity. If titulars dragged their feet over evaluation, the commissioners could act at the request of the affected ministers, and Charles directed that the figure of 800 merks not be regarded as a ceiling for a stipend—though in fact most augmentations were close to that figure. If a titular chose to assign part of a teind to a minister, he could not be compelled to sell it to the heritors. The teind commission ruled in June 1634 that in those parishes where the small (or vicarage) teind still belonged to the minister, it was to be valued, and its worth taken into account in calculating the heritors' obligations. Charles overturned this decision: the vicarage teind was not to be valued in such cases, lest the minister be awarded less out of the great teind. The king's prodding paid some dividends, in that the commissioners, in spite of the continuing problem of getting a quorum to attend meetings, did act somewhat more expeditiously than before, especially in augmenting stipends, and caused, predictably, a good deal of grumbling on the part of those whose interest suffered. The earl of Lothian, for example, complained that the loss of the superiority of Newbattle cost him £800 a year, and Aberdeen officialdom protested noisily over the rumor that the bishop of Ross was working toward persuading the king to raise the salaries of ministers in the kingdom's principal towns. Their ministers already got well over the minimum, they said; any increase would mean an intolerable burden for the town. The protest was vain; in May 1637 Charles ordered them to increase the ministers' stipends and finance the increase in whatever way they saw fit. The burghs were also aggrieved at the teind commission's decision prohibiting the use of the teinds of one parish to increase the ministerial stipend in another, a right they had sought to acquire. This was a matter of particular concern to Edinburgh, whose parishes, limited as they were by the ancient boundaries of the town, were geographically small.[55]

As an illustration of the sorts of problems that might arise, consider the parish of Abercorn. The earl of Abercorn was patron of the living and tacksman of the teinds, which he agreed to sell to the twelve heritors of the parish for 20,000 merks. If this was nine years' purchase, the teinds were worth some 2,200 merks a year. In 1633 the heritors agreed to augment the minister's stipend of 350 merks and 24 bolls of oatmeal by 150 merks and half a chalder of beir, which would bring it close to the prescribed 800-merk minimum. But there was a complication. Prior to the Reformation the parish had been appropriated to the bishopric of Dunkeld, and the bishop was suing to recover both patronage and teinds. The earl had to agree to bear the expenses of the lawsuit, and to refund the purchase price to the heritors if the bishop was successful.[56] Given the extent to which Scottish parishes had been appropriated before 1560, it is not surprising that tacksmen and heritors alike were cautious about striking bargains which might be subject to future litigation.

Even more alarming to the aristocracy than the behavior of the teind commission was the king's policy respecting monastic property: it was to be gotten into his hands and then used to endow bishoprics, with all the transactions passing through the hands of Laud. No infeftment in such property was routine any more; the king ordered the exchequer to pass only those personally signed by him. The lands of two abbeys, Holyrood and Newabbey, formally dissolved, were placed unreservedly in Charles's hands by act of parliament in 1633; he used them to endow his new bishopric of Edinburgh.[57] The two leading courtier Scots, Lennox and Hamilton, sold the king their rights in the priory of St. Andrews and the abbey of Arbroath, their lordships of erection, so that the king could endow the archbishopric of St. Andrews and the bishopric of Brechin respectively. Such behavior might be expected of courtiers, and, no doubt, as Burnet said, Charles persuaded them to behave thus in order to persuade other holders to sell cheap. The fate of those who did not was indicated in Charles's instructions to Traquair to deal with Viscount Stormont regarding Scone: if his terms for surrendering the abbey lands were unreasonable, he was to be proceeded against at law, by a process of reduction. Stormont duly acquiesced, and agreed to surrender his interest in return for assurance of his liferent. Given time, Charles's policy of endowment would doubtless have strengthened the position of the bishops; in the short run they suffered from the perception that they had urged this policy on the king out of greed. The king's own officials were as uncooperative as they thought they could safely be. For example, in February 1634 the bishop of Edinburgh tried to block the ratification of some sales of teinds by Lord Holyroodhouse to certain heritors on the ground that Holyroodhouse had resigned his rights to the crown. The exchequer commission ignored the bishop and issued the ratifications. An English Puritan, Sir William Brereton, who visited Scotland in the summer of 1636 reported that he was told that the bishops would swallow abbey lands and revenues "as that they will in a short time possess themselves of the third part of the kingdom."[58]

This sort of use of monastic property was disquieting enough; a move with still more sinister implications was the attempt in 1635 actually to create a new abbot. Andrew Learmonth, minister of Liberton, near Edinburgh, a brother of a member of the court of session and a supporter of the king's church policy, was to become abbot of Lindores, "with power to quarrel all feus."[59] The proposal, which, Laud later said, came originally from Learmonth himself, created an uproar, and the king drew back. Laud wrote waspishly to Spottiswoode, who had conveyed the protests to him, that Charles had decided not to proceed until he could consider the legal aspects of the situation. Spottiswoode was told in no uncertain terms that Charles had only the best interests of the church at heart, and if he, or any other churchman, doubted it, "you will not only do His Majesty wrong, but hurt your selves, and the Church which you seek to benefit." But it was apparent, from the letter, that the project was dead.[60]

Spottiswoode and his colleagues in the government might well be excused for wondering if Laud and his master had taken leave of their senses in entertaining this proposal. In the first place, the affairs of Lindores were in an incredibly tangled condition, owing in part to the spendthrift behavior of the current Lord Lindores, who had sold off a good part of the lands. Secondly, one of those with an interest in the property was the earl of Rothes, Lord Lindores's first cousin; this made the king's action in creating an abbot of this particular abbey look like a piece of political vengeance, like the attack on Balmerino. Other holders of abbey lands might well tremble for their holdings. But the implications of this abortive appointment went far beyond the question of property. Everybody knew that abbots were entitled to sit in parliament, and that the General Assembly of the church itself had declared, in 1598, that the church should have fifty-one representatives there; it now had fourteen. Brereton reported the rumor that forty-eight abbots would be restored, to assure clerical control of parliament.[61] Everybody also knew that the clerical estate had once held eight of the fifteen seats on the court of session; it now had none.[62] Titular abbots, tame henchmen of the king and Laud, could be put to a great many uses. But even Charles, insensitive though he was to the feelings of his Scottish subjects, could hardly be unaware of the unpopularity of this ploy, and he abandoned it. And so, as with the prosecution of Balmerino, the king had the worst of both worlds: he reaped all the odium of a dangerously unpopular policy and none of the benefits.

The king continued to pay little attention to Scottish economic development in these years. He did suggest to the burghs that something be done to increase manufacturing; he wrote to Louis XIII asking for the renewal of Scottish trading privileges in France; and he showed some interest in proposals to create Scottish overseas trading companies. Nothing came of any of this. Those areas in which the king's activity did produce results created unhappiness in landowners and burgesses alike. His decision in 1634 to double the export duty on coal was very damaging to the coal owners; his candor in avowing that he was taking the action at the behest of English coalmining interests, which were being undersold in the foreign market, did not improve the political climate in Scotland. Nor were the coal owners pleased when, in April 1636, Charles raised the levy on salt, restricted the amount that could be imported into England, and ordered the formation of a corporation of saltmasters on the English model.[63]

The burghs did not object to the increased duties on coal, since reduced exports might help keep the price low at home, but the prospect of higher duties on other goods such as salt, and especially fish, which cut into their own export trade, distressed them exceedingly.[64] In the matter of government regulation the burghs consulted their pocketbooks; they wanted government action, or inaction, as their economic and financial interests dictated. On the one hand, Aberdeen was anxious that the government act to limit the export of English cloth to Scotland, and to require Scotsmen to wear clothes made of Scottish materials—their export business in plaiding, they said, was falling off owing to the competition of their neighbors. On the other hand, the burghs wanted no part of a government proposal to establish (at their charges) an overseer for the ferries of the kingdom, who, it was alleged, was needed because so many ferrymen were dangerously incompetent or dishonest—the king was particularly concerned about those who plied between Portpatrick and Ireland, since they brought in large numbers of Irish beggars.[65]

As has been said, the burghs objected in the parliament of 1633 to the appointment of Lord Spynie as muster-master general. Given the opportunity, in 1634, to spell out those objections to the council, they did so, at length and in detail. As was true in England, their principal concern, after they got finished with the details of training, schedules, and equipment, was the expense: "the said muster master should be paid out of his Majesty's own rents."[66] The complaints and protests, taken together with those voiced at parliament in 1633, evidently made an impression. Spynie decided that there was nothing to be gained from the job; the next we hear of the muster-master general comes in October 1636, when Charles appointed General Patrick Ruthven, a professional soldier who had spent some thirty years in the Swedish service, to the post.[67] The terms of his commission were still unsettled when the troubles began.

Of all the government's economic policies, the most disliked was the granting of monopolies. In 1632, as has been said, the convention of royal burghs ordered that all burgesses take an oath that they would participate in no new monopolies, which did not, of course, prevent Charles from granting new monopolies or continuing old ones. Occasionally he did put an end to one—in May 1634, for example, he ordered the exchequer not to renew Lord Erskine's tanning patent when it expired.[68] But such an action was exceptional, and relief in this case was a long way off, since the patent would not expire until 1651. The two monopolies which caused the most controversy in the mid-1630s were the much-disliked fishing association and a new grant, in 1634, of a tobacco monopoly to one of Charles's bedchamber people and a servant of the marquis of Hamilton. The ostensible purpose of the latter grant, which was to run for seven years, was the preservation of the nation's health, which was being endangered by the "ungoverned sale and immoderate use" of tobacco that was often "corrupt and rotten." The original grant was followed by a series of proclamations spelling out what constituted a violation of the monopoly; one such was the sale of "tobacco cut small or pulverised by the name of sneissing." The monopoly turned out to be completely unenforceable; violators, the council complained, used all sort of subterfuges to effect sales, including the use of their children as peddlars. The burghs did not like the monopoly, and in 1636 petitioned for its repeal. In spite of promises of rewards to informers, of threats that the heads of households would be held responsible for the behavior of their children and servants, and of numerous prosecutions of offenders, the illicit trade went merrily on.[69]

As for the fishing association, it continued to enjoy Charles's support, but as time went on it became increasingly apparent that his dream of creating a great and profitable industry was just that—a dream. The burghs continued to press for restrictions on the association's activities.[70] In the western isles the landlords were exacting payment of duties from members of the association and were using foreigners to fish the water illegally—or so Charles charged in May 1634. The council commissioned Lord Lorne and the bishop of the Isles to investigate; they did so, and reported that the chiefs stated that they charged only what they were entitled to charge under the terms of an old agreement with the burghs, and denied the presence of foreign fishing vessels there. This bland response hardly satisfied the association, which complained bitterly about the behavior of Scottish admiralty officials and asked Charles to be allowed to appoint judges to settle disputes—in other words, to be judge in its own cause. Charles acceded to this extraordinary request, but without effect. The council's response was to issue a proclamation against violence, and to order the landlords in the isles to keep their followers under control. It also reiterated the ban on fishing by foreigners, though "friendly" aliens—undefined—could fish if they paid duty to the admiralty. The king's authorization of these changes in August 1636 meant that Charles had, in effect, conceded that his plan had not proved workable. Until such time as it did, the government would revert to the old, hitherto unsuccessful policy of trying to make the Dutch pay for the right to fish in British waters, in the hope that Dutch involvement in the European war, which necessarily reduced the naval protection available to their fishing fleet, might make the republic more amenable to this demand. In June 1637 the king instructed the council to consider the question of how best to make the foreigners pay.[71]

The occasional violence done to the members of the fishing association in the western isles paled beside the growing lawlessness in both the highlands and the borders. By the middle years of the 1630s conditions in both areas were worse than they had been at any time since the union of the crowns; they resembled those of the early 1590s, when the north was rent by the bloody feud between Huntly and Moray, and when King James's cousin Francis Stewart, earl of Bothwell, the alleged patron of the North Berwick witches, defied the king and his enemy, Lord Chancellor Maitland, from his border fastnesses. Lawlessness and brigandage were increasing, wrote the Jesuit Andrew Leslie in October 1635, and even if the brigands were caught they were often able to escape punishment because they, or their friends, had influence with various councillors[72]—one more indication of the collective demoralization of the privy council. On the border the situation had been slowly deteriorating ever since the abolition of the border police force in 1621. Hitherto Charles had not acted on the Scottish council's request, made early in his reign, to revive the joint Anglo-Scottish commission for the middle shires, which had done such useful service in King James's time. The disorders there, which Menteith's visit to Jedburgh and Dumfries in 1630 had temporarily stifled, broke out again. Finally the king acted. The proclamation of January 1635, which at last reestablished the joint commission, spoke of armed bands roving freely over the afflicted area by day and by night, robbing and ravishing.[73] Other proclamations followed in the course of the next fifteen months, spelling out procedures to be followed when malefactors were seized, including, notably, provisions for a speedy trial and for more careful scrutiny of travelers to Ireland, who included not only members of robbery gangs but also defaulting tenants absconding with money owed to their landlords. Traquair, who came from the border area, had pushed hard for this action, and was the key man among the Scottish commissioners; of the others, only Roxburgh and Annandale were men of any political importance, and they were now both elderly men, relics of the Jacobean past. The commission would put an end to the widespread theft, Traquair wrote Hamilton in November 1634, by putting a stop to criminals' ability to skip from one jurisdiction to another. It was now up to Traquair to make it work; to that end, in January 1636 he asked for, and received, special power to arrest any fugitives from the border found lurking in Edinburgh.[74]

In his letter to Hamilton Traquair also remarked on the amount of disorder in the north, especially amongst the Gordons, which he attributed to lack of severity on the government's part. Disorder there certainly was, on an alarmingly wide scale, and, like that of the 1590s, it was touched off by a spectacular and fiery tragedy. On the night of October 7, 1630, there occurred a fire in an isolated tower in the courtyard of the home of James Crichton of Frendraught. Eight men who were spending the night in the tower were burned to death, including John Gordon of Rothiemay and a son of the marquis of Huntly. The Crichtons claimed that the fire was accidental, but neither Huntly nor Rothiemay's mother, who held the laird of Frendraught responsible also for the death of her husband earlier in the year, was disposed to believe this. Nor were they satisfied with the conviction and execution for this crime of one John Meldrum, a former hanger-on of Frendraught's who had become his enemy and allegedly stole two of his horses. The result was relentless harassment of Frendraught by assorted Gordons with the connivance of Huntly, whose bland refusal to act allowed the lawlessness to go on. Huntly leveled no charges against Lady Frendraught, the alleged prime mover in the murders, if murders there were: she was a Gordon, and his cousin. Nor did he give any credence to the hypothesis that the fire was a belated and appropriate act of revenge on the part of his ancient enemy the earl of Moray, whose father Huntly had done to death after a fire at Donibristle forty years before, and with whom his relations were at best chilly: he blamed Moray for the loss of his hereditary sheriffdoms, and his eldest son blocked the renewal of Moray's commission of lieutenancy in the north. But the ravaging of Frendraught's property went on year after year; those ancient, nameless outlaws, the Clan Gregor, resurfaced again to take part in the harassment.[75]

By the time King Charles came to Scotland in 1633 the affair was ceasing to be a local nuisance and was turning into a major political issue. The question was clear: did the government have the ability to restore order in northeastern Scotland and bring the marquis of Huntly, that "great hidalgo," as Lord Chancellor Dunfermline had once called him, to heel? There had been petitions that the king should act, and parliament renewed the legislation against the Clan Gregor.[76] Meetings were held to discuss the problem; highland landlords were asked for their recommendations and to supply a list of broken men. The council ordered the king's subjects to obey the king's officials; failure to do so, it declared, promoted "thefts and other insolencies . . . to the high contempt of the law and misregard of his Majesty's authority"—a conclusion neither startling nor helpful. The council wrote politely to Huntly, who in December 1633 politely replied, denying that he had been negligent and promising to do all he could to pursue lawbreakers. Nothing happened. In August 1634 Frendraught, lamenting the woeful condition of his estates, asked for, and was granted, a commission to pursue lawbreakers on his own lands. This helped not at all; by the end of the year he had been driven from those lands, "forced to steal away under night and have his refuge to his Majesty's Council." At last the council, backed by Charles's specific instructions, summoned Huntly to appear. He did so, with a show of reluctance that bordered on contempt, in March 1635, three months after the date fixed for his appearance. He pleaded age, bad health, and bad weather; he gave assurances, in accordance with the law, in the name of all the Gordons—and was sent home with a commission to pursue lawbreakers! The result was to be expected. Twice more in the course of the year he was summoned, and on the last occasion, in September 1635, he was warded in Edinburgh castle. Six months later, having confessed to the king his error in not putting himself "to any pains or trouble for staying his [Frendraught's] personal harm or staying his estate or goods from the insolencies of others," he was released. In May 1636 he finally received permission to return home, and died en route to his mountain fastnesses. It was somewhat easier for the council to deal with Lady Rothiemay, who was accused of turning her house into a fortress garrisoned by armed ruffians; the council in March 1635 ordered the sheriff of Banff to seize the house, and the lady was held in Edinburgh.[77]

In spite of this flurry of activity Frendraught's miseries continued. In June 1635 he had to petition the council for relief from the actions of the sheriffs of Aberdeen and Banff, who had put him to the horn and were seizing his goods for non-payment of taxes. Six months earlier the council had been disposed to sympathize with Frendraught's pleas for relief; now it remitted the horning, but not the poinding of Frendraught's goods. The council's attitude hardened in other directions as well. Early in 1635 it ordered a number of aristocrats who held land either in the highlands or on the fringes to appear and provide caution for the good behavior of their tenants; later in the year it ordered that there were to be no exemptions from the obligations of the general band, which made landlords responsible for the conduct of those who lived on their estates, and began once more seriously to pursue the Clan Gregor. In December 1635 it brought a charge of willful error against an assize which had acquitted various Gordons accused of harassing Frendraught. In March 1636 it offered rewards of £1,000 for the capture of two leading MacGregor chieftains still at large. And in May it proclaimed the adoption of an entirely new method of dealing with the highlands, one which involved the use of the clergy in administration. Twice a year bishops and ministers in the highland parishes were to make up a list of indwellers in each parish. No highlander who was not a landholder would be allowed henceforth to travel more than three miles outside the parish without a license from the minister.[78]

The steadily increasing activity of the council in both highlands and borders after the middle of 1635 reflects the growing influence of Traquair in the aftermath of the conviction of Balmerino. His hand was felt in other directions also. He had now clearly triumphed in the competition to act as Charles's spokesman; he would, wrote Charles to the council in November 1635, reveal to them the king's views on various matters the council had brought to his attention. He also spoke for Laud; the archbishop wrote to Spottiswoode in that same month that Traquair would tell him about the decision respecting Lindores.[79] Two problems concerned him more than others. One was law and order. This was not a matter merely for the highlands and the borders. In Aberdeen, for instance, Charles's exclusion of Patrick Leslie from office on account of his opposition to the king's measures in the parliament of 1633 created division of opinion and disorder at the annual election of officials in 1635. Traquair wrote a long account of the troubles there to the marquis of Hamilton, advising him to urge Charles to act, to use his power to nominate officials, and prophesying administrative breakdown if nothing was done. Charles adopted this advice; the council, following his instructions, imposed Alexander Jaffray, one of the bailies, on the town as its provost. There were people in Aberdeen who evidently thought Jaffray unsuitable for the office, as he was the grandson of a baker, a member of a craft guild; they showed their displeasure by occasionally putting a baked pie on the provost's dais in church. Jaffray ignored the provocation. The king's intervention was apparently effectual; Aberdeen quieted down. It is worth noting, perhaps, that in the troubles which lay ahead Jaffray refused to sign the Covenant, while Leslie became a zealous Covenanter.[80]

The crown's perennial financial problems were of even greater concern to Traquair than the maintenance of order—finance was, after all, his official concern as treasurer depute. The collection of the tax voted in 1633 was carefully monitored, and in January 1634 Charles authorized the appointment of a commission to audit the treasurer's accounts—the first step in the campaign to ease Morton out of his office. Another commission to pursue and arrest tax delinquents was appointed. Traquair compelled the judges of the court of session to make tax payments that, they complained, were illegal. He was in all probability responsible for the king's abandonment of the longstanding policy of buying up hereditary offices, on the ground of expense. Indeed, the policy was reversed: in January 1635 Charles made it clear that he would sanction hereditary grants, as long as the grant was redeemable by the refunding of the purchase price, and in 1636 and 1637 he made some hereditary appointments. Traquair argued against providing bishops with abbey lands, on the ground that the crown's income would suffer. He met with only partial success, however—the transfers of Arbroath and St. Andrews went through. In the end, his diligence and activity paid off: in May 1636 Charles appointed him lord treasurer in succession to Morton, who left office without regret—Morton preferred to live at court, and had not attended a meeting of the privy council since the summer of 1634. Traquair pretended, rather transparently, that he undertook the job reluctantly, at the behest of Lennox and Hamilton and other prominent aristocrats. Whether anyone believed this is hard to say. Bishop Maxwell of Ross, who had wanted the job for himself, was aggrieved. Huntly's wife wrote Traquair that the bishop had said that "he and the bishops should make you in that estate the earl of Airth was reduced to," and, according to John Row, Maxwell "vowed that either Traquair should break his neck, or he his"; the king had to smooth matters over. Maxwell's temper was not improved by Laud's instructions that Traquair should be consulted in church business, and that if there were a difference of opinion between Traquair on the one hand and either Spottiswoode or Maxwell on the other, he (Laud) and the king would adjudicate. Laud imposed this system, which, he said, was not to be made public, in the wake of the controversy over Lindores, which he did not want repeated. What this order indicated was that Laud had more faith in Traquair's ability to make sound political judgments than he had in that of his Scottish episcopal colleagues.[81]

So Traquair achieved his ambition: he was head of the king's administration in Scotland. The chancellor, the nominal head of the government, deferred to him: in April 1636 Spottiswoode, in advocating an increase in the lay membership of the council, addressed himself to Traquair rather than directly to the king.[82] Poor attendance, especially on the part of its lay members, was an indication of the demoralization of the council under Traquair; it was both inefficient and virtually incapable of taking initiatives. In October 1633, for instance, Charles ordered an investigation of the crown's rights and those of the earl of Seaforth in Lewis; he was planning partially to buy out the earl to improve the position of the fishing association. In May 1635 the order had to be repeated. Such delay might be, and frequently was, caused by opposition to the crown's plans; in this case, however, Seaforth was apparently quite willing to cooperate.[83] The council was also badly divided on account of the growing number of clerical members and their increasing employment in administrative and judicial tasks which the lay establishment regarded as its prerogative. Traquair shared these opinions, but he was prepared to cooperate, more so than Morton, who, when the opportunity arose in the following years, was not at all reticent in expressing himself on the subject of bishops in politics.[84] The new lord treasurer was, nevertheless, in an equivocal and difficult position. He was useful and diligent, and so the king had rewarded him. But he had come to power in part by paying court to Archbishop Laud, whose methods and policies he fundamentally disliked and opposed. Furthermore, he was strictly the king's man, in the sense that he had no party of his own in Scotland, no faction or connection upon which he could rely. He carefully cultivated Hamilton, but that enigmatic favorite's influence was entirely negative. Hamilton could and would damage a man he disliked, as Menteith's career had proved, but he did not exert himself to support any individual or group—he was not much interested. So the most Traquair could expect was that Hamilton would be not unfriendly, and this much he achieved. Now, he must go on being diligent and useful, so as to retain the king's favor, find some way of dealing with Laud and his Scottish followers, and prevent any lay rival to himself from emerging. It would not be easy.

NOTES

1. Edward, Earl of Clarendon, *The History of the Rebellion and Civil Wars in England,* ed. W. Dunn Macray, I, 143. William Laud, *The Works of . . . William Laud . . . Archbishop of Canterbury,* ed. W. Scott and J. Bliss (Oxford, 1847–60), III, 311.

2. See, e.g., Nov. 19, 1633, Stirling to Morton, NLS Mss. 81, no. 55.

3. Feb. 20, 1634, Charles to Hope and Kinnoul, *Stirling* II, 723.

4. G. Burnet, *The Memoires of the Lives and Actions of James and William, Dukes of Hamilton,* pp. 25–26.

5. HMC, 9th Report, app. II, p. 245.

6. Oct. 6, 1633, Charles to Kinnoul, *Stirling* II, 682.

7. *RPCS* 2nd ser. V, 190–91, 233, 240, 341–42, VI, 263–64.

8. *RPCS* 2nd ser. VI, 2.

9. Nov. 21, 1634, Traquair to Hamilton, SRO, Hamilton Papers, c. 1, no. 998. *RPCS* 2nd ser. VI, 94.

10. L. Taylor, ed., *Aberdeen Council Letters* II, 14–15, 17, 19–20.

11. *RPCS* 2nd ser. V, 178–79, 197–98. *Stirling* II, 699, 719–20, 793. HMC, 9th Report, app. II, p. 246.

12. Oct. 15, 1634, Charles to the teind commission, *Stirling* II, 788. Sir John Connell, *A Treatise on the Law of Scotland Respecting Tithes* I, 314.

13. *Stirling* II, 735–36.

14. See, e.g., SRO, P. S. 1/107, ff. 20b–21b.

15. The committee's report is in BL Add. Mss. 24,275, ff. 12b–15b; see also Sir William Purves, *Revenue of the Scottish Crown, 1681,* ed. D. M. Rose, pp. xlv–xlvi. NLS Adv. Mss. 32.6.8, ff. 94–95. *Stirling* II, 700, 720–21, 774. *APS* V, 55–57. Sir William Fraser, *The Scotts of Buccleuch* I, 279–82, II, 361–63, 435–36. On the matter of pensions see J. Imrie and J. G. Dunbar, eds., *Accounts of the Masters of Works* II, intro., pp. xxxv–xxxvi.

16. *Stirling* II, 523, 794, 821, 825. See also D. Stevenson, "The King's Scottish Revenue and the Covenanters, 1625–1651," *Historical Journal* XVII (1974), 21. The first part of this article, pp. 17–26, is an excellent brief account of the crown's financial condition prior to 1637.

17. HMC, 9th Report, app. II, p. 246.

18. Quoted in David Masson, *Drummond of Hawthornden* (London, 1873), pp. 239–40.

19. *Balfour* II, 220–21, accused Traquair of prompting the audit of Kinnoul's accounts for the tax of 1630 out of rage because the chancellor had overreached him in acquiring an heiress for a nephew of his. This is unjust: Kinnoul was in no sense singled out for a special audit.

20. *Stirling* II, 771. Nov. 23, 1633, Traquair to Morton, Dec. 23, Stirling to Morton, NLS Mss. 81, nos. 109, 61. Dec. 23, Charles to the court of session, *Stirling* II, 709.

21. *Stirling* II, 816, 817–18. Bishop Guthry argued that Lorne wanted the chancellorship, and that his subsequent actions sprang

from his disappointment at being passed over. Henry Guthry, Bishop of Dunkeld, *Memoirs of Henry Guthry,* p. 12. This is improbable: there is no evidence that anyone, including Lorne himself, thought of Lorne as a candidate for the post.

22. *Row,* p. 368.

23. *Ibid.,* p. 375.

24. HMC, 9th Report, app. II, p. 258. *RPCS* 2nd ser. V, 228, 378–91, 424–30. *Row,* p. 388, commented that a number of ministers declined appointment, but that some of the prelatically inclined accepted.

25. *Stirling* II, 682, 688–89, 704–5, 710, 772, 798, 829; NLS Adv. Mss. 32.6.8, f. 97. Sir William Fraser, *The Sutherland Book* I, 222–23.

26. Oct. 15, 1634, Charles to Hope, *Stirling* II, 789. See also *ibid.,* p. 724; NLS Mss. 81, no. 98. This letter, from Traquair to Morton, is undated; the context indicates that it was written in 1634.

27. *RPCS* 2nd ser. V, 193, 195, 201–4. D. Laing, ed., *A Diary of the Public Correspondence of Sir Thomas Hope,* pp. 11, 14, 24. Nov. 11, 1634, Charles to Traquair, *Stirling* II, 806. For Hope's relations with his colleagues see Laing, *Hope's Diary,* pp. 15, 18; Jan. 1634, Lothian to Ancram, *A&L* I, 79–80; May 13, Charles to Kinnoul, *Stirling* II, 745.

28. NLS Mss. 81, no. 51.

29. *Row,* pp. 395–96. *Stirling* II, 678, 739. Guthry, *Memoirs,* pp. 12–14.

30. For the first Lord Balmerino see M. Lee, Jr., *Government by Pen: Scotland Under James VI and I,* pp. 93–94; David Calderwood, *The History of the Church of Scotland* VII, 10–15.

31. Connell, *Tithes* II, 268–71. July 19, 1632, Charles to Hope, *Stirling* II, 607.

32. *Stirling* II, 734–35, 773–74.

33. *Row,* pp. 376–81.

34. *Ibid.,* p. 382. Gilbert Burnet, *Bishop Burnet's History of His Own Time,* ed. M. J. Routh, I, 40–41. John Rushworth, *Historical Collections* II, 281.

35. *RPCS* 2nd ser. V, 409–10.

36. For Lindores, see below, pp. 167–68.

37. *Balfour* II, 216.

38. HMC, 14th Report, app. III (London, 1894), p. 108.

39. Laing, *Hope's Diary,* pp. 16, 18.

40. Jan. 9, 1635, Charles to Spottiswoode, *Stirling* II, 823.

41. Dec. 8, 1634, Lauderdale to Hamilton, SRO, Hamilton Papers, c. 1, no. 8,310.

42. Mar. 2, 1635, Charles to Spottiswoode, Mar. 5, Charles to Errol, *Stirling* II, 838, 839.

43. The trial is in Thomas B. Howell, ed., *Cobbett's Complete Collection of State Trials* III, 591–712. See also *Balfour* II, 216–20, *Row*, pp. 381–88, *Burnet's History* I, 38–44. Burnet's source was his father, an intimate of Lauderdale's, from whom he got the papers relating to the trial.

44. Quoted in Masson, *Drummond of Hawthornden*, p. 238.

45. William Knowler, ed., *The Earl of Strafford's Letters and Dispatches* (London, 1739) II, 119.

46. See, e.g., the verses quoted in John Russell, *The Haigs of Bemersyde* (Edinburgh, 1881), p. 215, and Oct. 15, 1635, and Oct. 22, 1637, the earl of Ancram to Lord Johnstone, Sir William Fraser, *The Annandale Family Book* (Edinburgh, 1894), II, 290–91, 295. Johnstone had voted to convict.

47. *Burnet's History* I, 44. *Row*, p. 389.

48. *RPCS* 2nd ser. VI, 43–44, 47, 334. *Balfour* II, 219.

49. Howell, *Cobbett's State Trials* III, 690–91.

50. Burnet, *Hamilton*, preface, p. a4b.

51. *Stirling* II, 734.

52. *RPCS* 2nd ser. V, 463–64, 479–80, 534–35, VI, 38–39. *Stirling* II, 799, 810, 814. Dec. 23, 1633, Stirling to Morton, NLS Mss. 81, no. 61. SRO, Hamilton Papers, c. 1, no. 283. BL Add. Mss. 23,112, f. 20b. HMC, 9th Report, app. II, p. 256. The fact that in 1635 Antrim married the widow of Charles's great favorite Buckingham no doubt contributed to Lorne's initial apprehension.

53. For Laud's influence see Jan. 8, 1634, Stirling to Morton, NLS Mss. 81, no. 50. See also, e.g., the memorandum from Lord Kirkcudbright to Laud regarding church livings worth £150 sterling, which he was prepared to exchange for lands in Ireland. Knowler, *Strafford's Letters* I, 439.

54. Jan. 2, 1634, Charles to Spottiswoode, *Stirling* II, 711. For a general survey of the parishes before the Reformation see I. B. Cowan, *The Parishes of Medieval Scotland*, Scottish Record Society (Edinburgh, 1967).

55. *Stirling* II, 633, 647, 655–56, 681, 683, 684, 704, 741–43, 753, 763–64, 795–96, 797, 853. Connell, *Tithes* I, 269, 294, 345, 354–55, II, 90, 134–35, 249–51, 279–80. BL Add. Mss. 23,112,

ff. 21–21b. *RPCS* 2nd ser. V, 124, 141, VI, 192. HMC, 9th Report, app. II, p. 246. NLS Mss. 1,547, pp. 27, 30–31, 38; Mss. 3,012, f. 32; Adv. Mss. 25.4.7, f. 58b. Jan. 1634, Lothian to Ancram, *A&L* I, 79–80. Taylor, *Aberdeen Council Letters* II, 42–43, 68–69. For Edinburgh see Michael Lynch, "The Origin of Edinburgh's 'Toun College'," *Innes Review* 33 (1982), p. 6.

56. Sir James Dalyell and James Beveridge, eds., *The Binns Papers 1320–1864,* Scottish Record Society (Edinburgh, 1938), pp. 29–31.

57. *Stirling* II, 790. *APS* V, 54–55. *RMS 1620–1633,* pp. 750–51.

58. Burnet, *Burnet's History* I, 35. NLS Mss. 3,012, f. 32. *Stirling* II, 860. Nov. 10, 1635, Laud to Spottiswoode, Rushworth, *Historical Collections* II, 314–15. HMC, 9th Report, app. II, p. 248. Oct. 2, 1635, Andrew Leslie to the general of the Jesuits, W. Forbes-Leith, *Memoirs of Scottish Catholics during the XVIIth and XVIIIth Centuries* I, 171–72. P. Hume Brown, ed., *Early Travellers in Scotland* (Edinburgh, 1891), p. 138. NLS Adv. Mss. 32.6.8, f. 94.

59. June 18, 1635, William Maxwell to Sir John Maxwell, Sir William Fraser, *Memoirs of the Maxwells of Pollok* II, 254–55.

60. June 24, 1635, Charles to Traquair, *Stirling* II, 866. Nov. 10, Laud to Spottiswoode, Rushworth, *Historical Collections* II, 314–15. Laud, *Works* III, 312–13. Among those with an interest in the lands of Lindores was Sir James Balfour, which may help to explain his animosity toward the bishops and their supporters.

61. M. Lee, Jr., "James VI and the Revival of Episcopacy in Scotland: 1596–1600," *Church History* XLIII (1974), 60. Brown, *Early Travelers,* p. 138.

62. On this point see Burnet, *Hamilton,* p. 30.

63. *Stirling* II, 702, 721, 729–30, 732, 756, 760, 775–76, 781. *RPCS* 2nd ser. V, 217–18, 223–24, 258–60, VI, 139–40. Feb. 10, 1634, Stirling to Morton, NLS Mss. 81, no. 46. T. Keith, *Commercial Relations of England and Scotland 1603–1707,* p. 25. Taylor, *Aberdeen Council Letters* II, 36–37. HMC, 9th Report, app. II, p. 247.

64. See, e.g., Taylor, *Aberdeen Council Letters* II, 36–37, 40–41.

65. HMC, 9th Report, app. II, pp. 252–53. *RPCS* 2nd ser. VI, 304. Taylor, *Aberdeen Council Letters* II, 31–34.

66. Taylor, *Aberdeen Council Letters* II, 10–14. See also *RPCS* 2nd ser. V, 200–201, 237–38. For the English attitude see Robert Ashton, *The English Civil War: Conservatism and Revolution, 1603–1649* (New York, 1979), pp. 58–59.

67. *RPCS* 2nd ser. VI, 342–43.

68. *Stirling* II, 755.

69. *RPCS* 2nd ser. V, 271–73, 336–37, 393–94, 430–31, VI, 47–48, 62–63, 69–71, 298–99, 312, 380; *Stirling* II, 862. *RCRB* IV, 540–41.

70. See, e.g., Taylor, *Aberdeen Council Letters* II, 3–7.

71. *Stirling* II, 762. *RPCS* 2nd ser. V, 286–87, 414–16, VI, 93–94, 96–97, 279–80, 335, 346, 456–58. *CSPD 1635,* pp. 90, 130–32, 141, 264, 271, *1636–1637,* p. 96. Feb. 12/22, Apr. 1/11, 1636, Correr to the Doge and Senate, *CSP Venetian* XXIII, 519, 543.

72. Forbes-Leith, *Memoirs* I, 171–74.

73. *RPCS* 2nd ser. V, 496–99. See also *Stirling* II, 728, 807.

74. *RPCS* 2nd ser. VI, 161–65, 167, 198. SRO, Hamilton Papers, c. 1, no. 998.

75. There is a good brief account of the Frendraught business in D. Mathew, *Scotland under Charles I,* pp. 141–47. See also that in John Spalding, *Memorialls of the Trubles in Scotland and in England, A.D. 1624-A.D. 1645* I, 13 ff. Mar. 1, 1634, Moray to Morton, NLS Mss. 80, no. 82. From the first notice of the affair on Nov. 2, 1630, *RPCS* 2nd ser. IV, 49–50, the pages of the privy council register are full of references to it for the next five years.

76. July 31, 1633, Charles to the council, *RPCS* 2nd ser. V, 131. *APS* V, 44–45. *Stirling* II, 762, 809.

77. *RPCS* 2nd ser. V, 129–31, 135–36, 148–50, 175–76, 350, 405–8, 431–33, 436, 439–43, 450, 462, 467–69, 499–500, 507–9, 515–17, 521–24, VI, 16, 23, 45, 88–89, 103, 211–12, 244–46. Feb. 17, 1636, Huntly to Charles, HMC, 9th Report, app. II, p. 261.

78. *RPCS* 2nd ser. V, 470, 480–81, 490–91, VI, 20, 105–6, 142–43, 207–10, 215–20, 231–36. NLS Mss. 1,945, pp. 122–23.

79. *RPCS* 2nd ser. VI, 137. Rushworth, *Historical Collections* II, 314–15.

80. Taylor, *Aberdeen Council Letters* II, 24–25, 28, 29–31. John Stuart, ed., *Extracts from the Council Register of the Burgh of Aberdeen, 1625–1642,* pp. 80–88. *RPCS* 2nd ser. VI, 143–45, 172–75. Spalding, *Memorialls* I, 67–69. SRO, Hamilton Papers, c. 1, no. 984.

81. *Stirling* II, 720, 828. Burnet, *Hamilton,* pp. 25–26. *RPCS* 2nd ser. V, 478, VI, 226–27, 343. HMC, 9th Report, app. II, pp. 256, 258. C. A. Malcolm, "The Office of Sheriff in Scotland," *SHR* XX (1922–23), 305–6. *Row,* pp. 389, 395–96. D. Laing, ed., *The Letters and Journals of Robert Baillie* (Edinburgh, 1841–42), I, 7. Nov. 10,

1635, Laud to Spottiswoode, Rushworth, *Historical Collections* II, 314–15.

82. HMC, 9th Report, app. II, p. 256.
83. *Stirling* II, 690, 723, 739–40, 861.
84. Guthry, *Memoirs,* p. 23.

CHAPTER

6

"Laud's Liturgy"

FOURTEEN MONTHS elapsed between Traquair's appointment as lord treasurer and the uproar in St. Giles on July 23, 1637. They were not easy times. The famine which had been afflicting Orkney and Shetland in recent years was now spreading to the rest of Scotland. 1635 was a bad year. "This last year's famine," wrote Traquair to his ex-chief, Morton, in June 1636, "is like to be much increased by this extreme heat and dryness of the weather, by which both corn and grass are burnt up and consumed, and in my judgment if it shall not please God to have pity on us by sending of rain very shortly, there has not been such misery seen in this kingdom of a long time."[1] There also was plague: a brief outbreak in Cramond late in 1635, in Newcastle and Prestonpans in 1636, and then a serious infestation which spread northward from the border in the spring of 1637.[2] Against this depressing background Traquair worked hard to consolidate his position. His techniques were those of Dunbar: keeping the council impotent, running an efficient administration, destroying opposition by means of terror or entrapment. It all seemed to be working well enough, until the fatal miscalculation which led to his ruin and that of the house of Stewart.

Keeping the council impotent was easy enough. In England, by the 1630s Charles had restored the cohesiveness and activity of the privy council after its eclipse in the days of Buckingham, but he never showed any interest in following a similar line in Scotland: there were to be no new Dunfermlines or Melroses to create difficulties for him. In the interest of promoting docility Charles kept increasing the large clerical contingent until it included ten of the fourteen bishops;[3] the lay members of the council were naturally jealous, and this division meant that any concerted opposition to Traquair was most improbable. Furthermore the bishops were preoccupied with the impending changes being prepared south of the border under the aegis of Laud, changes which entailed nothing more than formal action on the part of the council. Under these circumstances all Traquair had to do was to prevent any rival arising from the ranks of officialdom. He saw to it that no threatening new appointments were made. When the last of the old Jacobean triumvirate, Lord Privy Seal Haddington, finally died in May 1637, his replacement was not the Laudian Walter Whitford, bishop of Brechin, who wanted the job, but rather the aged earl of Roxburgh, whose willingness to surrender his abbey lands of Kelso to the crown may well have influenced the king in his favor.[4] Of Traquair's two lay colleagues with brains and energy, one, Lord Advocate Hope, he did not get on with at all. There were repeated disputes over property which, Hope believed, Traquair was improperly and maliciously trying to get away from him; he also believed that Traquair was trying to saddle him with an unwanted deputy, a post that Hope wanted for his son.[5] But, although he was well connected in the Edinburgh legal fraternity and with a number of aristocratic families whose man of business he was, Hope posed no serious threat. No mere lawyer could aspire to political influence; he needed either an aristocratic leader, or, as was Haddington's case in King James's time, the personal friendship of the king. Hope had neither. Traquair's other prospective rival, Clerk Register Hay, was too closely associated with the bishops to be dangerous unless the latter came completely to dominate, apparently a by-no-means-impossible circumstance, given all Scotmen's perception of the role of Laud in England. Traquair was well aware of the potential danger here.

Generating administrative efficiency was rather more difficult. Traquair did what he could by proclamation. In January 1636, for example, the council issued a general warning, repeated in June 1637, to the justices of the peace not to neglect their duty. In the highlands the old difficulties continued, made only marginally less awkward by the death of Huntly—we do hear less about the difficulties of Frendraught in these months, possibly because Lady Rothiemay was still in custody. In February 1637 Charles unwisely ordered her release; the council held her south of the Forth "until the 27th of July next," in other words, as long as they decently could. Lord Lorne laid hands on one of the most wanted MacGregors, was duly thanked and rewarded, and his captive duly hanged. Elsewhere, however, miscellaneous acts of violence continued and went unpunished: the captain of Clanranald, a MacDonald, and his accomplices looted an English ship that got into difficulties off the Irish coast; Cameron of Lochiel, released from ward in November 1635 because Morton and Lorne became his cautioners, and MacDonald of Keppoch were ordered a year later to produce a group of their followers accused of a violent act of cattle-rustling, which, said the council, would encourage "other thieves and limmers to do the like if this be suffered to pass over unpunished." On the borders things went rather better; Traquair had a direct interest in this area, and acted vigorously. In October 1636 a meeting of the revived joint commission took place in Dumfries and worked out a set of regulations formally promulgated by the Scottish commissioners at Jedburgh in February 1637. Licenses were required for travel to Ireland for everyone save "landed men or unsuspect persons." Innkeepers had to produce two witnesses to the fact that the meat they sold had been lawfully obtained. Wives and children of convicted thieves and fugitives from justice were to be expelled from their lands. There was to be no more collusion on the part of victims of crime who, in return for compensation, refused to go on with the prosecution. Resetters of thieves were to be punished. Much of this was familiar; more effective was the commissioners' action in hanging some thirty thieves, an action which earned Traquair a letter of commendation from the king. The English commissioners were active also, pursuing Scottish thieves across the border, bringing them back to England, and trying them there.[6] This was a good beginning, but no more than a beginning, and the outbreak of the troubles meant that, in future, the job had to be done all over again.

On another intractable difficulty, the reform of the coinage, some corrective action finally began. The two fundamental problems were the same as before: the circulation of foreign dollars whose value was extremely uncertain, and the excessive amount of copper, much of it debased, in circulation as a result of the king's grant to Secretary Stirling. Furthermore, by this time a good many of both dollars and coppers were counterfeit. Nothing was done about the copper. Charles was aware of the unpopularity of the "Stirling Turners," but on account of his commitment to Stirling he authorized the coining of 1,800 stone more in June 1637, though he did promise that this would be the last such order.[7] With the foreign dollars, however, remedial measures at last began. After prolonged haggling over the terms, Nicolas Briot accepted a temporary appointment in Scotland in the summer of 1636, and the necessary recoinage finally got under way. All the foreign dollars were to be called in, and a new issue struck. Briot also proposed a new technique for striking the coins, an idea which the workmen in the mint found distasteful but in the end had to swallow. Briot drove a hard bargain: not only were his methods to be used, but he was also to receive the normal profits of the crown for the first six months of his operation, in view of the expense to which he would be put in installing the new machinery. The council accepted this and gave the necessary orders in January 1637. Traquair, who had long recognized the need for action on the coinage, believed that this was a useful start, but that more still might be done. In June 1637 he arranged for a conference among a committee of the council, the officials of the mint, and the Edinburgh mercantile community on other methods of increasing the amount of money in circulation. The latter made three suggestions: the encouragement of manufactures, raising the rate of annualrents—a reference to the unpopular 8 percent ceiling imposed in 1633—and "the enlargement of trade by an ease of the customs."[8]

Customs duties were much on the merchants' minds at this juncture. As part of the continuing campaign to increase the crown's revenue, Charles in April 1636 authorized the revision of the book of rates, last overhauled in 1612. "Revision" meant revision upward, of course, and the burghs were predictably worried; at the meeting of the convention of royal burghs in July they offered a compromise. They would agree to a 2 percent rise in the rates if Charles would endorse the present book. They also asked the king to withdraw the tobacco patent and agree to authorize no new monopolies without consultation with the burghs. This was not enough for Traquair, who insisted on 2½ percent, though he did make some exceptions for individual items—salmon and plaiding, for instance, at the request of Aberdeen, on the ground that the consequence of the higher rate would be "evident wrack" for the town's trade.[9] And late in 1637 the tack for the wine impost was increased by more than one third. Traquair took the matter of increasing the king's revenues very seriously; it was, after all, the basis of his power. Spottiswoode, now chancellor, was no longer president of the exchequer: that function was left to the treasurer or his depute, and Traquair used it. The process of auditing accounts went forward, especially with respect to the new income generated by the act of revocation.[10] Traquair put an end to separate accounting for different branches of the revenue in 1635–36, thus greatly simplifying the auditing process. He made use of the parliamentary enactment of 1633 which gave the exchequer an expanded jurisdiction over cases involving the king's property, and he issued instructions that he and Hope were to be notified of any case taken up by the court of session which involved the king's property or income in any way.[11] In 1637, in response to an inquiry as to Prince Charles's prospective income— he was now seven years old, and his court was about to be formed—Sir James Balfour drew up a scheme to augment the size of the Principality of Scotland, a scheme which, if it became public knowledge, would certainly make the landholders in- volved very nervous indeed.[12] Above all, Traquair followed Charles's orders in cutting some pensions and fees, delaying pay- ment where he could, and abolishing unnecessary offices. This naturally made him very unpopular, especially with his fellow officials, who, like Secretary Stirling, frequently found their pay- ments held up pending an accounting for the money they might owe the treasury.

Traquair's policies were effective: he claimed to have raised the king's revenues by one third. The Scottish tax burden was not in fact enormous, and the crown's income, pitiful by comparison with that of England and less even than that of Ireland, clearly needed increasing. Charles was pleased with Traquair's accomplishments, and wrote him in December 1636 congratulating him on increasing the take from customs and crown rents without grievance to the prople.[13] Traquair's tactics were in fact deplorable, however, and certainly cost the government far more in goodwill than it gained in income. To the resentment occasioned by the increased tax burden voted in 1633 was added antagonism to what people regarded as a ruthless turning of the financial screws and to such tyrannical new methods as the use of the recently granted exchequer jurisdiction. Traquair was a man in a hurry. He wanted quick results, and so he abruptly introduced his new methods of accounting, making no effort to explain his policies to anyone, or to win agreement for what he was doing. Instead, he used the tactics of terror, browbeating people into compliance—"horrible fines," wrote Robert Baillie in 1637, were expected to be his normal method of procedure.[14] Since he was conscious of his comparative political isolation, Traquair may have thought such tactics necessary—or perhaps, as David Stevenson suggests, he thought of himself as the Scottish Wentworth, enforcing the policy of "thorough." And, like Wentworth, he seems to have enjoyed bullying people, including his colleagues.[15] Such tactics were extremely dangerous; they left their user without any reservoir of goodwill in the event of real trouble, as both Wentworth and Traquair would shortly discover. The popular view was expressed after the event by Sir James Balfour. Traquair, he said, "assumed to himself a boundless liberty of meddling and disposing upon men's estates, where he or his followers and supports could allege the King to pretend the very least interest, to great prejudice and utter undoing of the subjects." David Stevenson echoes this judgment: "Traquair's methods, his arrogance and impatience, made discontent much worse than it need have been."[16] The sense of increasing financial pressure, arbitrarily applied, which Traquair's policies and methods evoked in the propertyholding classes greatly helped to fuel the explosion over the equally arbitrarily imposed service book.

In the same letter which carried Charles's congratulations to Traquair on his financial success, the king added that Traquair was to refer to him any difference of opinion over how best to remedy the abuses of the teind commission. From the establishment of this commission there had been complaints about its decisions; in October 1636 Charles decided to suspend its operation, influenced, according to Baillie, by Bishop Maxwell of Ross's argument that the commission's work was very damaging to the long-range interests of the clergy since it meant permanent loss of such a great part of the total income from tithes. In December the commissioners protested the king's decision, on the ground that their work was far from done. If the commission were dissolved, many ministers would receive no augmentations, and others who had received augmentations as yet unassigned to localities would be unable to collect them; injustice would be done to various groups of titulars and heritors as well. Charles thereupon allowed the commission to resume; then, in July 1637, he suspended it again, and ordered Spottiswoode and Traquair to confer with other officials about the commission's abuses, with an eye to corrective measures. These maneuvers were Traquair's doing. He persuaded Charles to terminate the initial suspension on account of his rivalry with Bishop Maxwell, and he arranged the second one "to cross the Chancellor"—that is, in order to block the elimination of tacks of the teinds of parishes dependent on the priory of St. Andrews, newly transferred to the archbishop, which would have "much augmented his [Spottiswoode's] own rent." He also wrote scathingly to the king's confidant Patrick Maule, one of the courtier Scots, about the pitiful behavior of those bishops who thought only of their private gain, and not of the public good.[17]

In arguing for the suspension of the teind commission Traquair claimed that he was acting for the good of the church; Archbishop Spottiswoode's proceedings, he said, were prejudicing the king's plan to rebuild St. Andrews cathedral. Even Laud, who disliked the commission and was not sorry to see its work suspended, was dubious about Traquair's assertion on this point.[18] But what was not at all in doubt was that Traquair was determined to do everything he could to block the political influence of the bishops. They, and their tool, Clerk Register Hay, "a man," in Balfour's words, "altogether corrupt, full of wickedness and villainy, and a sworn enemy to the peace of his country," were his only serious rivals for power. "It is evident," wrote Baillie, "that he [Traquair] sets himself to cross their general designs, and almost professes to do particular despite to his antagonist Ross, also to Glasgow and St. Andrews."[19] At the end of 1636 a test case arose, in the form of a struggle over the vacant see of Argyll. Spottiswoode's candidate was Henry Rollock, an Edinburgh minister who was showing more enthusiasm than his colleagues for the king's ecclesiastical policy, and who was to preach in favor of the new service book before the fatal 23rd of July; he had the support of at least some of the Campbells. Traquair's candidate was his former teacher James Fairlie, also a conformist, an Edinburgh minister and professor of divinity at the university there. Spottiswoode and Archbishop Lindsay of Glasgow refused to include Fairlie's name in their short list at first. Thereupon Traquair, through Patrick Maule, informed Laud that the clergy at large thought well of Fairlie, and that his appointment would increase Laud's influence with the clergy. Also, of course, "it will contribute much to me in the opinion of the world." Fairlie got the bishopric.[20] Both he and Rollock turned out to be vicars of Bray; once they saw how unpopular the service book was, they repented of their previous behavior with sufficient conviction to be given parishes during the Covenanting period.

On balance Traquair was winning far more of his disputes with his episcopal rivals, actual and potential, than he was losing. Spottiswoode, wrote Baillie, was "terrified" of him; he "now guides our Scots affairs with the most absolute sovereignty that any subject among us these forty years did kyth [manifest]."[21] Traquair was a lot less certain of his absolute sovereignty than was Baillie, however. The bishops were still dangerous. He did not win all his battles. "I find not my Lord Treasurer much inclined to it," wrote Bishop Whitford in March 1637 of the impending annexation of the temporalities of Arbroath to his bishopric of Brechin.[22] Furthermore Traquair was in an awkward dilemma. He, along with most other Scottish officials, believed that Laud was all-powerful with Charles,[23] and so he could not afford to alienate the archbishop; yet it was Laud who was the patron of his episcopal rivals. So Traquair, with fatal lack of understanding, made no effort to alter the king's and Laud's decision to go ahead with the introduction of the new service book. Whatever happened, he thought, he was bound to be the gainer. If the book was accepted with a minimum of fuss, Spottiswoode, who had been urging that it be held back until the people were better prepared to receive it, would be made to look foolish. If, as was more likely, there was serious backlash, the bishops as a group would be discredited, especially Maxwell and the other recently appointed Laudians who had been urging prompt action, and Traquair would be rid of his last serious rivals. This was not treachery on Traquair's part, as both Bishop Guthry and Laud's biographer Peter Heylyn later asserted;[24] it was nothing more sinister than a devious and, as it turned out, mistaken political calculation.

What Traquair completely failed to understand was the extent and the depth of the Scottish political classes' discontent with the existing regime, and the extent and the depth of the king's commitment to his new religious policy. To be sure, Traquair knew that there was unhappiness in Scotland, and that Charles could be very stubborn. But for half a century now the Scottish government had been able to deal with discontent, and Charles in the past had been willing to make adjustments, concessions even, when he was convinced that they were necessary—witness his behavior over the revocation. There was no need to warn the king of possible trouble; his shock—and his anger at the bishops—would be that much greater. Traquair was in no doubt of his ability to handle the probable brouhaha. And so, as Bishop Burnet put it, he was "fatally caught in the snare laid for others."[25]

Traquair's most crucial error, which was in fact decisive, was his misreading of the nature and depth of Scottish religious sentiment. This stemmed in part, perhaps, from ignorance. There is no evidence that Traquair kept in touch with clerical opinion even to the extent that Menteith had; if he did, he chose to pay it no heed. In misjudging the situation he was not alone; everyone, including his opponents, shared his astonishment at the size and violence of the storm when it came. The difference in intensity of feeling between the generation that overturned the Roman church in the 1550s and that of the Covenanters is a commonplace among historians. The Reformation was the work of a minority, a coalition of enthusiasts and politic men; in the seventy years since the official establishment of Protestantism by law in 1567, Scotland had become thoroughly imbued, in the lowlands at least, with a form of Christianity quite different from that of the Roman church. Protestantism required each individual to assume responsibility for his or her own salvation, insofar as any individual could; the final decision, of course, lay with God. It was the Christian's duty to obey God's law, set forth in His word, and not only to obey it himself, but also to see that others did so too. This was the duty in the first instance of the godly prince, and then of the godly magistrates, but in the final analysis that of the godly people also. Godly discipline, exercised through kirk sessions at the local level, would impose and enforce this obedience to God's law. Since it behooved each individual to know that law through the reading of God's word and its explication by experts, education and preaching were essential to godliness. To a very great degree these essentials had been provided in Scotland by the 1630s, in the towns and in the rural areas in the lowlands and borders. There were ministers—enough ministers, and they were not absentees—and schools, and kirk sessions enforcing a severe discipline, especially in sexual matters, and, after a fashion, looking after the parish's poor. The principal offenses punished by the kirk session were fornication, Sabbath-breaking, drunkenness, and cursing; adultery, a more serious affair, was the province of the presbytery. The scope and authority of this discipline was so effective that "from 1560 up to about 1730, Scottish people were far more likely to find themselves in a church court than in a secular court."[26] There were exceptions, of course. If the description of their life-style in the *Privy Council Register* is to be believed, it is hard to see much moral improvement or piety in the swarms of vagabonds and beggars that still abounded in Scotland. The northwestern highlands and western islands were untouched, and there were in fact some reconversions to Catholicism, thanks to the work of missionary priests coming from Ireland.[27] A number of aristocrats were still Catholic, and it was difficult for the kirk to coerce them, though it never stopped trying—witness the repeated, and ultimately vain, efforts to force the marquis of Huntly, the most important of the lot, to conform. With other groups in Scottish society, however, especially the burgesses, and the lairds and their substantial tenants, the kirk's success was very great indeed. One authority has recently summed up that success thus:

> This primary Christianization . . . was characterized mainly by the systematic exposure of the laity to Christian instruction and moral exhortation through vernacular preaching, by an entirely novel shift from the idea that the religious life was to be lived only by religious specialists to the assumption that each individual was personally responsible for his own salvation. . . . In the fifty years following the Reformation, in those areas where Kirk sessions were set up and trained ministers sent, much of the populace was introduced through a most strenuous indoctrination of literacy, preaching, and the 'godly discipline,' to a basic Christianity and to concepts of moral behavior which would have been quite unfamiliar to their grandparents.[28]

This new-found religious enthusiasm was not unique to Scotland, of course. It could be found all through Protestant Europe, and in those areas of Catholic Europe where the Counterreformation had its greatest impact. It was particularly widespread in Scotland, however, thanks to the remarkable success of the kirk sessions in setting up schools, an activity which the king heartily endorsed.[29] Furthermore, to many Scots, notably the clerical followers and spiritual heirs of Andrew Melville, that is, the opponents of episcopacy, their Reformation was a unique event, because God viewed their unique church with particular favor. Christianity in Scotland long antedated the Roman usurpation there, and that usurpation had collapsed with remarkable speed and completeness when God finally stretched out His hand. The new church which arose was a particularly perfect church, the result of God's special covenant with His Scots; "Theirs, it seemed," writes S. A. Burrell, "was a more perfect reformation than that achieved by any other church in Christendom." And they looked forward to the time when that perfection would spread from Scotland to other lands.[30] The climax was reached in 1596. "The Kirk of Scotland was now come to her perfection," wrote the presbyterian minister David Calderwood, "and the greatest purity that ever she attained unto, both in doctrine and

discipline, so that her beauty was admirable to foreign kirks."
Then the rot set in, and proceeded apace: bishops, the banish-
ment of Andrew Melville and the rooting out of his followers, the
five articles of Perth, the corruption and then the end of General
Assemblies, Anglopiscopapistical men and doctrines flourishing
like the green bay tree. "In a word, the end of this year [1596]
began that doleful decay and declining of this kirk, which has
continued to this hour proceeding from worse to worse; so that
now we see such corruption as we thought not to have seen in our
days."[31] The Melvilleans inside and out of the ranks of the clergy
clung to their belief in the uniqueness of the Scottish church as
they watched the policy of assimilation to the church of England
go forward. "If anything," writes Burrell, "the strength and
vehemence of their convictions increased as their numbers
declined."[32]

One such Melvillean was Samuel Rutherford, minister of An-
woth in the diocese of Galloway, and what happened to him is
instructive. He did not conform to the five articles of Perth, but
his backsliding in this respect was overlooked by the Jacobean
bishop, Andrew Lamb. In 1634 Lamb died; his successor was the
Laudian Thomas Sydserf, translated to the diocese in August
1635. Within a year Sydserf had rid himself of Rutherford. The
High Commision, at Sydserf's instigation, condemned Rutherford not only for nonconformity but also, says Row, for a book
against Arminianism which made the Arminian bishops "gnash
their teeth." In July 1636 the Commission ordered him to reside
in Aberdeen; not even the influence of Lord Lorne, whose sister,
Lady Lochinvar, was Rutherford's friend, could prevent this. Robert Baillie, who regarded Rutherford as overzealous, though
godly and learned, regretted what had happened to him. Writing
in January 1637 to his cousin in Holland, he asked if there was a
chance of getting Rutherford a post in a Dutch university, since
he had no future in Scotland.[33] It was easy for Sydserf to oust
Rutherford. Given time, he would have been replaced at An-
woth—the clerical profession was becoming overcrowded in the
1630s, enough so, perhaps, to spawn a group of "alienated intel-
lectuals."[34] Baillie himself was a conformist; he disliked Arminianism, but he was willing to comply with the five articles of

Perth, and regarded those who were too stiff-necked to associate with those who were prepared to kneel at communion as schismatics. The universities were being carefully monitored, and their faculties filled with what their opponents called "corrupt professors" who preached Arminianism.[35] There is evidence, then, to suggest that, in Scotland as in England, time was on the king's side: in another twenty years a generation of conformists might well have monopolized Scottish pulpits.[36]

In the middle of the 1630s, however, the situation inside the Scottish religious community, both clerical and lay, was extremely explosive. The multiplying evidences of Anglicization of the church were extremely unpopular, a fact apparent even to Laud, who in February 1634 wrote to Bishop Bellenden of Dunblane, dean of the chapel royal, expressing the hope that some of the other bishops were also officiating in their whites, so that he would not bear the whole brunt of the criticism. Promotion nevertheless depended on conformity with Laud's views, however unpopular they might be. Bellenden was passed over for the bishopric of Edinburgh in 1634 because he did not use prayers according to the English liturgy in the chapel royal. In the following year he was more compliant. Laud wrote to praise him for wearing his whites "notwithstanding the maliciousness of foolish men." Bellenden therefore received his reward, in the form of translation to Aberdeen, where he almost immediately blotted his copybook by authorizing a public fast on a Sunday. Laud was outraged; he regarded such fasts as an "unworthy custom" and "contrary to the rules of Christianity." In future, he informed Archbishop Spottiswoode, there were to be no public fasts, on Sunday or any other day, without the king's consent.[37] "The discipline of the Church of England is much pressed and much opposed by many pastors and many of the people," wrote the English Puritan Sir William Brereton of his visit to Scotland in July 1636; the Catholic observer Andrew Leslie said much the same the year before.[38] The word "presbytery" vanished from the official vocabulary by Charles's order; he instructed Lord Advocate Hope to cease using the term in his writs, and to write "preachers" or "ministers" instead.[39]

Fear of Popery was genuine and growing. Menteith was, in a

Scottish Jesuit's words, "a bitter persecutor of the Catholics"; after his fall the official pursuit of Catholics ceased, and there were some reconversions. The increasingly Popish atmosphere of the royal court, and the crypto-Papalism of Laud, were commonplaces among the enemies of the king's religious policy on both sides of the Tweed. Had they known of Secretary Stirling's enthusiastic support of the Catholic marquis of Douglas's effort to get a cardinal's hat for George Con, the Scottish-born Papal agent at Charles's court, they would have been more uneasy still.[40] The policy of reendowing the bishops with abbey lands retrieved from their lay holders, and especially the incident involving Lindores, smacked of Popery; Bishop Burnet says that those who feared for their own property were particularly forward in instilling this idea in the minds of the lower clergy.[41]

As for the recent appointees to the bench of bishops, they did nothing to put the popular mind at rest. Bishop Maxwell of Ross preached *jure divino* episcopacy, according to Row, and "when Bishop Laud grew great," those who had counted his arguments "stark naught" before, "were all forced to adhere to Mr. Maxwell his divinity."[42] *Jure divino* episcopacy was a novelty, and bitterly resented. "Your majesty knows," wrote Alexander Henderson to Charles after the troubles began, "that King James never admitted Episcopacy upon divine right; that his Majesty did swear and subscribe to the doctrine, worship and discipline of the Church of Scotland"—an exaggeration, but on the point about episcopacy Henderson was right. Some of the king's religious opponents believed that Maxwell and his colleagues sowed confusion and division deliberately, in order to win people over to their allegedly Popish and Arminian views.[43] The contrast with a man like George Graham, appointed bishop of Dunblane in 1602 and translated to Orkney in 1615, was enormous. Graham was a member of a cadet branch of the house of Montrose, and was closely connected with the Murrays of Tullibardine, now holders of the earldom of Atholl. He was an easygoing man, concerned with making provision for his numerous children, not an extremist of any sort—on a visit to Glasgow he went curling on Sunday, to the annoyance of the local presbyterians. His qualities were not admired at court; he was one of the few bishops not appointed to the privy council. He was not, perhaps, a typical Jacobean bishop—he was one of three who renounced episcopacy as a system following the Glasgow Assembly. But he was the sort of man who, in his own person, provided a link between the ecclesiastical hierarchy and the ruling class of landholders. Given the very different situation of the church of England, Scotland's Anglicized king never realized the importance of such linkage.[44]

Under these circumstances the practice of holding conventicles, which had begun in the later years of King James's reign, after the adoption of the five articles of Perth, continued unabated. After the collapse of the effort to enforce the Perth articles in 1622 neither the government nor the episcopate was especially anxious to persecute those who attended such meetings; Lord Chancellor Hay's definition of a conventicle as a meeting which took place while a regularly scheduled church service was in progress was so narrow that most people could honestly deny that they attended them. The network of nonconformist ministers which presided over them was substantially reinforced in the mid-1630s because of the policy of Laud and his political ally Lord Deputy Wentworth in Ireland. From the early 1620s Ulster had been a place of refuge for Scottish clerics who either voluntarily or under duress left their parishes because of their opposition to the government's religious policy. These ministers used Ulster as a safe base from which to conduct intellectual forays into southwestern Scotland, preaching and holding conventicles there, and retreating to Ireland before the authorities could react. Their revivalist style of preaching was enormously effective; they organized private fasts every quarter, and occasionally induced fainting fits in their hearers, who had to be carried out of church—what was called "the Stewarton sickness." The Scottish bishops complained, and the Irish administration responded. By the mid-1630s, thanks to Wentworth, and the appointment of Laudians to the bishoprics of Raphoe and Down, Ulster was no longer a safe haven. Some ministers, including Robert Blair, a future moderator of the General Assembly, and John Livingstone, a redoubtable preacher, planned to migrate to Massachusetts, but what might be called a Protestant wind, in the form of an Atlantic storm, turned them back. God had other plans for them: they

eventually returned to Scotland. There they were to become major contributors to the success of the Covenanters' cause; years of
living under a lax administration in Ireland had made them far
less concerned about encroachment on the royal prerogative than
were their stay-at-home colleagues. By an unhappy coincidence
for the king, the strength and quality of the ministerial opponents of his policy were greater in the mid-1630s than at any
previous point in his reign.[45]

In 1637, then, the Scottish church was not in the best condition to act as the instrument of a forward ecclesiastical policy.
There was division of opinion at all levels. The Scottish bench of
bishops lacked cohesiveness; as was the case in England, Laud had
not as yet succeeded in remodeling the hierarchy in his own im-
age.[46] Most of the sees, including St. Andrews, were still in the
hands of Jacobean appointees. Only four of the fourteen bishops
could be considered Laud's men, owing their preferment to him
rather than to their senior colleagues, with whom they did not
get along very well. Furthermore, the bishops were overworked.
In addition to their clerical duties they sat on the council and the
teind commission, had appointments as justices of the peace in
their dioceses, as did many ministers, and they dominated the
court of High Commission, which had a very broad jurisdiction,
including, after Charles's grant of a new and broader commission
in 1634, the power to proceed against pamphleteers. People now
feared that the High Commission was likely to become more
active in rooting out clerical nonconformists and in acting against
those laymen who were "obstinate contemners of the discipline of
the church." Having so many jobs, the bishops necessarily did a
number of them badly: for example, very few of the lower clergy
wore surplices on the prescribed occasions, in spite of the king's
orders. The bishops did not, in fact, turn the High Commission
into an engine of oppression. Owing to the loss of its records we
know little about its proceedings, but it seems not to have been
very active. It apparently paid little attention to conventicles,
which, save in the southwest, were rather small gatherings. All
that is certain is that it cited and punished six ministers, including Rutherford, and deprived none of them.[47]

All this governmental activity on the part of the bishops antagonized the aristocracy, who resented what they regarded as their own steady loss of influence. They feared that their rivals wanted still more—control of the court of session for instance. They could not have been pleased at the king's order, acquiesced in by the council nineteen days before the uproar in St. Giles, that henceforth the archbishop of St. Andrews would take precedence over all other subjects in Scotland, including the chancellor—a posthumous defeat for Lord Chancellor Kinnoul.[48] Both Clarendon and Burnet regarded this resentment and fear as the chief cause of the aristocracy's alienation from Charles. In addition the lower clergy resented the newly exalted position of the bishops. They were too proud, said Burnet; the Laudians among them, wrote Henry Guthry, himself a parish minister in 1637, looked down on the ordinary parish minister.[49] Those ministers themselves were collectively less well off than they used to be; testamentary evidence indicates that in spite of the work of the teind commission, ministerial wealth, which had been rising since the turn of the century, was dropping in the 1630s.[50]

The policy which this divided and uncertain church was to be asked to promote was one which struck at the very root of the national identity of all Scots. Since the royal visit in 1633 Archbishop Laud had been issuing orders to the Scottish bishops as though he, not Spottiswoode, were their primate—always, he later claimed, at the king's instructions.[51] What these orders amounted to, what the Scots' alien, Anglicized king and his all-too-English archbishop were asking them to do, was, in effect, to conform to the church of England, to become, as Robert Baillie scornfully put it, a "pendicle of the diocese of York."[52] Furthermore, in the Scots' opinion this was a very different church of England from that of King James; the gulf between the views of George Abbot and those of William Laud was very great indeed. The nature of the new service book, and the fact that it was imposed by prerogative alone, were bound to arouse, directly or by implication, every existing fear among all the groups who counted in Scotland: fear of Popery, of clerical rule, of alien rule, of destruction of the political influence of the landed classes and further encroachments on their property, of the end of Scots law and Scots institutions, of Scotland as an independent entity. Every exposed nerve in Scotland was grated on at once by what came, perhaps wrongly, to be called "Laud's liturgy."

If the church was a weak reed, so too was the civil government. The council's collective impotence continued. Its spurts of other than routine activity depended on the presence, instructions, and uncertain judgment of Traquair, and where he did not give matters his direct attention, administrative inefficiency prevailed. Burghs such as Aberdeen and Edinburgh were aggrieved at royal interference in the choice of their officials. Furthermore, the summer of 1637 was a meteorological disaster, the worst of a series of bad years which necessitated extensive imports of grain from Ireland and the Baltic, with adverse effects on prices. "The earth hath been iron in this land . . . and the heavens brass this summer," wrote the earl of Lothian in October 1637, and now, at harvest time, there were high winds and floods.[53] The author of the most recent work on Scottish agriculture argues that the 1620s and 1630s were "a period of modest prosperity"; it is also true, however, that there were crop failures. The price of oatmeal in Fife equaled or exceeded that of the disastrous famine year of 1623 four times in the 1630s, and hit a new high in 1637.[54] The adverse effect of sudden shortages of food at a time of political crisis has been repeatedly demonstrated. In short, not only were Charles's judgment and timing bad, so also was his luck.

The decision to compile a new service book and a set of canons was taken in 1634. By October of that year the king and Laud had decided to accept the Scottish bishops' argument that the English Book of Common Prayer could not simply be imposed, and they authorized the compilation of a new liturgy which was to be based not on the old Jacobean draft of 1619 but on the English book, which it was to resemble as closely as possible. In the meantime the bishops and the universities were to use the English book on holidays and other ceremonial occasions.[55] The work of revision took about two years, with much traveling on the part of Bishop Maxwell. According to Guthry, Maxwell and Sydserf were the most enthusiastic forwarders of the project, though in fact many of the crucial suggestions for change came from Bishop Wedderburn, the new dean of the chapel royal, "a man," said Baillie, "set in the Chapel to be a hand to Canterbury

in all his intentions."[56] For Laud, Wedderburn proved an unhappy choice. He was a Scot, but was in Anglican orders; he had
spent most of his ministerial career in England, and could not be
expected to assess accurately what would and would not please
Scottish opinion. We cannot know what Maxwell told Laud in
private conversation; the surviving correspondence between the
archbishop and his Scottish colleagues indicates, however, that
the latter gave Laud no indication that they anticipated trouble,
only that full conformity between the churches would take
time.[57] The deviations from the English book were made at the
Scots' request, and were designed to make the book more acceptable there—the elimination of the term "priest," for instance,
and cutting back on the use of the Apocrypha. Laud was cheerful
enough about the changes. "Whereas you write, that much more
might have been done if the times would have borne it," he commented to Wedderburn in April 1636, "God be thanked, this
will do very well, and I hope breed up a great deal of devout and
religious piety in that kingdom."[58] The archbishop and his colleagues were not altogether impervious to the possibility of political backlash, however. Bishop Juxon wrote to Maxwell in
February 1636 that the book of canons was apt to make more
noise at first than those in Edinburgh castle, but, he felt, the
Scots would get used to them and ultimately find them useful.[59]

King Charles had instructed Laud and Juxon to peruse the
proposed book of canons to be sure that it resembled the English
as closely as possible. They did so. The canons appeared in January 1636, and Charles expressed his pleasure at the result.[60] The
code assumed that bishops had authority in their dioceses, and
made no mention of presbyteries or of the General Assembly. In
the words of Rosalind Mitchison, it "thus directly confronted the
presbyterian system." It also reaffirmed the five articles of Perth,
prohibited extempore prayer and the preaching of clergy in parishes other than their own without episcopal license, and commanded acceptance of the forthcoming liturgy. It was imposed by
virtue of Charles's royal prerogative; as Row put it, not even a
"conventicle of bishops and doctors" had met to give it the rubber
stamp of their approval.[61] This was something that had never
happened before; King James, although he claimed the power to

make changes in the church on his own authority, had always taken care to get clerical approval for what he wanted to do, even though this involved him in considerable political effort and manipulation. James's difficulty in securing approval for the Perth articles may well have prompted Charles's decision; "Things had prospered so ill in General Assemblies," wrote Burnet, "that they thought of these no more."[62] Laud, when later taxed with having altered the title from "Canons agreed on to be proponed to the several Synods of the Kirk of Scotland" to "Canons and Constitutions Ecclesiastical, etc., ordained to be observed by the Clergy," agreed that he had done so. His explanation was that the book was about to go to the printer, and that one did not print rough drafts; there was nothing, he said, to prevent the bishops from discussing the canons with their synods.[63] This was very lame; there can be no real doubt as to Charles's and Laud's policy on this point. It was an unwise policy. As Clarendon commented, Charles's methods gave the enemies of bishops and government the opportunity to argue that "here was an entire new model of government in Church and State." Yet there was no immediate backlash, which Clarendon attributed to those enemies' "wonderful power and wonderful dexterity."[64] What it probably showed was not so much dexterity as the difficulty of finding a way to attack the canons, and a forum in which to do so. The greatest innovation here was procedural rather than substantive. Furthermore, everyone knew that the service book was in the works: it was apt to provide far more ammunition than the canons.

The comparatively quiet acceptance of the canons did nothing to discourage Charles and his allies from proceeding with the service book, and imposing it in the same way. They were, perhaps, even encouraged to do so by the appearance in August 1636 of David Calderwood's bitter attack on the General Assembly at Perth, an indication of the difficulty the liturgy would probably encounter if submitted to such a body. The service book was all but complete by October 1636, when Charles wrote confidently to Archbishop Spottiswoode ordering its use, and that each parish should have two copies; the tone of the letter is that of a man expecting no difficulty. The same orders went to the council, which on December 20 issued the appropriate proclamation.[65]

The book was not yet off the press, but rumors as to its nature were flying, and those who knew about it could foresee the storm. In July 1636 James Baird, a lawyer and a member of Edinburgh's ecclesiastical bureaucracy, wrote to his cousin in Banffshire that "it may be before long ye see work among the Rufflers and Joiners, and it may be that men who dream security to themselves be awakened through their sleep."⁶⁶ Robert Baillie was anxious to see a copy; he had heard that it was more Popish than English, with "a very ambiguous prayer . . . looking much to Transubstantiation;" he feared for the peace of the church.⁶⁷ Baillie wrote in January; in the following month Charles, once again by fiat, ordered the use of a new translation of the Psalms, partly the work of King James; Charles had been considering this, off and on, since 1630. The introduction of the Psalm book became one more count against the poetical Secretary Stirling, who had helped James with the versification. He is "extremely hated of all the country," wrote Baillie in 1638, "for his alleged bribery, urging of the Psalms and the Books for them, overwhelming us with his Black money."⁶⁸ When Stirling died in 1640, one of his critics had the following epitaph for him:

> Here lies a fermer and a millar,
> A poet and a psalme book spiller,
> A purchessour by hooke and crooke,
> A forger of the service booke,
> A coppersmith who did much evill,
> A friend to bischopes and ye devill.⁶⁹

For some months there was no clear indication as to when the new service book was to go into effect. The council's proclamation had declared that each parish should have its copies by Easter, and the original intention probably was to have it first used then. But the press run was delayed, some ministers refused to buy the book—the two copies cost £9, 12 shillings⁷⁰—and there was considerable criticism in various diocesan synods in the spring. Some bishops were willing to give their ministers until autumn to decide whether or not to accept the book, but Charles was impatient, as usual. And so, on July 16, 1637, the bishop of Edinburgh indicated that the book was to be used on the follow-

ing Sunday, July 23. According to a subsequent account, probably drawn up by Stirling, the reasoning was that the term of the
court of session ended on July 31. If the new service book was
quietly accepted in the capital, where trouble could be anticipated if trouble there was to be, all those folk who were in Edinburgh on legal business would spread the word of the
government's success in their own communities when they got
home. Baillie's explanation of the timing, written in October
1637, was different: the two archbishops were planning a journey
to court to complain of Traquair on account of those actions of his
which had deprived them of income, and they wanted something
positive to show Charles, to persuade him to listen to them.[71]

There was an element of calculated risk in the decision to use
the service book without any effort to deal with either the hostile
rumors or the criticisms voiced in the synods. But hardly anything else would satisfy the king, and Charles had been given no
reason to anticipate a serious reaction. After all, the canons had
been accepted, the English prayer book had been used in the
chapel royal for twenty years, and he had no reason to suppose
that people would regard as Popish anything endorsed by his
bishops, whom he knew to be as good Protestants as he himself
was. Furthermore he had authorized the bishops to dispense with
any part of the book about which they felt doubtful—though
Laud emphasized to Wedderburn that "His Majesty hopes there
will be no need of change of anything."[72] As S. R. Gardiner has
remarked, however, "Nothing can be more unfair than to argue
that the authors of this unlucky liturgy had any intention of
approximating to the Roman ritual; but they could hardly have
given greater offence if they had introduced the missal at once."[73]

Gordon Donaldson has argued that presbyterians like John
Row grossly misrepresented the changes in the liturgy, and that
the book was never considered on its merits. He is certainly right.
The most obvious example of this has to do with the words of
administration employed in the communion service. The Book of
Common Prayer runs thus: "The body of our Lord Jesus Christ
which was given for thee, preserve thy body and soul unto ever-
lasting life, *and take and eat this in remembrance that Christ died for
thee; feed on him in thy heart by faith with thanksgiving.*" At Wed-

derburn's suggestion, said Laud, the italicized clause was omitted from the Scottish book as not being in accord with Scottish doctrine, since it smacked of Zwinglianism. The decision was technically correct—according to Alexander Henderson the words commonly used were "take ye, eat ye, this is the body of the Lord which is broken for you"—and politically disastrous. The stress on the real presence, and the omission of reference to the commemorative aspects of the service contained in the Book of Common Prayer, made plausible the charge, by Row and others, that the communion service had "all the substance and essential parts of the Mass." Equally bad was the removal of the holy table to the east end of the church and the instructions to the minister to say the prayer of consecration in such a position as to have both hands free, implying that an act of elevation might take place. Row used these matters, and other things as well, to excoriate the liturgy as "this Popish-English-Scottish-Mass-Service-Book," more Popish than the Book of Common Prayer.[74] Laud and Wedderburn thus gave their clerical opponents an obvious point of attack. As Gilbert Burnet later said, the changes made in the English text "rendered it more invidious and less satisfactory" to the Scots.[75] However unfair their criticism of the details of the service book, the king's opponents were right on the general point that the new service afforded far less scope for *extempore* prayer on the minister's part, and shifted the emphasis away from the sermon to ceremonial routine. In that sense the essential nature of the kirk would be greatly altered: in future there would be, in the phrase of one group of protesters, "a reading, not a preaching ministry."[76]

Whether the new service book ought to be called "Laud's liturgy" is not altogether clear. There is little doubt that Laud was telling the truth when he said that at the beginning what he and Charles wanted was simply to impose the English prayer book, and Laud later claimed, in preparing his defense for his trial, that that remained his wish, "but some of the Scottish Bishops prevailed herein against me; and some alterations they would have from the Book of England."[77] The archbishop made this statement in connection with the change in the wording of the administration of the communion service; it was very much to his interest to avoid responsibility on this particular point. Laud never denied, however, that he approved of the whole Scottish service book, including this controversial phraseology. It has been argued, therefore, that once changes were decided upon, Laud worked through Wedderburn to make changes which he, Laud, regarded as desirable and which he could then impose on England in the name of uniformity.[78] This is an ingenious argument, but not, in the nature of things, provable, and it does not take very much account of the role of the king. Laud, at a time when it served his purpose to do so, minimized his own responsibility, claimed that he was simply following Charles's orders, and attributed the alterations in the English text to the Scottish bishops. There is certainly truth in this. It is also true that the initial impulse for the change in the Scottish service came from Charles and that, as Burnet said, the king's conscience determined his religious policy.[79] There is also no evidence of any disagreement between Charles and Laud. So it is not really possible to know how much credence to give to the archbishop's version of events, and how, finally, to allocate responsibility for religious policy between the two men. The essential point to grasp for an understanding of what happened, however, is that everyone in Scotland, including Traquair, believed that the impulse came from Laud. The timing of events gave plausibility to this view. The anti-clerical Menteith had been the king's friend, and during his days of power the bishops had no influence. Since the fall of Menteith in 1633 Laud had been the king's closest confidant: it followed that the new turn in religious policy was his. If that policy met with resounding failure, Laud's influence would be gravely weakened and something like the Jacobean status quo in religious matters might be restored.

So no one in Scotland undertook to warn the king that his cherished policy would lead to trouble, least of all Traquair. In fact he contributed to the mounting tension by circulating rumors that the High Commission's authority was about to be expanded in some unspecified way. But throughout these months, Traquair carefully avoided involvement with the canons and the liturgy save in the most formal way; there is no contemporary evidence to corroborate Clarendon's and Heylyn's assertion that he advised Charles to postpone the inauguration of the service book from Easter to July.[80] Traquair knew that there would be trouble. There was one official intimation of it: on June 13 the council issued a proclamation claiming that those ministers who refused to buy the service book were trying to "foster and entertain distraction and trouble in the kirk."[81] And, anticipating that trouble, Traquair imitated the behavior of a far abler politician than he, the Regent Moray, and made himself scarce. Pleading the necessity of attending a kinsman's wedding, he was not in Edinburgh on that fateful Sunday. This turned out to be a blunder: it gave his enemies the opportunity to point out, quite correctly, that he had foreseen the difficulties and had failed to warn the king.

Because he did not try to make the king listen, Traquair must bear his share of responsibility for the disaster. In his behalf it should be said that there is no evidence that the king *would* have listened; his warnings, like those of Spottiswoode, would almost certainly have been brushed aside. Unlike Menteith, Traquair was not the king's friend, and had no personal standing with him, though in this case even Menteith might not have dissuaded Charles. On matters on which he felt deeply—and this was certainly one—the king heard only what he wanted to hear, and, as was his wont, he expected his servants to carry out his orders, whether they approved of them or not. Commenting on Traquair's behavior in this whole matter Sir James Balfour wrote, "Fear of the King's and bishops' displeasure, on the one hand, and preferment on the other, did altogether extinguish that professed zeal (if any was in him) to the peace of his native country."[82] This verdict is unduly harsh. Traquair was unscrupulous, to be sure, but he did not expect his country's peace to be permanently disrupted. In this situation his principal fault was that of everyone else in the government: miscalculation.

Two weeks after the riot Laud wrote to Traquair that it had been a mistake to announce in advance that the new service book would be used on July 23; this gave the ill-affected a chance to organize, which, said the archbishop, they obviously had. Laud was certainly right. The protest on the 23rd was planned, though it seems unlikely that the violence was; all that we can be certain of was that there was to be a mass walkout.[83] In St. Giles on that day, however, in the words of John Row,

> So soon as the Bishop did open his Service Book, and began to read therein, and the people perceiving the Dean opening his book also, all the common people, especially the women, rose up with such a loud clamour and uproar, so that nothing could be heard; some cried, "Woe, woe!", some cried, "Sorrow, sorrow! for this doleful day, that they are bringing in Popery among us!" Others did cast their stools against the Dean's face, others ran out of the kirk with a pitiful lamentation, so that their reading upon the Service Book was then interrupted. . . . After sermon, when the Bishop came out of the pulpit, and went out of the kirk he found the street full of people, who ran about him, crying, That he was bringing in . . . Popery upon them. The Bishop, put in a great fear, ran up the nearest stair . . . crying to the people, that he had no wit of the matter.

The violence, bordering on physical assault, which some of them underwent, so shook the nerves of the hierarchy that it was on Archbishop Spottiswoode's initiative that the council on July 29 suspended the use of the book until the king's pleasure was known. Though no one knew it at the time, the revolution had begun.[84]

The larger question remains: was there a conspiracy? If so, who were the conspirators? When did their plotting begin? And what did they wish to accomplish? The king's supporters believed in the existence of a conspiracy. Clarendon is cautious: he writes of aristocratic discontent dating from 1633. The nobility had gone into debt by the time of the king's visit; they saw their power restrained in parliament, "the diminution whereof they took very heavily, though at that time they took little notice of it," and they looked with alarm at the growing influence of the bishops. So they awaited their opportunity to launch an effective attack on their rivals, which the bishops handed them, mostly through stupidity. The bishops, said Clarendon, should have warned Charles that there would be trouble; they knew it was coming, but they had too much confidence in the ability of the royal authority to produce acquiescence. As for Traquair, he was not disloyal, but his advice to delay the introduction of the book gave the malcontents time to prepare.[85] Burnet, though more even-handed in his analysis of the causes of the upheaval—he was not an enthusiast for any of the parties—was more critical of Traquair, accusing him of egging on the bishops in order to lead them to their destruction. Bishop Guthry, who, like Clarendon, dated active aristocratic discontent from 1633, went further and accused Traquair of deliberate treachery, out of his base ambition to wreck the bishops. Almost equally bad, in Guthry's view, was Lord Advocate Hope, the opposition's key strategist, who, to cover his tracks, used Balmerino and the minister Alexander Henderson as his front men. To Laud's biographer, Peter Heylyn, Traquair was indeed treacherous, but no more than a tool: the real culprit was the marquis of Hamilton, whose agent Traquair was. Hamilton wanted the throne; hence his wrecking of Menteith when the latter laid claim to the earldom of Strathearn, and his deliberate attempt to alienate the king from Montrose, the holder of the other Graham earldom.[86]

The most elaborate conspiracy theory was that spun by John Spalding, the clerk of the consistory court of the diocese of Aberdeen. There was a large aristocratic cabal, the ringleader of which was Lord Lorne. Lorne had a grievance against Bishop Sydserf, which had to do with Alexander Gordon of Earlston, the guardian of Lorne's nephew the laird of Lochinvar. Earlston had said that to kneel at communion was idolatry. Sydserf's diocesan court fined him 500 merks for this, which Lorne paid, and banished him briefly to Montrose. This, and Sydserf's disciplining of Lorne's sister's friend Samuel Rutherford, irritated Lorne. So he picked a quarrel with Sydserf, who was hot-tempered, and provoked him into making a comment in council which Lorne could construe as an insult to the nobility as a class, to give color to the aristocratic malcontents' stories of the threat the bishops posed to their political and economic position. The conspiracy included Traquair, "a great enemy to the bishops," Balmerino, and Rothes, among others, "not but [without] advice of the Marquis of Hamilton and divers others," along with a group of Puritan ministers. The disgruntled noblemen sounded out their English counterparts, found them equally discontented, and signed an agreement with them for the purpose of abolishing episcopacy and eliminating parts of the royal prerogative.[87]

It was in the interest of the king's defenders, then and later, to support a conspiracy theory, just as it served the purposes of the king's opponents to argue for a theory of spontaneous reaction to intolerable provocation. The creeping power and untoward ambition of the bishops were to blame, wrote the earl of Rothes; with their canons and their Popish service book they "loosed the flood of illegal violence, to overflow the truth of religion and liberties of the subjects."[88] The truth lies somewhere in between, as truth often does. There is no evidence of any long-range planning, though it is certainly likely that malcontents, in Scotland as in England, met with each other to air their grievances. The most significant group of malcontents was the aristocracy; in Scotland, this was a group closely connected through personal acquaintance and intermarriage. As an example, consider some of the connections of Charles Seton, second earl of Dunfermline, the son of James's chancellor, who became a Covenanter and, later, a royalist. His mother, the chancellor's third wife, was a Hay of Yester, who, after her husband's death, married the first earl of Callendar. Seton's wife was a daughter of the former Lord Treasurer Morton, which made him Lorne's brother-in-law. His half-sisters were married to the eldest son of the earl of Kellie, the earl of Lauderdale, the earl of Seaforth, Lord Lindsay of Balcarres, and his mother's brother Lord Hay of Yester. His first cousins were the earls of Winton, married to the earl of Errol's daughter, and Eglinton, married to the earl of Linlithgow's daughter; a female cousin married the eldest son of the "wizard" earl of Bothwell. His father's first two wives had been a Drummond and a Leslie, which connected him with the earls of Perth and Rothes. This genealogical excursus could go on, but the point has been made. The aristocracy rapidly assumed leadership of the protest movement after the riot in St. Giles, and on the first occasion on which they took the initiative, in the framing of the supplication of October 18, 1637, there came the first direct attack upon the bishops.[89] These were the circumstances which gave rise to the theory of aristocratic conspiracy.

Before the explosion in July 1637, however, the solid evidence that we have of cabaling and defiance points to the discontented among the clergy. By the beginning of 1637 the imminent introduction of the service book was known, and so was the general nature of its contents. Guthry alleges that Alexander Henderson and David Dickson, the radical minister of Irvine, met with Balmerino and Hope in April, secured their approval for an attack on the book, and then worked out the tactics: the women would start the protest and the men finish it.[90] Whether such a meeting actually occurred is doubtful; it is unlikely that the canny lord advocate would make any commitment, even a verbal one, to such a trio at this stage. Much better documented is a meeting of a dozen or so ministers, including Henderson, Dickson, and Calderwood, on July 6, at which it was decided to prepare a written attack on the book's "corruptions," to stage a mass exodus when the book was first used in Edinburgh and boycott it thereafter, and to petition the council to suspend any order to buy and use the book on the grounds that it was Popish and had not been approved by either General Assembly or parliament.[91] What can be deduced from this is that the protesters' aim was to convince the king that he should restore the Jacobean status quo in the church. The demonstration was carefully organized, and involved a number of the same people who had taken part in the last series of religious disturbances in Edinburgh back in 1624.[92] The violence, which occurred in other churches besides St. Giles,[93] was unplanned, and caught the organizers themselves by surprise. They quickly recognized it for what it was: an indication that the depth of the discontent they themselves felt was greater and more widespread than they had thought, and they knew how to turn it to account.

After the event the recriminations began. Within a week the council authorized suspension of the use of the service book, at the suggestion of Spottiswoode and the other bishops, pending instructions from the king. The bishops wrote to Charles, accusing Traquair of negligence in taking no precautions against the possibility of riot; Traquair in his turn laid the blame on the bishops—"the folly and misgovernment of some of our clergymen," as he put it to Hamilton. In writing to the king, however, he took care also to blame puritan-minded people, "from whose sect I have seldom found any motion proceed but such as did smell of sedition and mutiny"; they worked effectively on the popular fears which the folly of a handful of clergy had created.[94] Traquair had the better of this preliminary skirmish. In September Laud wrote to Spottiswoode, criticizing him not for introducing the service book, but for not having forced a public statement of support from the lay members of the council beforehand, and, rather unfairly, for not ridding the Edinburgh ministry of all nonconformists: most Edinburgh ministers did conform, and were deprived when the Covenanters achieved power.[95] Traquair's victory over the bishops did him no good, however. Charles's blank refusal to compromise, which may have been prompted initially by reports minimizing the significance of the riots,[96] rapidly hardened into a fixed determination to have his way. Traquair had not expected this, and he found himself in a hopeless position. In a desperate effort to persuade the king to give ground, he told Charles how widespread the opposition was—as Stevenson put it, he "seems to have regarded telling the king the truth as a last resort only to be used when all else had failed."[97] Charles was unmoved.

One factor in the king's behavior which historians have not sufficiently stressed is that English court circles knew very little about what was going on in Scotland, and tended to dismiss it as unimportant. Clarendon points out the general ignorance of and indifference to Scottish affairs in England, and his opinion is strikingly confirmed by the *relazione* written by the Venetian envoy Anzolo Correr at the end of his stay in England. It is dated October 14/24, 1637, and has much to say about religious divisions in England and even mentions the Puritans in America. But Correr said nothing of the Scottish troubles; he evidently thought them no more than a passing annoyance, an attitude which reflected that of the English court.[98] Traquair therefore found no English support when he urged the necessity for timely concessions. And so he was caught between his unbending master and the growing and increasingly organized Scottish opposition, whose position was strengthened by the king's intransigence, and which caused even Traquair's predecessor as lord treasurer to waver.[99] Traquair's effort to curry favor with both sides cost him the confidence of both; by the end of the year his influence was gone. He clung to office until 1641, but he was a spent force.

It took sixteen months for Scotland to move from riot to rebellion, to that direct defiance of the king at the Glasgow Assembly in November 1638 which made resort to force inevitable.[100] The slowness of the process—it took about the same length of time in England—is a testimony to the inherent strength of the Stewart monarchy. During those months Charles let slip one opportunity after another to make the concessions that would have averted the disastrous confrontation, even after he was made fully aware of the strength and character of the opposition. "The Scottish resistance seemed to him so entirely incomprehensible," writes S. R. Gardiner of the aftermath of the Glasgow Assembly, "that he could not account for it, except on the supposition that Richelieu was at the bottom of the whole movement, stirring up rebellion in the North, in order to keep England from interfering on the Continent." Bishop Guthry believed that all that Charles had to do to put an end to the troubles was promptly to withdraw the service book after July 23. It was not, perhaps, quite as simple as that, but the clergy's initial reluctance to support the aristocrats' attack on the bishops as a group in October 1637 is evidence that at the beginning the polity of the church was not the central issue. The bishops suffered, and ultimately were swept away, not because the majority of Scots were dyed-in-the-wool presbyterians, but rather because the bishops were the agents of a desperately unpopular policy; furthermore, everyone in Scotland was convinced that the king and Laud would, in time, fill the bench with men who shared their completely unacceptable religious views—the possible implications of Traquair's victory over the bishops in getting his man James Fairlie appointed to the see of Argyll were either not noticed or discounted. Even the National Covenant, though thoroughly anti-episcopal in tone, did not explicitly condemn episcopacy as an institution—though Spottiswoode was right when he despairingly remarked, on hearing of the events in Greyfriars' churchyard, "Now all that we have been doing these thirty years past is thrown down at once."[101]

In December 1637 Lord Loudoun, in a speech to the council

which Balfour thought worth reporting as nearly verbatim as he could, summarized the situation thus:

> The subject of our complaint and controversy is religion, and laws of the kingdom, upon which dependeth both the welfare of the church and commonwealth, our condition of life, our liberty and fortune in this transitory world, and the eternal happiness in the life to come. . . . In (the) service book are sown the seeds of diverse superstitions and heresies, that the Roman mass, in many and substantial points, is made up therein; which service book and other innovations have neither warrant of general assembly nor of act of parliament, but contrary to both are introduced by the bishops.[102]

As this speech indicates, the king's procedure was in fact more damaging to his cause than the changes he wished to make. Loudoun repeated the (by then) standard argument that the service book was the Mass in disguise, but he clearly was more concerned with what he regarded as the illegality of the way in which it was introduced. Submitting the service book to a General Assembly would have entailed a long delay, but would have permitted its few advocates to make the argument that the book was not Popish, and might even have produced enough change to bring about an acceptable compromise. Assemblies could be packed, after all, and the king's authorization to the bishops not to use parts of the book about which they felt doubtful indicated that he was not wedded to the text as it stood. All this is highly speculative, of course. Charles had already made a number of concessions; some matters about which he felt strongly, such as the inclusion of some of the Apocrypha, were very objectionable to the Scots; and, as Donaldson points out, "extensive changes in a puritan direction would have encouraged the malcontents in England."[103] But the king never gave the traditional procedures a chance to work, and once the issue became that of obedience to his orders, Charles became inflexible, as was his wont. His behavior in all of this was reminiscent of that with which he opened his reign, that of the revocation. Though no Bourbon blood flowed as yet in the veins of the royal Stewarts, Charles had evidently learned nothing of how to govern after twelve years on the throne.

His policies and his methods had alienated every group in Scotland that counted for anything; they could, and did, all coalesce in opposition to a "Popish-English-Scottish-Mass-Service Book" imposed by fiat, with its galvanic picture of a "presbyter" in a surplice standing at an altar with his back to the congregation, mumbling prayers, and with both hands free to elevate the elements. Fear for religion, for property, of arbitrary government and of loss of national identity all came together; all had to come together to produce an explosion of this magnitude.

As a straw in the wind, there was a distant reminder of another explosion, one that did not happen. On November 11, 1637, the town council of Glasgow, which in October had referred to the king's "gracious answer" to the petitions respecting the service book, voted that it would not be at any charge hereafter for celebrating the 5th of November, "being the King's night."[104] By this time the Scottish government was virtually paralyzed, and its king almost friendless. If Charles's authority was to be restored in his ancient kingdom, his English subjects would have to do the job. Thus the stage was set for that more famous drama which would now unfold south of the Tweed, and which would end, to the outrage of virtually all those now in revolt against their sovereign, on the scaffold outside the Banqueting House at Whitehall.

NOTES

1. NLS Mss. 81, no. 76. *RPCS* 2nd ser. V, 660–61. For Orkney and Shetland see *ibid.*, pp. 284–85, 659–60. *Stirling* II, 857–58.

2. *RPCS* 2nd ser. VI, 122–28, 130, 246–49, 429 ff.

3. The four non-members were the bishops of Argyll, Caithness, Dunkeld, and Orkney, all Jacobean holdovers. The bishop of Argyll died in 1636; the others were the only three bishops to renounce episcopacy after the Glasgow Assembly of 1638.

4. SRO, GD 45/14/17. William Laud, *The Works of . . . William Laud . . . Archbishop of Canterbury,* ed. W. Scott and J. Bliss, III, 314.

5. D. Laing, ed., *A Diary of the Public Correspondence of Sir Thomas Hope,* pp. 53–58. HMC, 9th Report, app. II, p. 247.

6. *RPCS* 2nd ser. VI, 115, 132–33, 175–76, 221, 253–54, 256,

258, 276, 283–84, 301, 316, 337–38, 400, 404–9, 472. HMC, 9th Report, app. II, pp. 247, 261. *CSPD 1636–1637*, pp. 358–59.

7. *RPCS* 2nd ser. V, 437–38, VI, 91, 432–33. *Stirling* II, 692–93. See also R. B. K. Stevenson, "The 'Stirling' Turners of Charles I, 1632–39," *British Numismatic Journal* XXIX (1958–59), 128–51. Charles made Stirling Master of the Metals in 1635, as another way of helping him to recover financially. *RPCS* 2nd ser. VI, 23.

8. *RPCS* 2nd ser. VI, xv–xviii, 41, 98–101, 256, 258–59, 295–98, 322–24, 344, 350, 360–62, 464–66, R. W. Cochran-Patrick, *Records of the Coinage of Scotland* I, intro., pp. clxxviii–clxxx. Nov. 21, 1634, Traquair to Hamilton, SRO, Hamilton Papers, c. 1, no. 998.

9. The town thanked Traquair effusively for heeding its plea. L. Taylor, ed., *Aberdeen Council Letters* II, 55, 64–65. *RCRB* IV, 540–41. HMC, 9th Report, app. II, p. 247. Laing, *Hope's Diary*, p. 43.

10. See, e.g., *RPCS* 2nd ser. VI, 259–60, 293.

11. *APS* V, 35. NLS Adv. Mss. 32.6.8, f. 130.

12. The tract is in NLS Adv. Mss. 33.2.13. See also *Balfour* I, intro., p. xxvi; Sir Robert Sibbald, *Memoria Balfouriana* (Edinburgh, 1699), pp. 38–39.

13. HMC, 9th Report, app. II, p. 247.

14. D. Laing, ed., *The Letters and Journals of Robert Baillie* I, 8. Sir William Purves, *Revenue of the Scottish Crown, 1681*, ed. D. M. Rose, intro., p. lxvi. See, in general, D. Stevenson, "The King's Scottish Revenues and the Covenanters, 1625–1651," *Historical Journal* XVII (1974), 17–26.

15. Stevenson, "Scottish Revenues and the Covenanters," pp. 24–25.

16. *Ibid.*, p. 25. *Balfour* II, 377. For Traquair's methods see J. Imrie and J. G. Dunbar, eds., *Accounts of the Masters of Works* II, intro., pp. xxxvii–xxxviii.

17. Jan. 29, Oct. 4, 1637, Baillie to William Spang, Laing, *Baillie* I, 7, 17. June 26, Traquair to Maule, SRO, GD 45/14/14, no. 3. Sir John Connell, *A Treatise on the Law of Scotland Respecting Tithes* I, 152–53, II, 111–16. BL Add. Mss. 23,112, f. 71b. *RPCS* 2nd ser. VI, 533–34.

18. July 4, Aug. 7, 1637, Laud to Traquair, Laud, *Works* VI, 491–96.

19. *Balfour* II, 193. Laing, *Baillie* I, 8.

20. Dec. 23, 1636, Archibald Campbell to Sir Colin Campbell of Glenorchy, SRO, GD 112/39/665. Jan. 1, 1637, Traquair to Maule, SRO, GD 45/14/14, no. 2. Jan. 29, Baillie to William Spang, Laing,

Baillie I, 6–8. James Gordon, *History of Scots Affairs from MDCXXXVII to MDCXLI,* ed. J. Robertson and G. Grub, Spalding Club (Aberdeen, 1841), I, 4–5.

21. Laing, *Baillie* I, 6, 7.

22. SRO, GD 45/14/17.

23. See, e.g., Jan. 8, 1634, Stirling to Morton, NLS Mss. 81, no. 50.

24. Henry Guthry, bishop of Dunkeld, *Memoirs of Henry Guthry,* pp. 17–18. Peter Heylyn, *Cyprianus Anglicus,* pp. 328–29.

25. Gilbert Burnet, *Bishop Burnet's History of His Own Time,* ed. M. J. Routh, I, 46–47.

26. Bruce Lenman and Geoffrey Parker, "Crime and Control in Scotland 1500–1800," *History Today* 30 (June 1980), 16. This is also, of course, a commentary on the nature of secular justice. For particulars of ecclesiastical discipline see J. diFolco, "Discipline and Welfare in the Mid-Seventeenth Century Scots Parish," *RSCHS* XIX (1977), 169–83.

27. On this point see D. Mathew, *Scotland under Charles I,* pp. 193–96; D. Stevenson, *Alexander MacColla and the Highland Problem in the Seventeenth Century,* pp. 53–54.

28. C. Larner, *Enemies of God: The Witch-hunt in Scotland,* p. 157. For an excellent brief discussion of various aspects of this "primary Christianization" see T. C. Smout, *A History of the Scottish People 1560–1830* (Edinburgh, 1969), chap. 3.

29. W. M. Campbell, *The Triumph of Presbyterianism* (Edinburgh, 1958), p. 5.

30. S. A. Burrell, "The Covenant Idea as a Revolutionary Symbol: Scotland, 1596–1637," *Church History* XXVII (1958), 344–45. See also his "The Apocalyptic Vision of the Early Covenanters," *SHR* XLIII (1964), 1–24.

31. D. Calderwood, *The History of the Kirk of Scotland* V, 387, 388. Calderwood returned to Scotland in 1625 after an exile of eight years—he had tried King James's patience too far in 1617 on the subject of obedience due to a king. See M. Lee, Jr., *Government by Pen: Scotland under James VI and I,* pp. 168–69. There was no hope of his regaining a parish charge; he spent his enforced leisure compiling his *History.*

32. Burrell, "Apocalyptic Vision," p. 15.

33. *Row,* pp. 396–97. John Willcock, *The Great Marquess,* pp. 32–33. Laing, *Baillie* I, 8–9.

34. On this point see W. Makey, *The Church of the Covenant 1637–1651*, p. 102.

35. NLS Mss. 3,926, p. 367, *RPCS* 2nd ser. VI, 311–12.

36. Cf. Burrell, "Covenant Idea," p. 346.

37. John Rushworth, *Historical Collections* II, 206. Laud, *Works* VI, 409, 419–20, 443–44. Laing, *Baillie* I, 432–33.

38. P. Hume Brown, ed., *Early Travellers in Scotland*, p. 147. W. Forbes-Leith, *Memoirs of Scottish Catholics during the XVIIth and XVIIIth Centuries* I, 171–72.

39. *Stirling* II, 725. See also Apr. 6, 1634, Laud to Traquair, HMC, 9th Report, app. II, p. 258.

40. Forbes-Leith, *Memoirs* I, 143, 171, 196–97. T. H. McGrail, *Sir William Alexander*, pp. 175–78. For Charles's court and Con see Caroline Hibbard, *Charles I and the Popish Plot* (Chapel Hill, 1983), chaps. 2 and 3.

41. Burnet, *Burnet's History* I, 40.

42. *Row*, pp. 353–54.

43. See NLS Mss. 3,926, pp. 361–63. Henderson is quoted in Mathew, *Scotland under Charles I*, p. 269.

44. See the brief sketch of Bishop Graham in Mathew, *Scotland Under Charles I*, pp. 31–33.

45. Guthry, *Memoirs*, p. 13. *Row*, pp. 397–98. D. Stevenson, "Conventicles in the Kirk, 1619–1637," *RSCHS* XVII (1972–74), 99–114, esp. pp. 107–9. W. L. Mathieson, *Politics and Religion: A Study in Scottish History from the Reformation to the Revolution* (Glasgow, 1902), I, 359–60. J. M. Barkley, "Some Scottish Bishops and Ministers in the Irish Church," in D. Shaw, ed., *Reformation and Revolution*, pp. 141–59. M. Perceval-Maxwell, "Strafford, the Ulster-Scots, and the Covenanters," *Irish Historical Studies* 18 (1973), 528–29.

46. See the interesting analysis of the episcopate in Mathieson, *Politics and Religion* I, chaps. 10 and 11, esp. pp. 355–59.

47. Laing, *Baillie* I, 424–28. Rushworth, *Historical Collections* II, 386. *Stirling* II, 724–25. *RPCS* 2nd ser. V, 424–30. *RMS 1634–1651*, pp. 93–94. Thomas McCrie, ed., *Life of Mr. Robert Blair*, Wodrow Society (Edinburgh, 1848), p. 137. George Grub, *An Ecclesiastical History of Scotland* (Edinburgh, 1861), II, 346. G. I. R. McMahon, "The Scottish Courts of High Commission 1610–1638," *RSCHS* XV (1966), 201–3. In some places ministers were made coveners of the justices; see, e.g., *RPCS* 2nd ser. VI, 426–27. It was possible for a minister to avoid service on the commission of the peace, if the council

excused him; see the case of William Row, *ibid.*, pp. 278–79. As Row was the brother of the historian, and himself became a zealous Covenanter, the council's action is not altogether surprising.

48. *Ibid.*, p. 471. See above, chap. 4, p. 129.

49. Edward, Earl of Clarendon, *The History of the Rebellion and Civil Wars in England*, ed. W. Dunn Macray, I, 116–17. G. Burnet, *The Memoires of the Lives and Actions of James and William, Dukes of Hamilton*, pp. 29–30. Guthry, *Memoirs*, pp. 14–15.

50. Makey, *Church of the Covenant*, pp. 121–22.

51. Laud's account of his "Troubles and Tryall" is in *Works* III, 273–462.

52. Laing, *Baillie* I, 1–2.

53. *A&L* I, 93–99.

54. Ian Whyte, *Agriculture and Society in Seventeenth-Century Scotland* (Edinburgh, 1979), pp. 154–55. R. Mitchison, "The Movements of Scottish Corn Prices in the Seventeenth and Eighteenth Centuries," *Economic History Review* 2nd ser. XVIII (1965), 283.

55. Oct. 20, 1634, Charles to Spottiswoode and Lindsay, *Stirling* II, 797. G. Donaldson, *The Making of the Scottish Prayer Book of 1637*, pp. 43–44. This is the authoritative work on the subject; much of what follows is based on Donaldson's excellent account.

56. Guthry, *Memoirs*, p. 16. Laing, *Baillie* I, 168.

57. Apr. 2, 1635, Spottiswoode *et al.* to Laud, *CSPD 1635*, p. 4.

58. Laud, *Works* VI, 455–59.

59. Laing, *Baillie* I, 438–39.

60. Feb. 17, 1636, Stirling to Bishop Maxwell, NLS, Wodrow Folio, LXVI, f. 38. Feb. 18, Charles to Spottiswoode and Lindsay, BL Add. Mss. 23,112, f. 29.

61. *CSPD 1635–1636*, p. 260. R. Mitchison, *Lordship to Patronage: Scotland 1603–1745*, pp. 38–39. *Row*, pp. 391–95, contains a list of what Row calls "impieties and absurdities" in the book of canons.

62. Burnet, *Hamilton*, p. 30.

63. Laud, *Works* III, 322–23.

64. Clarendon, *History* I, 140–42.

65. NLS Adv. Mss. 33.2.22, ff. 27–27b. *RPCS* 2nd ser. VI, 336, 352–53. For Calderwood's work see *Row*, p. 397.

66. W. N. Fraser, ed., *Genealogical Collections Concerning the Sir-Name of Baird*, p. 74.

67. Jan. 2, 1637, Baillie to William Wilkie, and Jan. 29 to William Spang, Laing, *Baillie* I, 1–2, 4.

68. *Stirling* II, 462, 591, 620–21, 815–16. *RPCS* 2nd ser. VI, 409–10. Laing, *Baillie* I, 77.

69. Quoted in Mathew, *Scotland under Charles I,* p. 288.

70. NLS, Wodrow Folio LXVI, f. 87.

71. Laing, *Baillie* I, 15–18, 444–45.

72. Gordon, *History of Scots Affairs* I, 6–7. Rushworth, *Historical Collections* II, 387. Laud, *Works* VI, 459.

73. S. R. Gardiner, *History of England 1603–1642* VIII, 311.

74. *Row,* pp. 398–406. Donaldson, *Prayer Book,* pp. 52, 69. Donaldson's analysis is in *ibid.,* pp. 60–83.

75. Burnet, *Hamilton,* p. 30. See also Rushworth, *Historical Collections* II, 396; Laud, *Works* III, 355–57.

76. J. M. Henderson, "An 'Advertisement' about the Service Book," *SHR* XXIII (1925–26), 204.

77. Laud, *Works* III, 356.

78. Hugh Watt, "William Laud and Scotland," *RSCHS* VII (1941), 171–90. As evidence for the rightness of his view Watt points to the violent language Laud used about Scotland and Scots in his letters to Wentworth in 1638. This is not very convincing; Laud, and everyone else in Charles's inner circle, had ample reason to fulminate against the Scots by then.

79. Burnet, *Hamilton,* p. 29.

80. McMahon, "Courts of High Commission," p. 208. Clarendon, *History* I, 143. Heylyn, *Cyprianus Anglicus,* pp. 328–29.

81. *RPCS* 2nd ser. VI, 448–49.

82. *Balfour* II, 257.

83. Rushworth, *Historical Collections* II, 389–90. Henderson, "Advertisement," pp. 203–4.

84. *Row,* pp. 408–9. *RPCS* 2nd ser. VI, 490.

85. Clarendon, *History* I, 107–8, 116–17, 137–43, 148.

86. Burnet, *Burnet's History* I, 46–47. Guthry, *Memoirs,* pp. 8, 17–18, 22. Heylyn, *Cyprianus Anglicus,* pp. 328–29, 347–51. Guthry and Clarendon also had their doubts about Hamilton, though they made no such claim as did Heylyn. Guthry, *Memoirs,* pp. 34–35. Clarendon, *History* I, 108.

87. J. Spalding, *Memorialls of the Trubles in Scotland and in England, A.D. 1624-A.D. 1645* I, 76–79. Laing, *Baillie* I, 16.

88. John, earl of Rothes, *A Relation of Proceedings Concerning the Affairs of the Kirk of Scotland,* ed. James Nairne, Bannatyne Club (Edinburgh, 1830), pp. 1–2.

89. David Stevenson, *The Scottish Revolution 1637–1644,* pp. 72–73.

90. Guthry, *Memoirs,* pp. 20–21.

91. Henderson, "Advertisement," pp. 199–204.

92. Stevenson, "Conventicles," pp. 111–12. See above, chap. 1, p. 12.

93. See Stevenson, *Scottish Revolution,* pp. 60–63.

94. *Ibid,* p. 63. *RPCS* 2nd ser. VI, 490. HMC, 9th Report, app. II, p. 258. Burnet, *Hamilton,* pp. 31–32.

95. Rushworth, *Historical Collections* II, 397.

96. Clarendon, *History* I, 148.

97. Stevenson, *Scottish Revolution,* p. 66.

98. Clarendon, *History* I, 145–46, 148. *CSP Venetian* XXIV, 259, 266, 273, 294, 295–308. Cf. also C. V. Wedgwood, *The King's Peace 1637–1641,* Book II, chaps. 1 and 2.

99. Guthry, *Memoirs,* p. 23, emphasizes Morton's complaints about the bishops. Rothes worked carefully but unsuccessfully on Morton, stressing the nature of the service book; "there be things in it your lordship would be unwilling to hear or practice." NLS Mss. 81, no. 14. Morton remained a royalist.

100. For a detailed narrative see Stevenson, *Scottish Revolution,* chaps. 2 and 3.

101. Gardiner, *History of England* VIII, 382. Guthry, *Memoirs,* pp. 24–25, 30. Stevenson, *Scottish Revolution,* pp. 73, 85. Of the fourteen Scottish bishops, eight, including both archbishops, were Jacobean holdovers. Of the other six, four, Maxwell (Ross), Sydserf (Galloway), Wedderburn (Dunblane), and Whitford (Brechin) were Laudians. Bishop Campbell of the Isles was a deracinated Scot who had held an English living before his election in 1633; the sixth was Fairlie, who received his appointment on July 10, 1637.

102. *Balfour* II, 240–41.

103. Donaldson, *Prayer Book,* pp. 60–61. For the extent of Charles's responsibility for the text of the service book see *ibid.,* pp. 41 ff.

104. J. D. Marwick, ed., *Extracts from the Records of the Burgh of Glasgow* I, Scottish Burgh Record Society (Glasgow, 1876), 385.

7

"The Nobility's Covenant"

O̲N SATURDAY, MARCH 30, 1639, the cavalry of the Covenanting army clattered into episcopalian Aberdeen, the only major town in Scotland which had not yet accepted the Covenant
and the decisions of the Glasgow Assembly. Following the cavalry
came the pikemen and musketeers, well armed, well provisioned,
and on parade—the city had surrendered without firing a shot.
Three days later the earl of Kinghorne, in the name of the Covenanters' commander, the earl of Montrose, demanded that the
town dismount its cannon and deliver them, and its powder and
shot, to the army; on the following day "the provost intimated to
the town convened by drum in the Greyfriars Kirk that they are
required by the nobility to subscribe their covenant." A week
later they did so: "After sermon made by Master James Row,
minister, the town for the most part subscribed the nobility's
covenant."[1]

"The nobility's covenant." The preceding pages have demonstrated that as far as the reign of King Charles is concerned, the
term is appropriate enough. Charles's alienation of his aristocracy
was at the root of his troubles; in that sense Sir James Balfour's
oft-quoted comment on the revocation of 1625 is accurate.[2] But
the problem is not as simple as that. Whether one wants to call
what happened in Scotland after 1637 a "revolution" or not, there
was certainly a major upheaval, and any historian nowadays who
asserted that responsibility lay solely at the door of one inept king
and let it go at that would be a very rash person indeed. The
question of long-range causes must be addressed. The upheaval
in Scotland was the work of the landed classes, the lairds and

especially the aristocracy; they dominated it and led it, though they had support at all levels of Scottish society. This was no bourgeois revolution; the Scottish middle class, though growing in importance and having its own grievances, mostly economic, was not yet capable of precipitating or leading a national movement. Still less was it a Jacquerie. And though "Laud's liturgy" triggered the upheaval, and religious concern ran very deep and produced the necessary ideological enthusiasm, and so was vital to success, religious discontent by itself could not have galvanized enough of the people who counted to produce a successful uprising.[3] The covenanting idea was in existence in the 1590s,[4] and Andrew Melville was a far more dynamic leader than Alexander Henderson or Samuel Rutherford, but the Edinburgh riot of 1596 was a damp squib and Melville died in exile. By 1637, however, the coalition of nobleman and kirkman which had been so instrumental in overturning Charles's unhappy grandmother had formed again. So the problem that must be addressed is whether by the time of Charles's accession the position of the nobility had undergone so much long-range deterioration that, sooner or later, they would have lashed out at a crown which was steadily, inexorably, grinding them down, as other aristocracies had done at other times, notably in the Netherlands—the Scots, with their numerous economic and intellectual ties with the Dutch republic, were very familiar with the parallel between Charles I and Philip II, the Hispaniolized son of a native-born father who had gone on to a greater throne.

It is certainly true that the power of the Scottish aristocracy vis-à-vis the crown had been slowly but steadily eroding ever since the second quarter of the fifteenth century. Previously, for a century and more, that power had grown. The aristocracy had been indispensable in the fight to maintain Scottish independence from England in the fourteenth century, and three successive aristocratic families, Balliol, Bruce, and Stewart, had been elevated to the kingship. The first two Stewart kings were both feeble and incompetent, and the third, at his accession, was a captive in the hands of the "auld enemy," King Henry IV of England, who, ironically enough, was himself an aristocratic usurper. During the regency for that absent boy, presided over by his uncle Robert, duke of Albany, the power of the crown reached its nadir. "It was hard," writes Gordon Donaldson, "to see the King even as *primus inter pares* in relation to magnates with territorial possessions and ancient titles which gave them numbers of dependents among whom loyalty to the crown was secondary to loyalty to their lords."[5]

Scotland was, in fact, a thoroughly feudal country at the beginning of the fifteenth century, feudal in the senses that there was a great deal of overlapping of public office and private right, and that the king was completely dependent on the landed classes for his army. The financial resources of the crown were not large; grants of regality and hereditary sheriffdoms meant that control of the local community, especially in matters of justice, was in the hands of the magnates. The power and influence of these men was not limited to the authority they derived from their position in the feudal hierarchy. There were also the ties of kinship, and, in addition to them, the creation of relationships between greater men and lesser by means of bonds of manrent, which might be characterized as a species of artificial kinship. The chief purpose of these bonds was to strengthen the great man's position in the locality; they were not designed to be a weapon against the crown—though no doubt, from the aristocrat's point of view, it was preferable that the primary loyalty of his following be to him rather than to the king: it was a form of insurance.[6] Such ties did not depend altogether on written agreement, nor were they limited to the unsophisticated. In the later sixteenth century John Knox was willing to perform a service for the earl of Bothwell because "my grandfather, goodsire, and father have served your Lordship's predecessors, and some of them have died under their standards; and this is a part of the obligation of our Scottish kindness."[7] George Buchanan, the great humanist, possibly the most cultivated Scot of his time, a man of letters with a European reputation, regarded himself as a Lennox man. After the murder of Darnley he turned venomously on Queen Mary, whom he had previously praised, because he held her responsible for the crime, and in the pages of his *Detection* and his *History* did his best, and with some success, to vilify her, and—vainly in this case—to persuade the world that Darnley was a fine, upstanding young man. That men like Knox and Buchanan could feel as they did in the 1560s and 1570s is a measure of the magnitude of the task the kings of Scotland faced in their efforts to become more than *primus inter pares*.

With the return of James I from his English captivity in 1424 that task began to be tackled. This took a long time to accomplish, and it should be stressed that in the 200 years and eight generations of kings that ran from the reign of James I to that of Charles I, most of the confrontations between crown and aristocracy were due to royal initiative: in this sense, at least, Charles was following in the footsteps of his ancestors. James I, whom Donaldson accurately characterizes as "an angry man in a hurry," put a stop to the policy of dissipating the crown's resources in the form of patronage, which had been followed by previous governments, including, notoriously, that of the Regent Albany. Instead, instructed perhaps by what he had observed in England, he set out to acquire land and keep it in order to improve the crown's financial position.[8] By the time of his death he had made virtually a clean sweep of the ancient territorial earldoms. His ruthlessness conjured up enemies, especially among his kinfolk the Stewarts, toward whom his ruthlessness reached the level of vindictiveness. They murdered him in 1437, but his successors continued his policy. James II was able to destroy the greatest of his over-mighty subjects, the earls of Douglas, killing one of them with his own hand in 1452, an act comparable—without the element of sacrilege—to Robert Bruce's murder of the Red Comyn in 1306. This was an extraordinary thing to do, yet James got away with it. "He was saved from the consequences of his own action," writes Jenny Wormald, "because the magnates were prepared to support him."[9] The Douglases met their final destruction in 1455, fighting alone, without support from their fellow magnates, and in that same year the act of annexation and other legislation declared that crown lands were henceforth inalienable save by act of parliament. Future alienations were cancelled; the king was empowered to resume alienated lands without the necessity of legal process, and the holders of such lands were obligated to refund their profits. All grants of heritable offices made since the death of James I were revoked, and no new regalities were to be created save by act of parliament. Here, in broad outline, is the policy of Charles I's revocation: no more than an aspiration, perhaps, in 1455, but altogether feasible in 1625.[10]

What the career of this adroit and successful royal homicide demonstrates is that in the fifteenth century the Scottish crown had elements of strength in its position out of all proportion to its material resources. At that time Scottish monarchy was personal monarchy; everything depended on the person of the king, his character and his abilities. If he was weak, like the first two Stewarts, then individual aristocrats, including members of the royal family, could behave like gangsters and get away with it— witness Robert III's brother Alexander Stewart, the Wolf of Badenoch, who burnt Elgin cathedral in 1390 because the bishop of Moray would not pay him protection money. If the king was strong, like James II, then he could get away with murder. The relationship between the crown and the aristocracy as a class was normally not adversarial, though more often than not the king was at odds with one lord or another, or one noble faction or another. The king needed consent in order to govern, and by and large he got it: most of the nobility was prepared to cooperate with firm royal leadership most of the time. The crown's ability to survive repeated minorities and emerge with its strength almost unimpaired is a demonstration of this. As was to be true of his predecessor and all of his successors down to James VI, misfortune overtook James II early: at age thirty he was blown up by the explosion of one of his own siege guns. Of the first five Jameses and Mary, the oldest occupant of the throne was James I, who was murdered at forty-three. The other Jameses died at ages ranging from thirty to forty; Mary lived to the age of forty-four, but she was deposed at twenty-four. For about half of the years of both the fifteenth and sixteenth centuries the crown was in the hands of a minor or an absentee, and the country was governed by others in the king's name.

The aristocracy took advantage of these frequent minorities to feather their nests, but the process of strengthening the power of the crown went on nevertheless—the nobility acquiesced, after all, in the king's right to issue an act of revocation after he came of age. New earldoms were created in the fifteenth century, but they were personal rather than territorial, and no earl ever again posed the kind of threat which the Black Douglas had.[11] In the reign of James III Donaldson detects a shift in the nobility's attitude and policy: "The crown was now far superior in wealth to even the greatest of the nobles, and it may therefore have seemed a more profitable policy to control the crown, which enjoyed so much landed wealth and the influence which went with it, rather than to take action which would lead to the dissipation of its resources."[12] James III and James V were acquisitive and unpopular. The former's erratic and high-handed behavior eventually undermined the aristocracy's willingness to follow his lead, and he "happened to be slain" after a clash with a rebel army which had secured the person and perhaps the support of his son and heir. James V, at the end of his reign, was courting the same fate. By contrast, the apogee of the Scottish kingship as personal monarchy came in the reign of James IV, the last of the pre-Reformation kings. His immense popularity with all classes of Scottish society caused his aristocrats to do what they had never done since the disaster of Neville's Cross in 1346: follow their monarch eagerly on an invasion of England, and, unfortunately, to even worse disaster at Flodden.

As was true of everything else in Scotland, the position of the aristocracy was enormously affected by the Reformation. In a sense the Reformation was the work of that handful of godly magistrates whose shilly-shallying so irritated John Knox but upon whom, in the end, he did not call in vain. But it was not their work alone; they had supporters among the lairds and the inhabitants of the burghs, and, finally and indispensably, the backing of the English government. In many ways the Reformation strengthened the position of the aristocracy. It rid them of their clerical rivals for office and royal favor; no cleric was to hold a major office in the state until Charles's reign. The nobility, as godly magistrates—most became nominally Protestants, and many genuinely so—had a duty to advance the work of the Lord, so nobly begun, in the absence of a godly prince, and there was no godly prince for a quarter of a century after the triumph of the new religion. Protestantism thus provided the magnates with an ideological justification for their position in the state which they had not hitherto possessed. It also enabled them to consolidate their grip on church property, especially episcopal and monastic lands. Previously they had been feuars, tacksmen, hereditary bailies; now, in addition, the most favored of them became lords of erection. They also, in the vast majority of cases, succeeded to the patronage rights of the bishops and abbots of the old church in their appropriated parishes. And, as has been said, they became tacksmen of teinds. Knox's railing at the greed of the Scottish aristocracy may have been exaggerated, but it was far from completely unjustified.

At first the crown profited but little from a religious upheaval which had been made against its wishes. Furthermore, the peculiar circumstances surrounding the replacement of a Catholic sovereign by her Protestant son in 1567 led to an appeal, both to history and to political theory, which threatened to weaken the position of the monarchy still further, with the undermining of the idea of personal monarchy which had sustained the kings of the fifteenth century. James II could get away with murder; a century later his great-great-granddaughter could not. The deposition of Mary could not be justified merely on the grounds that she had connived at the murder of her husband and then married the murderer, however. The case against her, while probably true, was not susceptible of proof, and even if it were, by what right did subjects pass judgment on their sovereign? Knox's argument that the godly magistrate (and people) had the right—nay, the duty—to revolt against an ungodly sovereign would not do. Mary had always been ungodly in the Knoxian sense; her godly subjects should never have acquiesced in her rule. George Buchanan, the tutor to the new king, came to the rescue of the Protestant party. Reviving the theories propounded by his old teacher John Mair and by Hector Boece in the first half of the sixteenth century, Buchanan argued that the Scottish constitution was not contractual, that the sovereign was nothing more than an agent whose principal responsibility was to do justice. He or she, if unsatisfactory, could be dismissed like any other delinquent servant, as, occasionally, highland clans still ousted a chief who had been found wanting. Buchanan appealed to Scottish history, especially its mythical history as expounded by Boece, to prove his case. Many times in the past, said Buchanan, the Scots, led by their nobility, who had chief responsibility in this matter, had divested themselves of an unsatisfactory king.[13] From the establishment of the modern Scottish kingship under Malcolm Canmore in the eleventh century to 1567, this had happened twice, to John Balliol and to James III. Balliol's deposition was unarguable; he had given away his kingdom, after all. But the case of James III was far more difficult, and it is no accident that it was in the decade after the ouster of Mary that the climax of the blackening of this king's historical reputation was reached, in the writings of Buchanan and of Robert Lindsay of Pitscottie, a Fife laird and a zealous Protestant apologist. By 1580 the James III of legend was fully created: an incompetent, avaricious, cowardly king, addicted to low-born favorites and unmanly pursuits, and so rightly deposed by his outraged aristocracy—a Scottish Richard II. Small wonder that in 1584 James VI regarded Andrew Melville's sermon comparing him to James III as seditious. There was more to it than that, however. As Wormald has put it, "The rebellion of 1488 could be transformed into a great constitutional act. Even more important, so could the events of 1567."[14] If the monarch's role was now a matter of constitutional definition, what then became of the idea of personal monarchy?

In some respects the triumph of the Reformation also weakened the position of the aristocracy. John Calvin himself may have preferred aristocratic government, but Calvinism, with its emphasis on the inability of prince and pauper alike to do anything meritorious in God's eyes, is the least hierarchical of all the established forms of sixteenth-century Christianity. By the 1580s it had developed what might without too much exaggeration be called a quasi-democratic form of church polity, at the hands of Andrew Melville and his fellow authors of the Second Book of Discipline. It was a polity which the aristocracy found it difficult to cope with. The role of the godly magistrate was very important to the reformers, but as Knox, Melville, and the others conceived it, the proper function of that godly magistrate was to take his marching orders from God's spokesmen, the clergy. This the nobility would not do, not even genuinely pious men like the Regent Moray; much less would hard-bitten and worldly Protestants like the Regent Morton, who once remarked to Melville, "There will never be quietness in this country till half a dozen of you be hanged or banished."[15] So the aristocrats held aloof from the kirk sessions, which filled up with lesser proprietors, lairds and feuars. As the kirk sessions grew in influence in the localities as administrators of the kirk's discipline, the local influence of the aristocracy correspondingly diminished. Indeed, the nobility was faced with a classic example of Hobson's choice: had they joined the kirk sessions on the kirk's terms, their influence might have diminished even more rapidly.

The widespread development of the feu farm was also a consequence of the Reformation, and this too was deleterious to the power of the aristocracy in the long run. Feuing was beneficial to those who became feuars of church or crown lands, but much less so to those who set their own lands in feu. The possession of a feu gave the holder a great deal of independence, and many feuars were small men, below the class of laird. Proprietorship created assertiveness, and also, for lesser men, the opportunity to participate on an equal footing with their superiors in the social hierarchy as elders in the assemblies of the reformed church. "The beginning of the seventeenth century," writes Margaret Sanderson, "was the great age of the portioners and the bonnet lairds [small proprietors], and the feuars who, given the chance, began to climb the social ladder."[16] The fact that the feuar paid a fixed rent was enormously beneficial also, especially if he paid it in cash rather than kind, given the inflation and currency debasement which racked Scotland in the later sixteenth century. The feuing of secular lands does not seem to have been extensive, but all sorts of tenants, not just feuars, were achieving greater security. "Copyhold tenures, rental and tack, based on the principle of 'kindness' [a claim to inheritance based on kinship with the previous holder], gave almost as much security in practice as the feudal tenures and created an assertive spirit among the kindly tenants."[17]

The consequence of these developments was that the lords' grip on their followers and kinsmen began to slacken. There was, lamented Sir Richard Maitland, "Na Kyndnes at Court without Siller"[18]—his kinsman at court paid him no heed until he opened his purse—but at court there seldom is. More disturbing was the weakening of ties in the local areas, which the great lords attempted to shore up by means of bonds of manrent. John Knox might have been willing to do a favor for the earl of Bothwell for the sake of "our Scottish kindness," but the earl's marriage to Queen Mary, by Protestant rites, did not convert Knox into a supporter of the queen and her new husband. Furthermore, while the victorious Protestant party had aristocratic leadership in both 1560 and 1567, its success was due to the support of the lairds and burgesses. The appearance of some hundred lairds at the Reformation parliament of 1560 was a portent, as was the fact that in 1568 more higher aristocrats supported Mary's—i.e., the losing—cause than that of the Regent Moray.

The extent of the weakening of the aristocracy's position must not be exaggerated, however. The Reformation and its consequences did not beget class antagonisms; no more did the civil war. Leaving the years of English military rule aside, there was one regime during the civil war period which was not dominated by the nobility, that of the kirk party between September 1648 and September 1650. The dominant elements of this regime were the clergy and the lesser lairds and burgesses. Its policies could hardly be called radical with respect to the Scottish class structure. Its agenda was for the most part that of the kirk: an intensified pursuit of sinners of all classes and varieties, including witches; the abolition of lay patronage; provision for compulsory assessment for poor relief if voluntary contributions were insufficient. These last two policies affected the nobility, of course. But the only actions which might be labeled anti-aristocratic were the appointment of a parliamentary committee to look into the grievances of tenants, who had suffered owing to "the guiltiness and sins of your Lordships and such as rule in the land," and, ironically, vigorous support of what had been Charles's policy of ending the feudal superiorities of lords of erection. During the troubles Charles, in an effort to buy support, had reversed himself and made new grants of superiorities and feu duties to various nobles. In 1649 these were for the most part nullified, and the crown's right to purchase feu duties from the lords of erection was reaffirmed. Where the crown had not already done so, the feuars themselves were granted the right to purchase the duties if they wished, without prejudice to the crown's ultimate right to acquire them—though, as David Stevenson remarks, "the lairds must have hoped that the effect of the act would be to free them from all feu duties on kirklands."[19] It is a commentary on Charles's ineptitude as a politician that he was not able to make allies of the feuars of church lands in the years before 1637, although they had a common goal.

The chief significance of the Reformation for the Scottish aristocracy, then, was that it could no longer take its position of leadership vis-à-vis the other groups in Scottish society for granted. Some of these other groups, the clergy and the lairds in particular, were becoming more assertive and developing their own agendas, which in some respects ran counter to the interests of the nobility as a class. Those interests were not exactly being threatened, but their automatic priority was now in question. Some of the nobility, at least, were aware of the subtle change in their position. So too were some outside observers. "Methinks I see the noblemen's great credit decay in this country," wrote the English resident in Scotland in 1572, "and the barons, burghs, and such-like take more upon them."[20]

The policy of James VI between 1585, when he began to govern for himself, and 1603 was admirably calculated to exploit the weaknesses in the aristocracy's position in order to reassert royal control over them and all other groups in Scottish society. James's position was complex and in some ways unprecedented. Unprecedented in its opportunity: before James's eyes there always shimmered the glittering prospect of the English crown and the measureless (by Scottish standards) wealth and power that went with it. But unprecedented also in its dangers: the pupil of George Buchanan understood very well that he could not count on the kind of loyalty that went with the old idea of personal monarchy. His nobles, suffering from their own new insecurities, might be tempted to treat him as an unsatisfactory servant, as they had done with his mother. They could no longer be depended upon to be automatically loyal, especially if they listened to critical preachers who, under the new dispensation, claimed the God-given right to say what they liked in the pulpit. The series of aristocratic coups to which James was subjected between 1578 and 1585, a total of seven, six of which were successful, was clear evidence of the nobles' undependability as a class. And even as individuals: James's boyhood friend and schoolmate, with whom he grew up, the earl of Mar, Jock o' the Slates, had a hand in the majority of them. James was fond of Mar and forgave him, but he had no intention of being as dependent as his predecessors had been on the goodwill of the aristocracy as a class for the success of his rule.

And so James set to work. His treaty of alliance with England in 1586, which was useful enough to survive the shock of Mary's execution, effectively cut off from dissident aristocrats their most obvious and convenient refuge and source of support. From the days of David II and Edward Balliol to James's own time English governments had patronized disgruntled Scots noblemen, paid them, even given them military support. The coup which overthrew James's favorite, James Stewart, earl of Arran, in 1585 and inaugurated his own personal rule had been hatched on English soil, where many of its devisers were refugees. With the treaty of alliance, that sort of thing would no longer happen. James's entente with the kirk, into which he entered rather reluctantly, at the behest of his political mentor John Maitland of Thirlestane, freed his hands so that he could attmept to get control of his government and bridle his magnates, which, he and Maitland agreed, were his most pressing political problems. The key stroke was the annexation of the temporalities of benefices to the crown in 1587. This pleased those elements in the kirk, Andrew Melville and his allies, who were anxious to eliminate episcopacy altogether; for this reason among others James came later to regret his action. But for the position of the crown vis-à-vis the aristocracy the act was enormously helpful. It gave the king a new and powerful source of influence over all lay holders of church lands, since he was now in a position, if he would, to confirm them in possession of these lands, and convert them into hereditary temporal lordships. It also gave him a means of rewarding loyal service, of building a *noblesse de robe* out of the ranks of lawyers, lairds, and younger sons and cadet branches of the great houses. At the same time, in 1587, he brought the lairds into parliament.

James's policy was highly successful. His government was full of "new" men, men of talent whose first loyalty was to the king and who received their rewards from him. The magnates were not shut out. James did not attack their local power: they retained their places on the privy council, and they came to court, where their gregarious and friendly king cosseted them and made much of them. So, sooner or later, most of them, with an eye to the future, when their king would (most probably) succeed to the throne of the ageing virgin in Whitehall, agreed to play the game on James's terms: to trade obedience for a place at court and access to the royal ear. The one aristocrat who absolutely refused to accept the new dispensation was James's cousin Francis Stewart, earl of Bothwell, who called Maitland a toadstool and for some years waged a kind of private war against him. In the end Bothwell was forfeited and driven into permanent exile. Having achieved this, James next turned his attention to the kirk and began the process of getting it under control. After some experimentation he opted for the restoration of diocesan episcopacy; he had not yet finished the job when he became king of England in 1603.

James accompanied his practical political success with a new theory of the nature of the Scottish kingship. In James's opinion, the two theories current in Scotland in the 1580s were very dangerous to the position of the monarchy. Buchanan's doctrine reduced the king to a mere agent, accountable to his people and liable to be dismissed by them. Andrew Melville's theory of the two kingdoms relegated King James merely to membership in the kingdom of Christ Jesus, namely the kirk. This theory also reduced the king to a mere agent, in this case of the kirk as represented by its General Assembly and by God's spokesmen the clergy, who thundered at James from the pulpit week in and week out, and claimed immunity from accountability to laymen for what they said while acting, as was said of John Knox, as members of God's privy council. To meet the challenge to kingship inherent in both these theories, James, in his *Trew Law of Free*

Monarchies, espoused the doctrine of the divine right of kings.[21] To the kirkmen he quoted Scripture, and in his favor was the fact that he was undoubtedly a godly prince. However much the kirk might complain of his "banning and swearing" and the peccadillos of his court, and of his deplorable fondness for Papists like the earl of Huntly and Lord President Seton, James's own Calvinist orthodoxy could not be challenged. To the believers in Buchanan's theory, which was entirely secular and historical and did not depend on God's providence, James opposed his own version of history. His ancestor King Fergus had come to Scotland as a conqueror; Scottish kingship therefore antedated the law, which, therefore, depended upon the king, not the other way around. A good king will obey the law and administer it fairly, wrote James, but his position as king is in no way dependent upon his doing so. Furthermore, asked James, who, under Buchanan's scheme of things, would make the determination that a king was performing unsatisfactorily, and upon what grounds? Such a theory leads straight to anarchy. In an age in which no one was prepared to agree, with Thomas Jefferson, that periodic rebellion was not necessarily undesirable, these were powerful arguments.

James thus provided the Scottish kingship with a new and very different rationale from that which had prevailed in the days of the Regent Albany and his Jacobean ancestors. The king now was far from being *primus inter pares;* he was no longer dependent on his personal skills, though James had those in abundance; he was God's agent, responsible to God alone and not to any of his subjects. It should be emphasized that James's role of political theorist was thrust upon him. Historians of England have been far too prone to assert that James's discourses on the nature of kingship were nothing more than self-indulgent displays on the part of a vainglorious pedant who liked to hear himself talk. What they do not understand is that in the Scotland of the 1580s and 1590s James's theoretical undertakings were vital to the strengthening of his position as king. And of course when he became king of England his already considerable power was enormously enhanced, in regard to the aristocracy and everyone else in Scotland. The union of the crowns was an event of immense importance for Scotland, far more so than for England. For the nobility in particular it was crucial, because at one stroke they had lost the ability to apply direct pressure on the king; all they could do now was ask rather than demand. It took some time, however, for the true significance of the change in the power position to become apparent to them. James's caution, his political skill, his intimate knowledge of the Scottish nobles as individuals, and the Scots' collective pride that their king was now ruling over the auld enemy combined to delay the magnates' realization of the extent to which their position had been altered.

For all of James's skills, however, his departure and his new and enhanced position had caused some strains to develop by 1625. Scotland saw him but once after 1603, and he did not encourage his Scottish subjects, nobility or anyone else, to come to court unless they had business there; English hostility to the Scots permanently resident there was bad enough without exacerbating it still further. Even if the king had been more forthcoming, the cost of visiting London often, or for any length of time, was very great indeed; an English traveler in Scotland in 1629 commented that the Scots were impoverishing themselves by going to court.[22] So for most of the Scottish nobility regular personal contact with their king was a thing of the past. James's plan for a closer union of the two kingdoms was hardly, if at all, more popular in Scotland than in England, and most of the people who counted on both sides of the Tweed were greatly relieved when it failed. James was a patient and persistent man, however. If union could not be achieved all at once, piecemeal change would pave the way for its eventual success—and such change always meant altering Scottish institutions and practices to make them conform to those of England. Most of James's changes had to do with the church; some of these, notably the most crucially unpopular, the order to take communion kneeling, directly affected everybody. Other changes, such as the creation of justices of the peace, threatened the grip of the aristocracy on the local community because it endangered their monopoly of the administration of justice. Still others, such as the steadily increasing burden of taxation, culminating in the unprecedentedly heavy tax of 1621, had an impact, and not a welcome one, on aristocrat, laird, and burgess alike.

Strains there were, then; but under James they had been kept under control. The removal of the court may well have "left a vacuum in political, social, and cultural life," as Wormald observes,[23] but as yet it was only a partial vacuum. The privy council was still an influential governmental body. Scottish magnates and gentlemen could still attract the king's attention, either through a member of the council or one of the many Scots at court. James knew them personally, or he had known their fathers, and James knew how to temporize. He may have talked and written of himself as God's lieutenant, but his policies, even his church policies, he adopted and advocated on grounds of convenience rather than conscience or divine law, and when necessary he was willing to make concessions to his opponents, or even to back down. The prevailing mood of the time was that expressed in the inscription which Lord Chancellor Dunfermline placed in his walled garden at Pinkie House in the second decade of the century: "For himself, for his descendants, for all civilized men, Alexander Seton, lover of mankind and civilization, founded, built, and adorned his house and gardens. . . . Here is nothing warlike, even for defense; no ditch, no rampart. But for the kind welcome and hospitable entertainment of guests a fountain . . . lawns, ponds, and aviaries." It was a confident expression of contentment with what Donaldson has called King James's peace, by a man whose own contributions to it were very substantial.[24]

After 1625, however, the position of the nobility deteriorated visibly and rapidly. Charles was a very different sort of man from James, much less accessible, unfamiliar with them both as individuals and as a class, and apparently uninterested in remedying that lack of familiarity. From the beginning, however, he was far from inactive. The revocation had an immense impact on the aristocracy because it brought starkly home to them the weaknesses in their position with respect not only to their now very powerful king but also to their more independent-minded inferiors. The fears expressed by Melrose in the opening phases of the implementation of the revocation with respect to the lairds may have been exaggerated,[25] but they were based on a clear-sighted appreciation of the possibilities of slippage in the aristocracy's position, of which he, as a newcomer to its ranks, was perhaps more keenly aware than most. Worse still, Charles acted without any of the customary forms of consultation which James had employed. The old king had made repeated use of parliament, for example. In the forty years of his personal rule parliament met fourteen times, and no more than five years elapsed between meetings. James's removal to England made no difference in this respect; parliament met seven times between 1585 and 1603, and seven times thereafter. The Scottish parliament may have had very little independent authority, but the fact that James consulted it so frequently after 1603 was psychologically important. The nobility, and the lairds and burgesses too, were fulfilling their traditional roles in the Scottish polity, not only in relation to the crown but also as links between the crown and the larger community of the realm. James did nothing of any importance without consulting either parliament or the General Assembly of the kirk, even though his enthusiasm for the latter body was minimal. Under Charles these links were snapped. In the twelve years between his accession and the riot in St. Giles, parliament met but once, in 1633, after a lapse of twelve years since James's last parliament, and the General Assembly did not meet at all.

That one meeting of parliament was anything but reassuring to the aristocracy. Increasingly, and especially after the traumatic events of 1633, they felt weak, powerless, frozen out, without a role to play. The promise of a return to Jacobean normalcy which the Menteith years had held out proved to be illusory. Many aristocrats were in an uncomfortable financial position; like Menteith, they had gone into debt in order to acquire property and/ or to engage in expensive building ventures. David Stevenson, the most recent historian of the Scottish revolution, characterizes the pre-1637 atmosphere thus: "The Scottish nobility had suddenly been transformed, in their own eyes, from the proud leaders of the society of an independent nation into a poor and provincial nobility. Their old reference group [the Scottish court] had been disbanded and they had not the resources to compete with the new one. They reacted with mixed envy and resentment."[26] The financial burden increased for everyone, and threatened to increase still further, to support an absentee and Anglicized king and his court, where the possibilities of gain for individual Scots grew increasingly slim. "Scotland," writes Stevenson, with reference to the court-country dichotomy so beloved of historians of early Stuart England, "was virtually all country and no court."[27] The extent to which the Scots, in 1603 and immediately thereafter, expected to profit from the union of the crowns is not at all clear—Stevenson believes that their expectations were high—but certainly few if any of them then thought that it would turn out to be deleterious. As the years of Charles's reign rolled on, however, the nobility and almost everyone else in Scotland came to believe that "the union undermined rather than strengthened the security of Scotland. Instead of helping to protect Scotland, the union was enabling absentee kings to introduce foreign influences and institutions, destroying in particular her religion. It was anglicizing policies that were mainly responsible for driving Scotland to rebellion in 1637."[28]

Much of Stevenson's analysis is persuasive, but this use of the word "kings" is an indication that he still follows the Whig tradition of S. R. Gardiner and his successors and fails to make sufficient distinction between James's policies and methods and those of his son, an error probably deriving, for historians of England, from the unique position of the duke of Buckingham in the English political scene from about 1620 to the time of his assassination in 1628. Whatever the truth of the English political situation—and the recent work of Conrad Russell and others on the politics of the 1620s in England accords greater importance to the change of monarchs than the schools of thought associated with either Gardiner or Christopher Hill have done—there can be no doubt of the significance of that change for Scotland.[29]

There were only two issues which, taken together, could have produced a successful Scottish revolt against Charles, for success depended upon a union of all the important groups in Scotland against this immensely powerful king. Both issues were present, one on the surface, the other just beneath it. The one that triggered the resistance was an issue of religious belief, and of belief on the part of both the king and his opponents. Charles, unlike his father, was sincerely convinced that the religious changes he wanted were divinely ordained, and he, like James, had the additional sanction of the divinity which doth hedge about a king. The other issue was epitomized in a letter written by Thomas Wentworth to the earl of Northumberland in July 1638. Wentworth wrote that he hoped that King Charles would subdue the Scots by force and impose not only the English prayer book but also English government and laws, and govern Scotland henceforth as Ireland was governed, by means of the English privy council.[30] Here was the hidden agenda that all Scots saw in Charles's religious policy. The service book represented the first step on the road to autocratic government from London and the destruction of Scotland as an independent nation. And so they united to oppose it.

Charles had committed a mistake in Scotland which abler rulers than he have made, both before and since his time. He had adopted a policy which he did not have the administrative, military, or fiscal resources to enforce in case of resistance.[31] And then, having precipitated that resistance on an unprecedented scale— no previous Scottish ruler had had so little support as Charles had in the late 1630s—he refused to make concessions until it was too late.

The crisis Charles provoked was in essence one of government, fueled by nationalistic enthusiasm and ideological revulsion. Its principal components were a regime perceived as alien and annexationist, an immensely unpopular religious policy, a financial policy regarded as extortionate and likely to get worse, and a ruling class which was shaken by the perceived weaknesses in its position and anxious to recover the ground it had lost. Overall, what happened in Scotland bears but little resemblance to the other upheavals that form part of what has been called the "general crisis" of the mid-seventeenth century; in all of the other confrontations, fiscal crisis induced by the strains of war or preparation for war played a predominant, perhaps a decisive, part. Parallels to some aspects of the Scottish situation exist elsewhere, to be sure—in Catalonia,[32] Ireland, Portugal, Bohemia, for example, though it is dismayingly superficial to lump these (save Bohemia) together with Scotland as "outlying provinces [which] rebelled against the centralizing process for fear of crushing tax burdens and interference in local liberties."[33] There is rather more to the position espoused by David Stevenson on the last page of his study of the years after 1637: "It could be argued that the Scottish revolution had more in common with the revolutions of the 1560s, when the quarrel between state and society was primarily religious in form . . . than with those of the 1640s, which [J. H.] Elliott sees as arising mainly from the fiscal demands of the state."[34] In that sense the conflict Charles provoked was one more installment of the wars of religion. The closest analogy is that of the Low Countries in the 1560s: Charles's policies and methods resembled those of Philip II, as did his foreignness, and caused the same sort of reaction. But even here the parallel is far from exact. The aristocracy of the Netherlands was far more alienated when Philip took over the government than was the case in Scotland in 1625. "In his (Philip's) absence [after 1559]," writes Pieter Geyl, "the high nobility entered into systematic opposition."[35] The religious situation in the Netherlands was far more complex than in Scotland, and, as H. G. Koenigsberger remarks with reference to the iconoclastic riots of the summer of 1566, "The real revolution was started by the lower classes in the towns."[36] More important, however, the Netherlanders' recent experience of the demands of war, and their fear of the consequences of further such demands, had a great deal to do with the attitude they adopted toward Philip and his viceroys. Uniquely, war and its strains played no part in precipitating the Scottish upheaval.

That upheaval was a conservative movement, as are all rebellions which are successful in avoiding class conflict. In many ways it deserves the label of "counterrevolution" as employed by Martha François to describe the revolts of this period.[37] The only fracture to appear before the final victory over the king was that between highlander and lowlander, and this particular fracture can be laid at the door of the Campbells: those highlanders who were aggrieved by the relentless expansionism of MacCailein Mór and his kindred formed the nucleus of Montrose's little army. In 1637 the aristocracy took the lead—it was indeed the nobility's covenant—and at the Glasgow Assembly, which restored Andrew Melville's presbyterian church structure, "the lay convenanters adapted the Melvillean church polity, which had been intended to challenge existing lay society, so that instead it reflected the structure of that society."[38] Power in society and the state was to remain with those who traditionally had held it, though the role of the lairds in the successive Covenanting governments grew steadily more important.[39] As has been said, it was not until very late in the day, in 1649, when the victorious coalition had been shattered on account of the triumph of the radicals in England, that there was anything resembling class legislation, and it was of a fairly limited sort. Even so, it made the nobility keenly aware of the dangers inherent in the policy of defying the crown in alliance with a kirk whose polity made it very difficult, if not impossible, to control on a permanent basis. "Argyll and others," writes Stevenson, "began to fear that by destroying the king's power they had begun a process which was now inevitably destroying the nobility and the whole social order. . . . The horrid example of England loomed large."[40] And, as in England, where the heirs of the Puritan gentry of the 1640s became the Tories of the 1680s, so the sons of Covenanting nobles became royalists and episcopalians after the Restoration.

King Charles was neither a wise nor a clever man. It was his misfortune that the circumstances in which he found himself magnified his weaknesses, and gave little or no opportunity for his virtues to display themselves. But it is hard to imagine circumstances prior to the reign of Queen Victoria which would have been propitious for the peculiar mix of qualities which made up his mind and character. He inherited problems and difficulties, to be sure—every monarch does—but what happened to him in Scotland was his own doing. It can be argued that he was ill served, and this is true; but the fact that he was ill served was his own responsibility. He ended his father's system of government, alienated the governing classes, and in the end was left with an administration made up of superannuated and/or deracinated men, and of men with no independent influence. He abandoned Menteith, the most useful man he ever found, when he need not have done so, and, ironically, pardoned him late in 1637, "contrary to the expectation of many,"[41] too late to do himself any good. The two able men the government still possessed in 1637, Traquair and Hope, disliked each other and had no commitment to their master's policy. From the beginning of the troubles Hope almost openly sided with the opposition, and Traquair was quickly exposed for the double-dealer he was. Scotland had had incompetent kings before, to be sure, and badly served ones to boot, and a few of them had been overturned. The enormous increase in the power of the Scottish crown during the long reign of Charles's father made such an outcome most unlikely now, however—and yet it happened. It is very difficult to make a convincing case for the proposition that what the theorists call "multiple dysfunction" had proceeded so far in Scotland by 1625 that Charles was as helpless as King Canute in the face of the incoming tide. The ingredients for an explosion may have been in existence when Charles succeeded to the throne; he nevertheless contrived to add a few more, and it was his hand which fashioned the charge. If ever a man brought ruin upon himself, that man was Charles Stewart.

NOTES

1. John Stuart, ed., *Extracts from the Council Register of the Burgh of Aberdeen 1625–1642,* pp. 154–57. There is no James Row listed among the Aberdeen ministers; possibly the clerk meant to write John Row, the son and continuator of the historian so often cited above. John Row became a minister in Aberdeen in 1641, and subsequently principal of Kings College there.

2. See above, chap. 2, p. 68.

3. On this point see the interesting discussion by Ian Cowan, "Church and Society in Post-Reformation Scotland," *RSCHS* XVII (1971), 185–201.

4. On this point see S. A. Burrell, "The Covenant Idea as a Revolutionary Symbol: Scotland, 1596–1637," *Church History* XXVII (1958), 341–42, and his "The Apocalyptic Vision of the Early Covenanters," *SHR* XLIII (1964), 12–13.

5. Gordon Donaldson, *Scottish Kings* (London, 1967), p. 44.

6. On bonds of manrent and kinship see Jennifer Brown (now Wormald), "The Exercise of Power," in Jennifer Brown (Wormald), ed., *Scottish Society in the Fifteenth Century* (London, 1977), pp. 56–65.

7. W. C. Dickinson, ed., *John Knox's History of the Reformation in Scotland* (New York, 1950), II, 38.

8. On this point see Craig Madden, "The Royal Demesne in Northern Scotland during the Later Middle Ages," *Northern Scotland* 3 (1977–78), 1–24. Donaldson's phrase serves as the heading for his chapter on James I in *Scottish Kings.*

9. Brown (Wormald), "The Exercise of Power," p. 49.

10. Madden, "Royal Demesne," pp. 18–19. *APS* II, 42–43. The general resemblance between this legislation and the main lines of Charles's revocation prompted the speculation (in chapter 1) that Sir James Skene, the lawyer son of an antiquarian father, was the originator of Charles's act.

11. For the changing character of the Scottish aristocracy in the fifteenth century see Alexander Grant, "The Development of the Scottish Peerage," *SHR* LVII (1978), 1–27.

12. Donaldson, *Scottish Kings,* p. 118.

13. Buchanan's historical account of the Scottish constitution, and also his political theory, depended on the genuineness of that long line of non-existent kings, "whose names read like a roll-call of Actaeon's hounds." This explains Buchanan's fury at the Welsh scholar Humphrey Lhuyd, whose *The Breviary of Britayne,* published in English in 1573, effectively destroyed them: "Their vertiginous alternations of election, fornication, and deposition had provided the historical basis of the alleged ancient Scottish constitution." See H. R. Trevor-Roper, *George Buchanan and the Ancient Scottish Constitution,* English Historical Review, Supplement 3 (London, 1966), esp. pp. 25–31. The quotations above are on pp. 24 and 27.

14. Jenny Wormald, *Court, Kirk, and Community: Scotland 1470–1625* (London, 1981), p. 147. For the legend of James III see Norman Macdougall, "The Sources: a Reappraisal of the Legend," in Brown (Wormald), *Scottish Society,* pp. 10–32, where he compares the growth of this legend with that of Richard III in Tudor England, and his *James III* (Edinburgh, 1982), chap. 12.

15. R. Pitcairn, ed., *The Autobiography and Diary of Mr. James Melvill,* Wodrow Society (Edinburgh, 1842), pp. 67–68.

16. Margaret Sanderson, *Scottish Rural Society in the Sixteenth Century,* p. 190.

17. *Ibid.,* p. 188.

18. W. A. Craigie, ed., *The Maitland Quarto Manuscript,* Scottish Text Society (Edinburgh, 1920), p. 30.

19. For the rule of the kirk party see David Stevenson, *Revolution and Counter-revolution in Scotland, 1644–1651,* chap. 4, esp. pp. 134–45. The quotation is on p. 139. See also Walter Makey, *The Church of the Covenant 1637–1651,* pp. 78–81.

20. Quoted in P. Hume Brown, *History of Scotland* (Cambridge, 1912), II, 117.

21. The text of the *Trew Law* is in C. H. McIlwain, ed., *The Political Works of James I,* pp. 53–70.

22. HMC, *Lonsdale Manuscripts,* ed. J. J. Cartwright, p. 83.

23. Wormald, *Court, Kirk, and Community,* p. 192.

24. Colin McWilliam, *Lothian* (London, 1978), p. 338. G. Donaldson, *Scotland: James V to James VII,* chap. 12.

25. See above, chap. 2.

26. David Stevenson, *The Scottish Revolution 1637–1644,* p. 320. For the nobility's financial position see J. Imrie and J. G. Dunbar, eds., *Accounts of the Masters of Works* II, intro., pp. xx, lxvi–lxxii.

27. Stevenson, *Scottish Revolution,* p. 324.

28. *Ibid.,* p. 313.

29. Conrad Russell's views are strikingly encapsulated in the last paragraph of his "The Parliamentary Career of John Pym, 1621–9," in P. Clark, A. G. R. Smith, and N. Tyacke, eds., *The English Commonwealth, 1547–1640: Essays in Politics and Society* (New York, 1979), p. 165.

30. Richard Bagwell, *Ireland under the Stuarts* I (London, 1909), 236–37.

31. J. H. Elliott believes that this was a factor in many of the revolutionary situations of the 1640s. See his commentary on Trevor-Roper's "general crisis" thesis in T. Aston, ed., *Crisis in Europe 1560–1660,* pp. 111–17.

32. J. H. Elliott, "The King and the Catalans, 1621–1640," *Cambridge Historical Journal* XI, no. 3 (1955), 253–71, draws a parallel between Scotland and Catalonia, where a revolt erupted in 1640. Anyone familiar with Elliott's later, full-scale work, *The Revolt of the Catalans: A Study of the Decline of Spain 1598–1640* (Cambridge, 1964) will be far more aware of the differences than of the similarities.

33. L. Stone, *The Past and the Present* (Boston, 1981), p. 138. Stone's phrase applies accurately only to Catalonia, which he discusses in a deservedly laudatory account of Elliott's *The Revolt of the Catalans.*

34. Stevenson, *Scottish Revolution,* p. 326. For J. H. Elliott's perceptive comparison of the 1560s and the 1640s see his "Revolution and

Continuity in Early Modern Europe," *Past and Present* no. 42 (1969), pp. 35–36.

35. Pieter Geyl, *The Revolt of the Netherlands (1555–1609)* (London, 1932), p. 70.

36. H. G. Koenigsberger, "Western Europe and the Power of Spain," *The New Cambridge Modern History* III (Cambridge, 1968), 269.

37. Martha François, "Revolts in Late Medieval and Early Modern Europe: A Spiral Model," *Journal of Interdisciplinary History* V (1974–75), 19–43. In common with other scholars who have addressed the "general crisis" theory (excepting Elliott and, of course, historians of Scotland like Stevenson), François does not discuss Scotland. For a summary of Stevenson's views see his *Scottish Revolution,* pp. 315–26. For further discussion of some of the issues raised in this chapter see M. Lee, Jr., "Scotland and the 'General Crisis' of the Seventeenth Century," *SHR* LXIII (1984), pp. 136–54.

38. Stevenson, *Scottish Revolution,* p. 107.

39. For the role of the lairds see the convenient summary in David Stevenson, ed., *The Government of Scotland under the Covenanters 1637–1651,* SHS (Edinburgh, 1982), intro., pp. xxii–xxiv.

40. Stevenson, *Revolution and Counter-revolution,* p. 214.

41. J. Spalding, *Memorialls of the Trubles in Scotland and in England, A.D. 1624-A.D. 1645* I, 83.

Index

Note on the author

MAURICE LEE, JR., is a widely respected scholar of Scottish history. He has been a faculty member of Princeton University, the University of Illinois, and is currently Distinguished Professor of History at Rutgers University. Among his many honors are a Woodrow Wilson Fellowship, a Guggenheim Fellowship, and the David Berry Prize of the Royal Historical Society for 1958. He is the author of *The Cabal, James I and Henry IV,* and *Government by Pen: Scotland under James VI and I,* among others.

DATE DUE

DEMCO 38-297